VÍA DE LA PLATA
WAY OF ST JAMES: SEVILLE/GRANADA TO SANTIAGO

About the Author

Alison Raju is a former teacher of French, German and Spanish to adults and the author of several other guides to pilgrim routes published by Cicerone Press: *The Pilgrim Road to Nidaros: St Olav's Way – Oslo to Trondheim* and *The Way of St James* (2 vols: *Le Puy to Santiago* and *Pyrenees–Santiago–Finisterre*).

VÍA DE LA PLATA
WAY OF ST JAMES: SEVILLE/GRANADA TO SANTIAGO

by
Alison Raju

CICERONE

2 POLICE SQUARE, MILNTHORPE, CUMBRIA LA7 7PY
www.cicerone.co.uk

A catalogue record for this book is available from the British Library

for Jim

Front cover: Santiago statue on south portal, church of Santa Marta de Tera

CONTENTS

Statue of Santiago Peregrino, cathedral chancel, Zamora

PREFACE

This is a new edition of the guide to the Camino Mozárabe de Santiago, or Vía de la Plata, first published in 2001. Since then many changes have taken place, both to the route and its infrastructure, making a new edition necessary. This edition also includes the alternative starting point in Granada and is, at present, the only printed guide (in any language) to cover this section.

Although every effort has been made to ensure that this new guide was as accurate and up-to-date as possible at the time of going to press, changes can occur (in waymarking and accommodation, for example), over which the author has no control. The publishers would welcome notes of any such changes.

Alison Raju

Map 1

Key

————	Road
– – – –	Route
	Boundary
- - - - -	Track
+++++++	Railway
	City
○	Town
♟	Church
	Water
	River

INTRODUCTION

HISTORY AND BACKGROUND

The Vía de la Plata, like the Camino Francés (from the Pyrenees to Santiago), is not simply a long-distance walk with a difference but a *pilgrimage* route. For although the so-called 'French road' is the most well-known, well-travelled and well-documented of the pilgrim roads to Santiago de Compostela (and to such an extent that for many people it is the only one) it was, in fact, only one of several used in former times. Pilgrims in the past obviously did not travel to Roncesvalles by train or bus to begin their journey there, as do their modern counterparts, but set out on foot from their own front doors and as well as the northern coastal route, for example, the Camino Aragonés

over the Somport pass to Puenta la Reina, routes from the east of Spain and several roads through Portugal, there was also the Camino Mozárabe or Vía de la Plata. This was so named, it is now thought, *not* because it followed the old Roman silver route from Huelva in the south to Astorga in the north but as a corruption of the Arabic *bal'latta*, used to describe wide, paved or public roads. This route, with its own network of tributaries, took pilgrims from Seville and other places, both along the way and adjacent to it, through Mérida, Cáceres and Salamanca to Zamora. (One of these feeder routes, from Granada via Córdoba to Mérida, is also described in this book.) From there many continued

Typical small Roman bridge (Puente Valimbre 6km before Astorga) (photo: author)

ahead via Benavente and La Bañeza to join the main flux of European pilgrims coming from the Pyrenees in Astorga. Others deviated via Puebla de Sanabria and Ourense to go directly to Santiago through Galicia. It is sometimes suggested that this was to avoid the Montes de León and the stiff climb up to Cebreiro, but as the route through the western part of Zamora and the province of Ourense is extremely strenuous and necessitates climbing up (and down again) both the Puerto de Padornillo (1368m) and then the pass at A Canda (1268m) on two successive days, this is not a very plausible explanation. There was also the option of going through northern Portugal, via Bragança, to rejoin the route through Galicia again in Verín. (Pilgrims interested in taking this latter option should consult the Confraternity of St James for information.)

The original Vía de la Plata was a Roman road, running in more or less a straight line south–north from Mérida to Gijón, and anyone walking the Vía de la Plata today will be very much aware of being in Roman Spain. It was in two distinct parts: a paved section as far as Salamanca and a compressed earth track from there to Astorga and onwards. A section of the original paved road has been restored, about a kilometre leading uphill out of the small spa town of Baños de Montemayor on the boundary between Extremadura and Castille-León, and gives us an idea of the surface on the first part of the route. The Romans also built innumerable bridges along the way, many of which are still standing. Some of these are quite simple ones, like those at Casas de Don Antonio and Valdesalor (both south of Cáceres), the one over the Río Turienzo near Estación

Group of miliaros, between Casar de Cáceres and the Embalse de Alcántara

Restored section of original calzada romana, *leaving Baños de Montemayor (photo: author)*

de Valderrey (shortly before you reach Astorga) or the much longer and more elaborate constructions such as the bridges over the Río Tormes in Salamanca, the Duero in Zamora and the Guadiana in Mérida, 792m long, with its 60 arches. (This is the way pilgrims enter the town. Mérida did not have just one Roman bridge, though, as pilgrims left the town by another one too – over the Río Alberragas to the north.)

The entire Roman route of the main Vía de la Plata was also divided into *mansiones* or stages of 20–25 Roman miles, with a *mansio* or place where travellers could rest overnight at the end of each one. The route was marked with *miliarios* (milestones), one every '1000 steps' or 1472m, and a number of them are still visible with their markings on them; these stood some 2ft 6in (76cm) high, like stone pillars, and were engraved with a Roman numeral. Several of them are still standing too, especially in the area near the Puente de la Magdelana, below Calzada de Béjar. Numbers CXLVIII (148) and CXLIX (149) were repositioned in 1994 by the local 'Amigos' (south of Fuenterroble de Salvatierra, some 50km south of Salamanca) and relevant *ayuntamientos* (town halls) have plans to reinstate others along the route as well.

The Romans did not invent this route completely from scratch, any more than the pilgrims, whether on the Camino Francés or the Vía de la Plata, created a completely new road to take them to Santiago, but they used and improved on existing paths and tracks

instead. (A lot of research done on the Vía de la Plata has been carried out by people interested in Roman roads rather than pilgrim routes.) The Romans who came to the south of Spain arrived by boat, from southern Italy, and could sail up the Guadalquivir river which at that time was navigable not only as far as Seville but beyond as well. The road that became the Vía de la Plata originally started in Mérida, the town known as Augusta Emeritus, which they developed for their emeritus or pensioned-off soldiers from the fifth and tenth legions, and this road was used as a means of moving troops northwards. Later on it was extended as far south as Seville. There are an enormous number of Roman remains all along the Vía de la Plata, starting with the city of Itálica on the outskirts of Seville, and especially in Mérida, with its theatre (still used for performances today) which originally held 3000 spectators, an amphitheatre with seating for 14,000 and a circus that could accommodate 30,000 people. It also has a splendid Roman museum and the so-called Acueducto de los Milagros (a look at it will reveal why) and its two Roman reservoirs, one of which, the Embalse de Proserpina, nowadays used as a recreation area, is a few kilometres to the north on the route of the Vía de la Plata itself. Anyone who is interested in things Roman could follow the Vía de la Plata (in a car, for example) just for this reason. The Roman aspects are not limited to the Seville–Astorga section either – the *termas* (hot springs) in Ourense, for example, were also in use in Roman times and, as already indicated, there are several bridges of Roman origin in other places along the route too.

So much for the Roman aspects. The route they established forms the physical basis of the one that interests us, the route which pilgrims in future centuries would take. Pilgrims from the south of Spain and other parts of the Christian Mediterranean (who travelled to Seville by boat), as well as Arabs and Orientals, apparently, made use of the existing Roman road infrastructure to take them to Santiago. This *camino* (the Vía de la Plata) – a great Roman engineering feat – also had its own network of tributaries, as explained above: from Córdoba, for example, and Granada, joining the route in Mérida, or from Toledo, where pilgrims joined it in Salamanca. It is often thought that pilgrims to Santiago only used the Vía de la Plata after the Reconquista (in 1492) but they actually began much earlier. The Vía de la Plata as a pilgrim artery began in the twelfth century, after the fall of Toledo in 1085, but especially after the political and religious annexation by Galicia of a large part of the western fringe of Spain through which the Vía de la Plata ran – the area around Salamanca, for example. Another important influence in 'getting the pilgrimage off the ground' along this route was the powerful Archbishop Gelmírez. It is already well known how he was responsible for promoting the Camino Francés across the north of Spain but under his rule the diocese of Santiago de Compostela, which already reached to Salamanca,

was extended as far south as Mérida in 1179. Spain was still under Muslim rule, of course, but during this period there was a degree of tolerance allowed to Christians – the Mozárabic ones, those living under Muslim rule (as opposed to the Mudéjar Muslims living later under Christian domination) – and the Vía de la Plata was the route these pilgrims took to Santiago, hence the name Camino Mozárabe. The Vía de la Plata was also the route used in 1062 (under Fernando I) to take the body of St Isidore of Seville up to León and after the Reconquest of Córdoba the bells of Santiago cathedral, which had been taken to the mosque in Córdoba 200 years previously by Al-Mansur, were returned via this route to their rightful home in Galicia.

The movement of pilgrims along the Vía de la Plata was never as great as along the Camino Francés but it too had its own infrastructure of pilgrim hospitals. The question is often raised as to the existence of Jacobean churches or other influences along this route. Once again, there are not as many as there are on the Camino Francés (one explanation that has been suggested is that the Mozárabic pilgrims were exiles/refugees and thus had no time to leave permanent traces of their passage) but there are certainly a significant number and the interested reader is referred to the summary in Appendix B. The other important factor to remember, when considering the historical aspects of the pilgrimage along the Vía de la Plata, is the role played by the Order of the Knights of Santiago, founded in Cáceres in 1170 and whose purpose was to protect pilgrims on their way.

LEGEND

Pilgrimages had been popular amongst Christians ever since Constantine the Great had the Church of the Holy Sepulchre built over the site of Christ's burial in Jerusalem, in AD 326, and the discovery, shortly afterwards, of the Holy Cross itself. Those journeying to this shrine were known as *palmeros* (palmers) whilst *romeros* went to Rome, the burial place of St Peter. But why did pilgrims want to go to Santiago? Those who have already walked or ridden the Camino Francés will very likely know something about the discovery of the body of St James in Galicia but for those who do not, the story begins after the death of Christ, when his disciples dispersed to different parts of the then known world, to spread the Gospel as they had been bidden. St James (son of Zebedee, brother of John and Christ's first cousin) went to Spain, we are told, where he spent a couple of years evangelising, apparently without a great deal of success. He then returned to Jerusalem but was beheaded by Herod shortly afterwards, in AD 44. Immediately following his martyrdom, however, his followers are said to have taken his body to Jaffa, on the coast, where a ship was miraculously waiting for them, and they set off back to Spain. They landed in Iria Flavia on the coast of Galicia, present-day Padrón, some 20km from what is now Santiago de Compostela, after a journey (and in a stone boat!) which is purported to have taken only a week, thereby providing proof of angelic assistance. The body was then buried in a tomb on a hillside, along with, later on, two of his followers, and then forgotten for the next 750 years. The story is, in fact, considerably more complicated than this; these are the bare bones.

Early in the ninth century Pelagius, a hermit living in that part of Spain, had a vision (which he subsequently reported to Theodomir, bishop of Iria Flavia) in which he saw a very large bright star, surrounded by a ring of smaller ones, shining over a deserted spot in the hills. The matter was investigated and a tomb was found there containing three bodies. They were immediately identified as those of St James and two of his followers and when Alfonso II, King of the Asturias (791–824), went there he declared St James the patron saint of Spain. He built a church and a small monastery over the tomb in the saint's honour, around which a town grew up. It was known as *'campus de la stella'* or *'campus stellae'*, later shortened to *'compostela'*. This is one explanation of the origin of the name. Another is that it derives from the Latin *componere* (to bury), as a Roman cemetery or early Christian necropolis is known to have existed under the site of the present-day cathedral in Santiago – and where the remains of St James are still believed to be housed today.

News of the discovery of the body of the saint soon spread, however, and

*Bas-relief of Santiago Matamoros,
Convento de Sancti Spiritu, Salamanca*

San Roque in pilgrim attire,
church of Santa María del Valle,
Villafrance de los Barros

led Santiago de Compostela to become the third great focus of Christian pilgrimage from the Middle Ages onwards. The spread of the news was encouraged, moreover, both by Archbishop Gelmírez and the cathedral authorities, who were anxious to promote the town as a pilgrimage centre, thus attracting money to the area, and later by the Order of the Knights of Santiago, who saw in it the opportunity to assist the Spanish Church in its long struggle against the Moors. Both factions were also helped by the fact that the Turks had seized the Holy Sepulchre in 1078, thus putting a stop to pilgrimages to Jerusalem, and because journeying to Rome had also become difficult for political reasons. However, Santiago was attractive as a potential pilgrim 'venue' in other respects too, as it fulfilled the various criteria necessary to make a pilgrimage there worthy of merit. It was far away (from other parts of Europe, for example) and difficult to reach, thus requiring a good deal of hardship and endurance to get there (and back again too, of course). It was sufficiently dangerous (wolves, bandits, fever, rivers that were difficult to cross) as well as being in a Spain locked tight in struggle with the Moors, and for this reason pilgrims often travelled in quite large groups. The road itself was also well enough supplied with shrines, relics and other sights worth seeing and as traffic increased roads were improved and bridges and hospices were built. Churches were dedicated to St James, too, whilst others contain his statue or depictions in paintings or tilework. As Santiago Apóstol he is portrayed bareheaded, with halo and a book (open or closed) in hand, but he more frequently appears as Santiago Peregrino in pilgrim outfit, with hat, stick, cape, gourd and satchel and with shells on either hat, lapels or both. His other common representation is as Santiago Matamoros (the moor-slayer), riding on a charger, with sword, shield and often a dead Moor or two falling at his feet. It is not unusual, however, to see a mixture of the apostle and pilgrim versions, with halo, book, stick and cockle shells, whilst there are also bareheaded pilgrim occurrences. Depictions of the Santiago sword, with bent handle, like a shepherd's crook, are also found in places associated in some way with St James.

A number of very tiny chapels *(ermitas)* built along the way were also dedicated to St Roch (San Roque in Spanish), the pilgrim saint from Montpellier. After a pilgrimage to Rome, St Roch devoted his life to caring for plague victims but withdrew to live in a forest when he contracted a disease which left him with an unsightly sore on his left thigh. For this reason he is depicted in art – and there are a number of St Roch representations along the *Vía de la Plata* – with the front flap of his coat turned back, to warn people to keep away from him, and is accompanied by the faithful dog, often with a loaf of bread in his mouth, who brought the saint his daily rations. Legend has confused him with Santiago Peregrino at times, and he not infrequently appears in a 'pilgrim version' as well, with added hat, staff and cockle shells on his clothing.

Why did people go on pilgrimages anyway? For a variety of reasons: as a profession of faith, as a form of punishment (a system of fixed penalties for certain crimes/sins was in operation during the Middle Ages), as a means of atonement, as a way of acquiring merit (and thus, for example, reducing or, in certain cases, cutting in half the amount of time spent in Purgatory) and as an opportunity to venerate the relics of saints available in shrines along the way. (Indulgences were also available from the cathedral authorities in Santiago to those who made the journey in Holy Years.) No doubt, too, there were some who were just glad of the opportunity to escape their surroundings. Those with the means to do so went on horseback and some wealthy people made the pilgrimage along with a considerable retinue. The majority of pilgrims went on foot, however, and even amongst the rich there were some who preferred to walk, rather than ride, because of the greater 'merit' they would attain afterwards.

The pilgrim in former times was not at all sure that he would eventually reach his destination, let alone return home in one piece, so before setting out he took leave of his family and employer, made his will and generally put his affairs in order. He (or she) obtained his 'credentials' (pilgrim passport) from his bishop or church, which he could then present in order to obtain

food and lodging in the many pilgrim 'hospitals' and other establishments along the way. This was both a precaution against the growing number of pseudo-pilgrims and as a means of providing proof of his journey: he had his papers stamped at different stages along the way so that once he arrived in Santiago he could obtain his *compostela* (certificate of pilgrimage) from the cathedral authorities there. This in turn entitled him to stay in the pilgrim shelters on his return journey as well as furnishing evidence, if needed, that he had actually made the pilgrimage successfully.

The pilgrim had his staff and scrip blessed in church before setting out and travelled light, carrying little else but a gourd for water and, on his return journey, his scallop shell. This singled him out as a pilgrim, rather than as any other type of traveller, and is the symbol embedded above doorways and in other places on the many and varied buildings that accommodated pilgrims along the different pilgrim roads. (Originally these were worn only by returning pilgrims but today they are common on hats, rucksacks and round the necks of those beginning their journey to Santiago, almost a required item of 'pilgrim uniform' for some.) Pilgrims with funds could obviously stay in inns and other publicly available lodgings (such as the *ventas* that lined the Vía de la Plata, often on the site of the former Roman *mansiones*) but there were also hospices and other facilities specially provided for them. Some of these were in towns, whether in the centre or outside the walls to cater both for latecomers and possibly contagious pilgrims, whilst others were in the middle of the countryside, often by bridges or at the crossing of important pilgrim feeder roads. Much of the pilgrim accommodation was provided by religious orders, by churches and civic authorities, as well as by benevolent individuals. The facilities offered varied considerably from one establishment to another and one or two such buildings are still standing, such as the one in Rionegro del Puente.

There are different explanations as to the origins of the scallop shell or 'coquille Saint Jacques' but one is that when the followers of St James arrived in the port of Iria Flavia with the apostle's body they saw a man riding along the beach (a bridegroom in some versions) whose horse took fright and then plunged into the sea. When they re-emerged both horse and rider were covered from head to foot in scallop shells (and even today the beaches in this part of Galicia are strewn with them). It was customary to set out in the springtime in order to reach Santiago for the feast of St James on July 25th and return home for the winter. This was especially true in Holy Years, those in which July 25th falls on a Sunday (after 2004 the next ones are in 2010, 2021, 2027, 2032, 2038 and 2049), the only time the 'Puerta Santa' or Holy Door of the Cathedral of Santiago is open. This is sealed up at the end of each such year and then symbolically broken down again by the Archbishop in a special ceremony in the evening of December 31st preceding the new Holy Year, one during which special concessions and indulgences were, and still are, available to pilgrims. On returning home many joined confraternities of former pilgrims, such as the *cofradías* in Castilblanco de los Arroyos and Rionegro del Puente, the forerunners of the modern-day associations of Friends of St James that now exist in several countries to support, promote and encourage the different routes to Santiago. Unlike the Camino Francés, however, from which there are a number of extant accounts of pilgrim journeys from the twelfth century onwards, there are no surviving writings documenting individual pilgrim journeys to Santiago along the Vía de la Plata.

THE VÍA DE LA PLATA TODAY

The route from Seville to Astorga has been waymarked (very thoroughly and clearly) since 1991, when the late Andrés Muñoz Garde researched the route and painted yellow arrows, like those on the Camino Francés, to guide a large group he was leading along this stretch of the Vía de la Plata. He was the one person who really set the route on its feet again in recent times. People living along the way are sometimes heard to remark 'Ah, yes, now there is a new route to Santiago,' assuming it must be something that has been invented recently, but although it has been waymarked for over 10 years very few pilgrims used it in the early years. The other catalyst was the very active group

Solitude in the springtime (photo: author)

of Amigos del Camino de Santiago in Seville, led by the late José Luis Salvador Salvador, who not only continued and maintained the waymarking but also visited all the villages along the way within reasonable walking distance of each other, talking to priests, *alcaldes* (mayors), the local police and so on to set up a network of very basic sleeping accommodation in parish halls, schools and sports centres, so that nowadays, apart from large towns, there is always somewhere (often very spartan, obviously) for pilgrims to sleep, apart from *hostales, fondas* and so on where these exist. The Seville 'Amigos' also produce a special *credencial*, a 'pilgrim passport' for the route (see below). There are also several other associations of 'Amigos de la Vía de la Plata' along the way (those in Fuenterroble de Salvatierra and Zamora are particularly active). The

group in Ourense played a big part in clearing and waymarking the route through Galicia while the 'Amigos' in Granada and Córdoba have been responsible for the section from Granada to Mérida. The 'feeder routes' from Huelva to Zafra and Jaén to Baños de Montemayor have also been waymarked by local associations.

In 1992 only about 50 people walked the route in a whole year (the author of this guide was one of them) and it was quite different then, not only from the well-travelled Camino Francés but also from the route today. Nowadays people living along the route know who pilgrims are, where they are going, what the yellow arrows are for and that they are living along an important pilgrim road to Santiago. There are also many more pilgrims – relatively speaking, of course. In 1993, a Holy Year (when July

25th, St James's Day, falls on a Sunday) there were about 100 (compared to 99,000 on the Camino Francés), some 450 in 1996 and what was often described by local people as *un montón* (a 'huge number') in the 1999 Holy Year – about 3000 altogether. In 2002 and 2003 respectively some 4000 and 5000 pilgrims were recorded by the cathedral authorities in Santiago as having arrived by the Vía de la Plata, swelling to 9309 in 2004 (compared to 138,397 on the Camino Francés). Many of these did not walk (or cycle) all the way from Seville but, like those who start in Sarria on foot on the Camino Francés in order to walk the minimum 100km required to qualify for their *compostela*, 5616 of them started in Ourense for the same reason. A lot of people also start either in or after A Gudiña because the Xunta de Galicia (regional government) has set up a network of *refugios*, which obviously makes it much easier to walk the route. There are still few *first time* pilgrims on the Vía de la Plata at present, however, and it is still surprisingly uncommon for people who live along the route itself to set out from their own front doors and make their first journey to Santiago along a *camino* which would lead them there directly. For some reason, perhaps because of the massive publicity during the nineties about the Camino Francés being THE Camino de Santiago, rather than just one of many routes to the 'city of the apostle,' people seem to think that they should go to Roncesvalles (from Seville, for example!) to set out on the 'proper' *camino*, though this is gradually changing. Others are misinformed, thinking that the route from Seville is not waymarked or that the Vía de la Plata is all road walking, since the N630, the main road which, in fact, follows the historical route taken by *the Vía de la Plata* is also, confusingly, named 'Ruta de la Plata.' Other people are unwilling to follow a route where 'there are no refugios.' In the past there were also no guidebooks; nobody, even priests and people with yellow arrows outside their doors, knew about the route or where it went, and anybody walking along with a rucksack bigger than a daysack was automatically considered either a 'hippie', a tramp or a *transeunte* (somebody walking from town to town theoretically in search of work) and looked at often very oddly by people in shops and places with accommodation. Unlike the Camino Francés, where the numbers of pilgrims has risen and fallen in different periods but where there has always been at least a continuous trickle, the pilgrim route along the Vía de la Plata came to a complete halt for a long time, possibly one or two centuries, and in the public eye, at least, it had disappeared into oblivion. It was heavily promoted for the 2004 Holy Year, however, to attract pilgrims (and tourists) away from the completely saturated Camino Francés and there are plans afoot to classify the Vía de la Plata as Patrimonio de Humanidad as well. As a result, in terms of pilgrim numbers and infrastructure, the Camino Mozárabe de Santiago along the Vía de la Plata today resembles the Camino Francés back in 1990.

The walk from Seville to Santiago, whether via Astorga or Ourense, can be completed in six to seven weeks by anyone who is fairly fit and who also likes to visit places of interest along the way. Those who prefer to start in Granada, on the other hand, should allow seven to eight weeks, while pilgrims who wish to build several rest days into their journey, on whatever alternative, should obviously allow longer. The Vía de la Plata can be undertaken in sections, too, by those who lack the time to do it all in one go or would just like to cover certain stretches, and indications are given in the text as to how to reach (or leave) the main towns along the way. Those who 'turn left' at Astorga, to continue along the Camino Francés (this option is only recom-

mended for those who have not already walked this route) often find it quite a shock to be suddenly immersed in a sea of pilgrims after walking for so many weeks on their own and feel strangers amongst all the others coming from the east who already know each other. The same applies, too, to those who continue through Galicia, however, and several pilgrims have commented that they found their arrival in Santiago somewhat depressing, particularly if they have already walked or ridden the Camino Francés. One suggestion for dealing with this problem has been to continue on foot to Finisterre, using the three or four more days of walking (described in Appendix A) as a quieter epilogue to the pilgrimage, akin to the often solitary character of the Via de la Plata.

Oak trees between Almadén de la Plata and the Finca Mateos Arroyo

Anyone in Britain who is thinking of walking any part of the route should certainly consider contacting the Confraternity of St James for advice and membership (see Appendix D for contact details) – their annually updated guide to accommodation and services is extremely useful.

The present guide is intended principally for walkers but as a large part of the route is suitable for mountain bikes (though definitely NOT touring bikes), indications of unsuitable stretches and their alternatives are provided in the text. (Cyclists may find it helpful to go through the text in advance and highlight aspects relevant to their needs.) Pilgrims on bikes should be aware, however, that they will not normally be able to travel very fast on the walker's route ('speed merchants' should stick firmly to the roads), that they may have to get off and push from time to time (and will therefore need suitable footwear) and that in Spain all types of cyclist are required by law to wear helmets. Details of bike repair shops are given where known.

Like the Camino Francés, which many pilgrims on this route have already walked or cycled, people make the journey along the Vía de la Plata for a variety of reasons – historical, cultural, religious, as a(nother) significant action or event in their lives – and late twentieth and early twenty-first century pilgrims are people from all walks of life. Many are Spanish, of course, but there is also a significant proportion from Belgium, the Netherlands, France and Germany, as well as from Britain and places much further a field. Many of those who make the journey along the Vía de la Plata travel alone, others in twos or threes, others in quite large groups, particularly those on foot. Many complete the entire route in one stretch; others, with more limited time, cover only a part of it or do it a section at a time over several years. Most who go to Santiago along the Camino Mozárabe, and especially those who have been able to do the whole route in one go, would probably agree afterwards, however, that like their (probable) earlier journey along the Camino Francés, it has changed their life in some way, even though they may never have set out with this intention at all.

Most long-distance footpaths avoid not only large towns but even quite small villages as well. The Camino de Santiago along the Camino Mozárabe/Vía de la Plata, on the other hand, because of its historic origins (much of the original *calzada romana* is subsumed under the N630) and the need for shelter, deliberately seeks them out. However, one of the differences between the modern pilgrim and his historical counterpart, whether he walks, goes by bike or on horseback, is that very few return home by the same means of transport. The modern pilgrim route has thus become a 'one-way street' and it is unusual, today, to encounter anyone with either enough time or inclination to return to his or her point of departure by the same means as he or she set out. Moreover, since the

Yellow arrow (waymark) on rock (photo: author)

waymarking with yellow arrows is also 'one way only' it would be difficult to follow the Vía de la Plata backwards, though some sections of the Seville–Astorga route are waymarked (in white, and somewhat patchily) in reverse for use as a renewal of a *ruta de transhumancia*. This is a road (in this case from Gijón to Cáceres) used for droving animals in large numbers, and in 1995 the practice was revived and huge numbers of cattle were moved on foot to try and help restore the tradition, with white arrows painted to guide the drovers on their way.

The route is a varied one, in climate, scenery, history and architecture, and pilgrims see a big cross-section of Spain as they walk along it. The part from Seville to Astorga is not physically difficult to walk in that there are no stiff climbs but the distances between accommodation are often very long, though the situation is improving every year. It is also a solitary route, which some people obviously like, but quite a few people who have walked the Vía de la Plata after the *camino* from Roncesvalles have said that they did not like it at all because they rarely met anyone else or any other pilgrims. The walking (or cycling) is almost all on old tracks and paths, very often the sort that are used for transporting animals or, if not, on extremely quiet minor roads. The pilgrim is normally far away from other roads though, sometimes never seeing anybody at all, or any villages, all day long. (This obviously needs a certain amount of organisation if you are not to get caught without anything to eat when you are hungry or short of water as there are hardly any public fountains until you reach Galicia.)

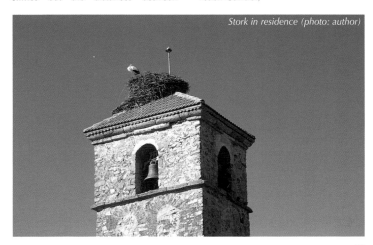

Stork in residence (photo: author)

Giant cactus, Sierra Norte de Sevilla (photo: author)

Those who decide to continue via Puebla de Sanabria and Ourense will find the route very strenuous, with a lot of stiff climbs and descents, but it is also very beautiful (in nice weather, of course). The route from Seville to Astorga is 722km (plus 250km more along the Camino Francés for pilgrims who choose this alternative) while the route for those who go directly via Galicia to Santiago is 1000km so there is little difference between the two options, in terms of distance. Pilgrims who start in Granada will need to be fit before they start, though, as this route (403km to Mérida) is extremely strenuous until Alcaracejos (three days after Córdoba), after which it flattens out. Some of the stages are unavoidably long and this option is, at present, at least, even more solitary than the main Vía de la Plata (not a route for those who don't

like their own company!) though people who live along the way seem to know where you are going.

TOPOGRAPHY, ECONOMY AND LANGUAGE

The Vía de la Plata leaves Seville, capital of the province of the same name and one of the eight that make up the autonomous *región* of Andalucia, crosses the Río Guadalquivir and leaves via the city's industrial suburbs to the northwest. To begin with the scenery is not particularly interesting: flattish landscape with scrubby vegetation and the ubiquitous *jara* (cistus) bushes that smell like church incense. You will also see very large cacti, interspersed with cotton fields, orange trees and, increasingly, plantations of cork trees with their bark often stripped bare, the more recently

Cork tree recently stripped of bark (photo: author)

removed a bright red-brown, the others already regrowing their coats (it takes seven years before they are ready to harvest again) a dull grey colour. After passing through Guillena – the first of several small towns with their character-istic white-painted houses with thick walls and wrought-iron bars at the windows, many of them single storey, their white-painted churches, public buildings and *frontón* (pelota court) all huddled close together – the route continues through the Parque Natural de la Sierra Norte de Sevilla to Castilblanco de los Arroyos along one of the first of many *veredas, cordeles* and *cañadas*. These routes were the highways of old and the classification of the different categories (which you will encounter in the names of some of the tracks you will take further on) was laid down by Alfonso X in 1284. The largest was the *cañada real*, 90 *varas* (75m) wide, followed by the *cordel* or *ramal*, 45 *varas* (33m), and the narrower *vereda* or *cordón*, 25 *varas* (20m) wide. Nowadays these old pathways are used mainly for the movement of animals but some of them have also been cleared and waymarked as recreational walking routes. However, since there are many extremely large estates *(cortijos)* in this part of Spain there are often few tracks and paths to walk on, open to the public or not, and for this reason you will sometimes have to use minor tarred roads (such as the 16km stretch between Castilblanco and El Berrocal, for example). The entrance gates to these *cortijos*, often quite elaborate white-painted constructions, are to be seen by the side of the road from time to time, though the farm buildings themselves are usually well out of sight.

Gradually the landscape becomes more undulating and the cork trees increase in number, as do the *encina* (holm oak) plantations. This is an ever-green relation of the *roble* (ordinary oak tree) and whose acorns provide food for the many hundreds of black, dark brown and grey pigs (the *cerdo ibérico*) that you will see grazing to either side of the walled lanes as you walk along – the 'source material' for the *embutidos* (sausage – literally 'stuffed' or 'packed in') for which Extremadura is so well known (along with its wines). However, while the landscape may have changed by now, the regional accents have not and the pilgrim will have to wait awhile before hearing the sort of Castilian he or she has probably been taught in language classes. One reason why local people you encounter may be difficult to understand, apart from sheer speed of delivery, is that in Andalucia and many parts of Extremadura all intervocalic and terminal 's's disappear so that *dos meses* (two months), for example, will sound like 'doh may'.

The Vía de la Plata from Seville enters the province of Badajoz (one of the two, together with Cáceres, that form the autonomous *región* of Extremadura) just south of Monesterio. Here the land-scape becomes hillier, with mules and donkeys working in the fields and mountains away in the distance, before opening out into the fields full of grass

Camino through encina (holm oak) plantations, Extremadura (photo: author)

(and wild flowers in the springtime), vineyards and olive plantations that characterise the scenery between Fuente de Cantos and Mérida.

However, for the pilgrim starting his or her journey in Granada the landscape is far from flat and is, in fact, extremely hilly almost from the outset. The route (and the waymarking) begins at the Real Monasterio de las Madres Comendadores de Santiago in the old Realejo district of Granada and leads northwest through the hills via the hilltop fortress towns of Alcalá la Real, Alcaudete, Baena and Castro del Río to Córdoba (much of this section follows the Ruta del Califato, a long-distance footpath following a historic route, in reverse). The route passes through seemingly endless olive plantations where you will hardly see anybody at all: nowadays all the work is done by one or two people on tractors, in contrast to former times when veritable armies of *braceros* (day labourers) performed the tasks by hand. The landscape in the first part of the route in particular (where you may see eagles if you are attentive) is dotted about with small fortresses and lookout towers on its hilltops, but because of the nature of the terrain you do not have the vast, distant, map-like panoramic views that characterise the flatter route from Seville to Astorga. After Córdoba the *camino* continues via Cerro Muriano through the Sierra Morena to Alcaracejos, after which the landscape opens out, becoming a lot flatter, before passing through pasture and then agricultural land to Hinojosa del Duque,

Castuera and Don Benito. From there it continues through the fortress town of Medellín, where it crosses the seventeenth-century bridge over the Río Guadiana. After that the pilgrim reaches Mérida where, as indicated above, he or she can join the main Vía de la Plata and continue on from there to Santiago. The route from Granada, unlike (normally) that from Seville, also requires the fording of several rivers and large streams, wide but shallow.

By the time the pilgrim approaches Cáceres (whose temperatures can rise to $50°C$ in the summer) the terrain becomes more barren, several castles are visible in the distance and the Vía de la Plata crosses the two big rivers (the Almonte and the Tajo) that combine to form the Embalse de Alcántara (a very large reservoir). The route continues to climb, up to the Puerto de Cañaveral and through the walled town of Galisteo, after which the landscape changes again for a while; it is a well-irrigated area planted with tobacco and sunflowers and with brick barns and farm buildings not encountered elsewhere. The *camino* leaves the province of Cáceres just after the spa town of Baños de Montemayor with its traditional *balneario*. ('Taking the waters' is not, perhaps, a phenomenon the reader would initially associate with Spain but there are, in fact, many such places in the provinces of Salamanca, Ourense and parts of northern Portugal.)

After crossing the border between the *regiones autónomas* of Extremadura and Castille-León (this is one of the

Arcaded village street, Calzada de Béjar

largest, with nine provinces), just below the Puerto de Béjar, the pilgrim will notice that the style of house-building has altered. The white-painted houses have disappeared, for the most part, and the adobe or stone constructions which replace them have wooden exterior balconies running along them at first floor level. It is here, too, that you will begin to encounter public fountains and *lavaderos* (places to launder clothes, often on two levels, the lower pool to wash, the upper to rinse) in the villages. You will see *cruceiros* (wayside stone crosses) there too and as you cross the wide, high, flattish plateau land between here and Salamanca (at nearly 800m) you will see large herds of jet black and dark grey cattle, as well as brown ones, all with enormous horns, grazing to either side of the *camino*. By this time, too, the linguistically-observant pilgrim

will have noticed several placenames whose composition includes 'del Camino,' 'Calzada de' or 'Calzadilla de', indicating the passage of an important route and thus the line of Roman and pilgrim roads.

After Salamanca the route passes through the area known as the Tierra del Vino which, as its name suggests, is reputed for its wine production. Beyond Zamora, after crossing the Duero, it enters the Tierra del Pan, with its seemingly endless undulating cornfields, reaching into infinity and beyond. However, those who continue north from here, via Benavente and La Bañeza to Astorga, will find, after crossing the Puente de la Vizana and entering the province of León, that the scenery changes dramatically, with its lush green fields well watered by an extensive system of irrigation canals. Those who

Camino in the Tierra del Pan (photo: author)

opt to go via Puebla de Sanabria and Ourense, on the other hand, will not encounter much change until they reach Mombuey, when the oak and chestnut woods begin, the terrain becomes very hilly and they find themselves, in spirit if not yet in fact, in Galicia.

After the hilltop town of Puebla de Sanabria and the passes of Padornelo (1350m) and A Canda (1250m), the Vía de la Plata leaves the province of Zamora and the autonomous *región* of Castille-León and enters Galicia, comprised of the provinces of Lugo, Ourense (which you enter here), Pontevedra and La Coruña. It has its own language (not a dialect), related to Portuguese, and which together with *castellano* (Spanish) is used as an official language in the región. As a result you will find that not only will people reply to you in *gallego* but that all road signs, official notices and so on appear in both languages. The spelling of place names often varies between the two languages, however, and as at present the *castellano* forms have not yet been officially standardised, the names you see on maps and notices may differ from those you see on signposts and on entry to villages big enough to have place name boards. Some of the more common phonetic differences between the two languages, such as the interchange of 'e' and 'ei' and 'o' and 'ue', are given in the glossary in Appendix D, together with other linguistic information the pilgrim may find useful.

Galicia is a very verdant area for the most part, with the highest rainfall in Spain. Unlike the south of Spain with its enormous *latifundios* (very large properties), the land in Galicia is divided (and subdivided) into tiny, often uneconomic individual holdings *(minifundios)*, the result of centuries of sharing out land among its owner's descendants. As a result you will frequently see people working in the fields (many of whom are women) doing tasks by hand that would elsewhere be done more economically by machine. Unlike Andalucia, Extremadura and Castille-León, where villages are often very far apart but whose buildings are tightly concentrated together, those in Galicia (the *aldea* or hamlet rather than a full-blown *pueblo*) are often tiny, not far from each other and much more spread out so that you are not usually very far from a building of some kind. The region is also criss-crossed with a veritable maze of *corredoiras* (old green lanes), which wend their way through fields separated from each other by dry stone walls or stone boundaries made of large slabs set on end, like rows of giant teeth, so that without some kind of waymarking system this *camino* would be almost impossible to follow.

Traditional vernacular architecture is also much more evident in Galicia than on the earlier part of the route and as well as innumerable fountains and *lavaderos* (not infrequently still in use), one of the characteristic features of its countryside is the *hórreo*. This is a long rectangular granary, of stone or sometimes brick, raised up on pillars and used for storing potatoes and

33

Punta da Barca, Muxía (photo: author)

corncobs. They have slightly pitched roofs with a cross at one end and a decorative knob at the other. *Hórreos* vary greatly in length, from those that are only 3–4m long to enormous structures with two or three compartments and that stretch for 20–30m; all of them are listed buildings, though, so that if they need to be removed (e.g. for road building) they have to be sold, dismantled and then set up again elsewhere. (You may see one from time to time with a *'Se Vende'* – 'for sale' – notice on it.) On this part of the route you will also encounter innumerable *cruceiros* (wayside crosses) with sculptures on one or both sides on the cross itself and often other figures or decoration on the shaft, small stone bridges, houses with a *patín* (stone outside staircase with a landing halfway up to access the first-floor accommodation) and a number of *pazos* (large country manor houses; the Pazo de Oca near Bandeira – open to the public – is worth a visit). There are also

villages which still retain their communal oven building, the occasional watermill in working order, a *galpón* (building used for holding local fairs under cover) and dozens of often very tiny granite Baroque-style churches. And in the area between Verín and Ourense you will also see the hilltop remains of several fifteenth and sixteenth-century fortified castles.

Due to its location Galicia remained isolated from the influence of much of what was happening to the rest of Spain in former centuries and as a result retains evidence of its Celtic origins. There were many *castri* in the area around Xinzo de Limia, traces of which can still be detected, while traditional Galician music uses the *gaita* (bagpipe). (Anyone interested in the architecture, working life and customs of Galicia should visit the Museo do Pobo Galego when they reach Santiago.) Galicia is also a very heavily wooded area, many of the trees centuries old, and as a result is very pleasant to walk in, even in the height of summer. Unfortunately, however, in recent years, large areas of its forests have been devastated by an epidemic of huge fires, suspected to have been started deliberately but quite why or by whom no one seems to know. Those who continue on to Finisterre and Muxía will also see something of the Galician coastline, with its *rías*, the fiord-like inlets along the Atlantic from the border of Portugal to the province of Asturias on the Costa Verde.

PLANNING YOUR JOURNEY

As indicated, Seville to Santiago can be walked comfortably in six to seven weeks and Granada to Santiago in seven or eight, by anyone who is fairly fit, leaving plenty of time to visit places of interest along the way. Allow plenty of time when planning your itinerary, especially if you are not an experienced walker. Those starting in Seville and who are not experienced walkers or are not very fit have the advantage of being able to find accommodation at 20–25km stages, more or less as far as Mérida, so that by then, when you need to walk longer distances, you will already be fit and into the swing of things. Those who begin in Granada, as already indicated, will need to be fit *before* they start.

Try not to plan too tight a schedule but allow plenty of time and flexibility to account for unforeseen circumstances (pleasant or otherwise). Where

BEFORE YOU GO

a) Read up as much as you can about the route, its history, art, architecture and geography; a short bibliography is given in Appendix C.

b) Do not expect anybody – anybody at all – to speak English. You will have to communicate in Spanish all the time, for everything you need, however complicated, so if you are not already fairly fluent consider a year's evening classes or home study with tapes in your preparations: you will find life complicated if you are unable to carry out practical transactions and will feel very isolated on what is already a solitary route if you are also unable to converse with the Spanish pilgrims and other people you meet along the way. (Those without a reasonable command of Spanish will find the Granada–Mérida section particularly difficult.)

c) Decide what type of footwear you will be taking – for example, walking shoes, lightweight boots, heavy (thick-soled) trainers, and break them in before you go. Likewise, if you purchase a new rucksack for the journey, go out walking with it (fully laden) on as many occasions as you can before you set off.

EQUIPMENT

1. **Rucksack** At least 50 litres if carrying a sleeping bag.
2. **Footwear** Both shoes to walk in and a spare pair of lightweight trainers/sandals for rest periods.
3. **Waterproofs** Even in summer it may rain, especially in Galicia. A 'poncho' (cape with a hood and space inside for a rucksack) is far more useful (and far less hot) than a cagoule or anorak.
4. **Pullover/fleece** Much of the route is high up and as you go further north it can get cold at night, even in summer.
5. **First aid kit** (including a needle for draining blisters and scissors). The type of elastoplast sold by the metre is more useful than individual dressings.
6. High-factor **sunscreen** if you burn easily.
7. **Large water bottle** Carry at least two litres if walking in hot weather.
8. **Sleeping bag** Essential if staying in *refugios* or other very basic accommodation.
9. **Sleeping mat** Also essential for basic accommodation where you will have to sleep on the floor and useful for siestas in the open air.
10. **Stick/trekking poles** Useful for fending off/frightening dogs and testing boggy terrain.
11. **Guidebook**
12. **Maps**
13. **Compass**
14. **Torch**
15. **Sun hat** (preferably with wide brim)
16. **Small Spanish/English dictionary**
17. **Mug, spoon and knife**
18. If you are addicted to tea/coffee or can't get going in the morning without a hot drink a 'camping gaz' type **stove** is a great advantage, even though it will add extra weight to your luggage. This is especially useful in seasons when you will probably set out very early to avoid the heat, since although bars and cafés open early in Andalucía the further north you go the later they open, rarely before 8.30 or 9am except in big towns and, while in small places they may in fact be open, many bars in Castille-Léon and Galiciado not serve hot drinks until the early afternoon. (A few of the *refugios* along the route have cooking facilities but not all.) If you do take a camping gaz stove make sure it uses the 200g cylinders – smaller ones are not readily available in Spain.

Note: A **tent** is not worth the trouble as rooms are usually available (in bars, cafés) if you are not staying in the more basic accommodation, and campsites in Spain (of which there are few along the route anyway) can also be relatively expensive.

In general, travel as light as you can, not just for the weight but because of the long distances, the constant hills on the Granada–Mérida route, in Galicia and, according to the season, the heat.

and how many rest days you take is up to you (though Seville, Mérida, Cáceres, Salamanca, Zamora and Ourense are 'musts'), as is also whether you include several short days' walking in your programme, arriving at your destination during the late morning so as to have the remainder of the day completely free. If you are extremely tired, or having trouble with your feet, a complete day off works wonders (particularly in a small place with no 'sights' to be visited) and is well worth the seeming disruption to your schedule. Allow at least three days to visit Santiago at the end – there is plenty to see – and you may well meet up again with other pilgrims you encountered along the way.

THERE AND BACK

How to get there

Seville and Madrid: by air direct from London (the most practical option for cyclists) or by easyJet to Málaga from where there are frequent buses to Seville; by train from London via Paris; by coach direct from London. Seville can also be reached by bus from Madrid

and other parts of Spain.

Granada: The quickest and cheapest way to get there is to fly to Málaga with one of the budget airlines and then take the coach (frequent service). Otherwise you can fly to Madrid or Seville and continue by train or coach. There is also a Eurolines bus service from London, twice a week or more frequently, according to the season.

Other places along the Way (for those who are only doing a section) such as Córdoba, Mérida, Cáceres, Salamanca and Zamora are most easily reached by bus via Madrid.

How to get back from Santiago

Air: there are Iberia flights from Santiago to Heathrow, and Ryanair now flies from Santiago to Stansted. Otherwise go to Madrid or Bilbao by coach or train and fly from there.

Train: to Paris, leaves at 9am every day, arriving in Hendaye late evening, in time for the connecting train with the overnight for Paris, arriving early the following morning.

Coach: to Paris two to three times a week, depending on the time of year. This is a cheaper, comfortable and

Church of Nuestra Señora de Gracia, Almadén de la Plata

slightly shorter trip than the train journey. The journey takes 24 hours and arrives at the Porte de Bagnolet bus station from where you can continue to London. (You can no longer book straight through to London.)

Finally, a very pleasant but slower way to return (and with more time to 'come back down to earth') is to take the FEVE narrow-gauge railway along the north coast from El Ferrol to Bilbao; you can get more information about this from the tourist office in Santiago (note that the FEVE is not part of the RENFE network). You can then continue (from Bilbao) on the equally picturesque TOPO (mole) train to San Sebastián and Irún/Hendaye. (Cyclists: note that the RENFE regional trains and the FEVE are more bike-friendly than the mainline Talgo/AVE.)

BEING THERE

Accommodation

Various types of accommodation are available along the way, ranging from luxurious five-star hotels (such as the state-run *paradores* established in redundant historic buildings) down to very basic accommodation provided on the floor in community centres, former schools, sports halls and so on. As the availability of accommodation changes rapidly, however, it is suggested that you either contact the 'Amigos' in Seville for the latest information, particularly about the very basic variety, or obtain the Confraternity of St James's annually revised guides to all types of accommo-

dation on this route (see Appendix D for addresses).

Hotel usually implies a higher standard of accommodation than that found in a *hostal* which, in turn, normally offers more facilities than a *fonda* or *pensión* (*hospedaje* in Galicia) and a *casa huéspedes*. (*Residencia* after either hotel or *hostal* means it only provides accommodation: neither meals nor breakfast are available.) There are also an increasng number of *casas rurales* (CR) springing up along the way in country areas; these provide bed and breakfast, often an evening meal, but some of them have cooking facilities as well. (Do not confuse these establishments – moderately priced in the main – with a *hotel rural* (HR), a newer category of accommodation whose meals, in particular, are often very expensive.) A number of bars also provide rooms (*habitaciones* – *camas* means 'beds') so it is worth asking about these, even if there is no sign or notice to say so. However, a word of warning: if you intend to stay in any of these and want to leave early in the morning to avoid walking in the heat, make sure you arrange to pay the previous evening and retain your passport and check how you will actually get out of the building the following morning (which doors or entrances will be locked and how they can be opened), otherwise you may find yourself unable to leave until at least 9am. (Some former pilgrims have also suggested asking for rooms at the back of the building, or as high up as possible, in order to have a quieter night's rest.) Note too that you will find it difficult to find accommodation during the *semana santa* (the week before Easter Sunday), not only in places like Seville, Granada, Córdoba, Mérida, Cáceres and Zamora, which are well known for these celebrations, but elsewhere as well. (It is also almost impossible to find anywhere to stay in Zafra during the *feria* (agricultural fair), which lasts for the whole of September and the first week in October.) In general, the commercially available accommodation listed in this guide is at the middle to lower end of the market, especially where there is plenty of choice.

A *refugio* (also known as an *Albergue de Peregrinos* – not to be confused with either an *albergue municipal*, which is a night shelter for the itinerant homeless, or an *albergie turístico*, an establishment for tourists but often with a special pilgrim price) is simple accommodation set up especially for pilgrims on foot or by bike (but not for those accompanied by a back-up vehicle) and is only for those holding a *credencial* (see below). (This is to ensure that these facilities are not used by 'pseudo-pilgrims,' backpackers or other travellers.) *Refugios* are provided by churches, religious orders and *ayuntamientos* (town halls or local authorities) and are gradually being set up in different places along the route. At present there are such facilities in Castilblanco de los Arroyos, Zafra, Aljucén, Alcuéscar, Casar de Cáceres, Galisteo, Cañaveral, Grimaldo, Aldeanueva del Camino, Baños de

Montemayor, Calzada de Béjar, Fuenterroble de Salvatierra and Villanueva de Campeán on the route before Zamora. There are also *refugios* in Villabrázaro, Alija del Infantado, La Bañeza and Astorga itself on the Astorga option and in Tábara, Santa Croya de Tera, Lubían, A Gudiña, Laza, Vilar de Barrio, Xunqueira de Ambía, Veríin, Ourense, Cea, A Laxe and Capilla de Santiaquiño on the Ourense route. Note, however, that *refugios* are NOT provided as cheap substitutes for hotels but as alternatives to sleeping rough, places to shelter pilgrims from the elements, so you cannot expect anything more than that they are clean and that the facilities on offer work; there are few at present of the type found on the Camino Francés. In many other places there are places to sleep on the floor or on mattresses with a sleeping bag, with basic washing facilities, and these are indicated in the text as 'R&F' (roof and floor), though in several places they offer more than just that, so you cannot expect anything more than that they are clean and that the plumbing works. Unlike hotels and *pensiones*, however, you will not encounter any difficulty in leaving *refugios* early and will find too that other people are doing the same.

There are no *refugios* at all on the Granada–Mérida route at present, and few R&F facilities for individual pilgrims either, especially in places where a *hostal* or *pensión* exists and despite what you may be led to believe by consulting the website (see Appendix D). This information was prepared by the group who walked the route when it was first waymarked, who met the press, gave interviews and were put up, on a one-off basis, by churches, townhalls etc and were provided with facilities which are not normally at the disposal of the pilgrim walking to Santiago on his/her own. This will therefore be a more expensive route (at present, at least) than the main Vía de la Plata. However, if there are two or three (or more) of you and you speak good Spanish there are some places where you may be able to sleep, such as sports halls or other equivalent facilities, in a few places. Where pilgrims have reported such experiences or where contacts have been suggested this information is given in the relevant sections of this guide [in square brackets]. Be prepared, however, in some places, for it to be in night shelter-type facilities

Planning the day
Long-distance walkers in Britain usually operate on a 'nine-to-five' basis, leaving their accommodation shortly after breakfast and returning in time for an early evening meal. There may be few, if any, places of historical, religious or cultural interest directly on the path, such as churches, cathedrals or stately homes, that require a detailed indoor visit (as opposed to historic bridges, fortifications, market crosses and so on that can be inspected fairly quickly from the route); in addition, many places of interest are open only 'nine-to-five', so that combining walking and sightseeing is difficult. Walkers in Britain, in the

main, tend just to walk. In Spain, however, not only are there an enormous number of places well worth visiting along the Vía de la Plata of outstanding artistic, architectural, cultural or religious interest, but they are also open at convenient times for the walker: as well as being open from 10am to 1pm, they normally open again in the evenings from 4 or 5pm to 8pm or later. Churches in big towns are usually open all day, but elsewhere those in small villages are nearly always locked, unless there is a service in progress However, it is often possible to visit during Saturday afternoons, when they are being cleaned in preparation for Sunday.

In July and August it is *extremely* hot along the Vía de la Plata during the day, and there is very little shade – except in many areas of Galicia The best way to avoid walking in the heat is to get up before it is light and set out at daybreak (though not before, or you will not be able to see the way). At this time of day it is cool and pleasant, and pilgrims have the advantage of being able to enjoy the scenery in the early morning light. It is also a good idea, in large towns and other places of any size, to go for a walk in the evening and check the route by which you will leave, so as not to waste time or get lost the following morning.

Rivers There are several places in the section after Córdoba on the Granada–Mérida route where you will have to ford rivers or streams at a crossing place. Most of them are fairly shallow and can often be negotiated via stepping stones but if it has been raining heavily on the previous or preceding days you may have to wade across. If you do have to do so, make sure you either keep your boots/shoes on or pack a pair of sturdy sandals in your luggage for this purpose (and have them easily accessible). Do NOT cross in bare feet as you may not always be able to see sharp objects or detect how clean the water is and with a heavy rucksack it is easy to over-balance If there is a strong current remember, too, to check first where you will 'land' on the other side as you may be taken further downstream that you expect This is not normally a problem on the Seville–Astorga section but given the numbers of streams and rivers in other parts of the route it may be worth considering taking a stick (e.g. a telescopic one), even though you may not normally use one, to test depth of water, current and to balance you better while crossing.

OTHER PRACTICAL INFORMATION

Shops (for food)

These are usually open from 9 or 10am and 2pm and then again between 5 and 8pm or later. In small villages they may be unmarked and you will have to ask where they are (though in such places bars often double up as shops) and in parts of Galicia, in particular, you will encounter mobile food shops as well as the bakers' vans found in most other parts of the route, all of which honk their

horns loudly to announce their arrival in the village centre. Except for large super-markets in some big towns, food shops close on Saturday afternoons and all day Sunday though bakers are often open on Sunday mornings if you can find them: there is usually only one in each village or district, they may not always be marked and may only have a small entrance on the street leading to the large baking area behind. The (mauve and yellow) *tabaco* logo on a building in a small place usually indicates that there is also a food and possibly a general store inside as well.

Meals

These are available between 2 and 3.30 or 4pm for lunch and 9 to 11pm for evening dinner, though you will find that in Galicia you can often be served as early as 1pm and 8pm respectively. However, as many bars in bigger places also provide *tapas* (different kinds of snack, both hot and cold) as well as *bocadillos* (sandwiches), you need not go hungry if you are feeling ravenous outside regular mealtimes (such places are referred to in the text as 'bar with simple food'). Breakfast in hotels and similar accommodation is rarely avail-able before 9am though in bars in Andalucía you can usually find *tostada*s and other things to eat as early as 6.30am Note, however (and this is customary in the rest of Spain – but not on the Camino Francés), the *menú del día* (fixed price menu) is often only avail-able at lunchtime in restaurants in small places (and not on Sundays either) so if you take your main meal in the evening it may be more expensive. Alternatively, you may prefer to have two breakfasts and eat your main meal at midday if you want to go to bed early at night.

Cafés and bars

These often close very late but do not normally open before 8.30 or 9am and in small villages do not always serve hot drinks all day. Remember that in Spain a *cafetería* is not a self-service restaurant but a bar that also serves things to eat for breakfast, such as cake, *tostadas* (toast with olive oil, tomato, jam or dripping, for example), sandwiches or hot *tapas*. And if you are wondering why the *hogar del pensionista* (old people's day centre) is indicated in a book of this nature, this is because, in small places, it may be the only place to get a drink and/or a snack: even if they have very few facilities for their clients there will always be a bar inside. You will also find bars in many sports centres and swimming pools and at least one in every village you pass through except in the very small ones in Galicia, though they may not always be marked. You will also find that many bars along the Vía de la Plata do not serve food or sandwiches, as they almost always do on the Camino Francés (where many of their customers are pilgrims) unless they are a restaurant as well; the vast majority of people who frequent the bars on the Vía de la Plata are local – they eat at home and so only go out to drink.

Water

There are few public fountains on the Seville–Astorga section of the Vía de la Plata, though they are fairly frequent on the Granada–Mérida route. Those left running permanently are usually safe to drink from (watch out for local people filling jugs and other containers at mealtimes as spring water tastes better than the chlorinated tap water) *Agua (non) potable* means that it is (isn't) safe to drink, and *agua non tratada* indicates that it is chlorine-free. Petrol stations on main roads are indicated in the text as they usually sell cold drinks, chilled (bottled) water and, sometimes, limited food.

As well as carrying plenty of water with you, make sure you drink plenty as well. When walking in hot weather it is important to avoid becoming dehydrated. It is difficult to do, but try to drink at least half a litre when you get up in the morning, as well as any tea/coffee you may have, as in this way you will be less likely to become dehydrated. Keep drinking at regular intervals, even if you don't think you are thirsty, because if you do get dehydrated it will then be too late to do anything about it, even if you have supplies with you. The best cure, when available, is large quantities of very hot drinks (e.g. herbal tea) and a lengthy bath/shower.

Prices

These have not been given in each individual entry but, in general, in 2004 a set-price *menú del día* cost between 6 and 9 Euros and a single room between

12 and 18 Euros per night in a basic *hostal* or *pensión*.

Changing money

Banks are only open from 8.30am until 2pm and only on Saturday mornings in large towns. However, there are cash dispensers (*cajeros automáticos,* indicated in he text as 'CD') in most places of any size and which accept a wide selection of cards. It is also possible to change money in post offices displaying the Deutsche Bank sign. In general, make sure you always have plenty of small change on you, both for drinks in small bars and for *donativos* in *refugios*.

Post offices

Apart from very large towns, where they are open continuously from 8.30 or 9am to 8pm or later in the evenings, post offices (*Correos*) are usually open in the mornings only, though stamps (as well as single envelopes) can also be bought in *estancos* (tobacconists).

Poste restante

If you want to send things to yourself further along the route (such as maps and guides) or have people write to you, you can do this via the *poste restante* system whereby you collect your mail (on presentation of your passport) at the post office. This service called *lista de correos*, is free, and items are kept for you for a month before returning them to the sender. Address the letter/parcel to yourself, Lista de Correos, postal code and name

of town and province. (The most likely places you will need will be 41080 Sevilla, 18080 Granada, 14080 Córdoba, 06880 Mérida, 10080 Cáceres, 37080 Salamanca, 49080 Zamora, 32080 Ourense and 15780 Santiago de Compostela.) If you decide (while in Spain) that you have too much in your rucksack it is considerably cheaper to post it to yourself this way in Santiago than to send a parcel home to Britain. Make sure, however, when collecting such items, that the clerk looks not only under your surname (*apellido*) but also under your first name (*nombre*); as the Spanish system of surnames is different you may find your mail has been filed in the wrong place.

Telephones

In Spain (which has one of the most expensive telephone systems in Europe) phone boxes usually take both coins as well as phone cards (available in newsagents in denominations of 6 and 12 Euros). Most Spanish area codes (for fixed line phones) begin with a 9, which is included when calling from abroad. (Mobile phone numbers begin with a 6.) The emergency number for the Guardia Civil is 062. Telephone books (*guía telefonica*) are by province (white and yellow pages in separate books) and entries are then arranged by town or population centre so that it is easy to locate, for example, hotels and *fondas* in a specific place. Postcodes are also included, as well as street plans for the larger towns.

OTHER PRACTICAL INFORMATION

Public holidays

There are more of these (*días festivos*) than in Britain: January 1st, Good Friday, August 15th, November 1st, December 5th, 6th and 25th. There are also three others which are taken locally and therefore vary from one area to another (e.g. San Mateo in the province of Jaén and San José in Extremadura has a holiday on September 23rd) as well as (especially in August) the *fiestas* in honour of a town or village's own patron saint and which can last up to a week in some places. Shops, including those for food (and sometimes bars and bakeries too), will be closed on these occasions or open only in the mornings.

Stamps for pilgrim passports

Modern pilgrims who seek proof of their pilgrimage also carry a *credencial* (pilgrim 'passport') which they have stamped (with a *sello*) at regular intervals along the way (such as *refugios*, churches, town halls, the local police or the tourist office) and which they then present to the pilgrim office in Santiago to help them obtain their *compostela* or certificate of pilgrimage. (However, try not to get too many stamps from bars as the cathedral authorities there will not be impressed if it looks as though your pilgrimage has been nothing more than a very lengthy pub crawl!) More information about the pilgrim passport is available from the Confraternity of St James or from the 'Amigos' in Seville. Alternatively, *bona fide* pilgrims can obtain their *credencial* and first stamp from the Cathedral in Seville; the office

is in the Puerta de la Campanilla and is open Monday–Friday only, 11.00–14.00 and 14.00–19.00.

Pilgrims starting in Granada should note that the practice of obtaining *sellos* is not yet so well-known as on either the Camino Francés or the main Vía de la Plata and as a result may well occupy quite a lot of your time.

Church services

Masses are usually held at 12 noon or 13.00 on Sundays, as well as on Saturday evening for Sunday. During the week there will normally be one at 8pm in places of any size and often at 8.30 or 9am too.

Dogs

Their owners nearly always tell you, 'he won't hurt you', though this is often hard to believe. They may tell you, too, that it is the rucksack that bothers them (and as dogs are reputed to see only in black and white there may be some truth in this, faced with mysterious humpback monsters on two legs) but it is not much comfort when faced with an aggressive one. They come in all shapes and sizes, live all along the route from Seville and Granada to Santiago, usually running around loose, hear you ages before you have any idea where they are and are often enormous (though the small ones are, in fact, a greater nuisance, as they have a nasty habit of letting you pass quietly by and then attacking from behind, nipping you in the back of your ankles). A stick is very useful, even though you might not normally want to

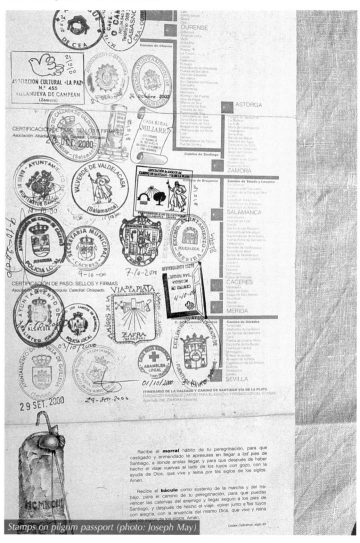

Stamps on pilgrim passport (photo: Joseph May)

46

walk with one – not to hit them with but to threaten. When you do meet them keep on walking at a steady pace (but do not run) and if you see flocks of sheep apparently alone give them a wide berth as they will be accompanied if not by two then certainly by four-legged guardians.

Remember, too, that though they may, in many cases, appear to be safely out of your reach, if there is a gap or hole in the fencing somewhere they will know exactly where it is and come rushing out to 'greet' you...

Road walking
In the short stretches that require walking on busy roads, remember to walk on the left, facing the oncoming traffic, though you will have to use your discretion if you encounter sharp bends that could obscure you from view.

Road signs
Brown for natural features (rivers, reservoirs) and purple for historic monuments.

Spectacles
If you wear glasses it may be a good idea to carry a spare pair or at least your prescription with you in case you lose/break them.

Waymarking
The route described in this book starts either at the cathedral in Seville or at the Real Monasterio de las Madres Comendadores de Santiago, in the old Realejo district of Granada, and ends at the cathedral in Santiago de Compostela (following the direction of the (modern) pilgrimage). It is described in one direction only. Those who would like to walk the route in reverse or return on foot will therefore find it extremely difficult – although the white waymarking in reverse, mentioned earlier, would help in the Seville–Astorga section, as would indications in the text such as 'track joins from back L', which are redundant for those walking only towards Santiago but helpful for the person going in reverse and faced with a choice of paths to select.

Waymarking *(señalización)* is in the form of yellow arrows *(flechas)*, familiar to those who have walked the Camino Francés, painted on tree trunks, walls, road signs, rocks, the ground, sides of buildings and so on, and are normally extremely easy to spot. They appear at frequent intervals, and the walker will not usually encounter any difficulty following them If, at any time, they seem to have disappeared, wherever you may be, this will normally be because you have inadvertently taken a wrong turning; retrace your steps to the last one you saw and start again from there, checking carefully. (Sections where it is known that waymarking is poor are indicated in the text.) In the provinces of Badajoz and Cáceres the Junta de Extremadura has positioned 400 granite 'camino cubes' with direction markers all along their 'patch,' from the entrance to Monesterio to the border of Castille-

*One of the 400 granite cube waymarks
in Extremadura (photo: author)*

Léon after Baños de Montemayor. In the province of Zamora the Fundación Ramos de Castro has placed terracotta information plaques in villages along the way, all in the same general style but each one explaining details about the history of the route in that particular area. In Galicia, in addition, there are standardised concrete marker stones, about the size of old-fashioned milestones, bearing an embossed conch-shell design and positioned at places where you make a manoeuvre from the path you are already on. In the province of Ourense there are also special carved slabs made by the local artist Carballo, with the stylised figure of a pilgrim indicating changes of direction; there are over a hundred of these, but although each one is slightly different they all have a common, easily recognisable style.

Pilgrims who start in Granada will find that, in a landscape often lacking in trees, buildings and convenient places to put yellow direction arrows, a large 'X' (also in yellow paint) is used at times to indicate the option you should NOT take Note, too, that from Córdoba onwards, and with the exceptions of Seville, La Bañeza and Ourense, on the main route there is no (systematic) waymarking in towns or other urban areas – though with the detailed route descriptions given in this guide (including the names of all the streets to take) you should have no problems in such places.

In general you will need to be more alert to waymarking on the Vía de la Plata than you may well have been on the Camino Francés.

Maps

Maps are a problem in Spain. It would be possible to follow the Vía de la Plata just with the waymarks and this guide but that would be very limiting. Maps are useful not merely as a means of finding the way when lost but also for situating the walk in the context of its surroundings and for making any diversions the walker might wish to make to visit places of interest within striking distance of the route. At present there are no comprehensive, up-to-date Spanish equivalents of the Ordnance Survey maps of Britain available for the whole country, though work on updating the existing 'military maps' is underway, and it is for this reason that sketch maps of the route are included with this text. To situate yourself generally, however (though not to walk from), three maps in the Michelin 1:400,000 (1cm to 4km) dark orange series are recommended: 578 (Andalucía), 576 (Extremadura, Castilla-La Mancha, Madrid) and 571 (Galicia). These cover the entire route (with street plans of large towns) apart from a 20km section just south of Zamora; if you want to include that section as well you will need 575 (Castilla-Léon) too. Such Spanish maps as are available in Britain can be purchased from, for example, Stanford's map shop in London, The Map Shop in Upton-upon-Severn, or from some of the larger general bookshops.

49

Textual description

Each section begins with the distance walked from the previous one, a description of the facilities available, a brief history, where applicable, and an indication of the places of interest to visit. (Pilgrims wishing to spend time in any of the larger towns should obtain information leaflets and a street plan from the local tourist office.) The text is – deliberately – not divided up into stages as in this way the walker (or cyclist) can decide for him or herself the distances he or she would like to cover each day. The figures after each place name heading indicate the height in metres where known and, in parentheses, the distance in kilometres from both Seville and Santiago via Ourense; the continuation from Granja de Moreruela to Astorga has just the totals going forwards – not in reverse – while those on the Granada–Mérida section refer to the distances left and to go between these two towns. Thus, for example, on the main Vía de la Plata, Santiponce is 10km from Seville and 990km from Santiago. In the case of large towns (Mérida, Cáceres, Salamanca, for instance), the distances to/from them start/end in their centres, normally at the cathedral. When a series of manoeuvres is given in quick succession this means that there is little space between them and for this reason distances are not given. Timings have not been given from place to place but 4km per hour, exclusive of stops, is often considered average, especially when carrying a heavy rucksack. However, a comfortable pace may often be more than this – a fit walker may well be able to maintain a speed of 5–6km or 3 miles per hour.

The term 'cross' used when referring to a river or stream means that there is a bridge for you to use. 'Ford,' on the other hand, means that there is not and that you will either have to use stepping stones or wade across.

Several parts of the route that were described as a 'track' or *camino de tierra* in the first edition of this guide have now been tarmacked, a process that is (unfortunately for the pilgrim) likely to continue. The descriptions given in the present guide were correct at the time it was prepared but the author cannot – obviously – be responsible for recent changes.

Place names

The names of towns and villages are in **green bold** type in green boxes, while other names that help in wayfinding (hamlets, street names, prominent buildings) appear in the text in **bold**. Route finding instructions are in normal type but introductory text is found in green boxes and more descriptive text is in *italics*. Note that 'river' in Spain rarely implies a wide, deep, fast-flowing stretch of navigable water such as the Guadalquivir or the Duero: many, if not actually dried up, are no more than narrow trickles at the bottom of a wide riverbed and may be non-existent at certain times of the year. The word *camino* refers to the Camino de Santiago. Some vernacular terms indicating features passed along the way (such as *hórreo, lavadero, cruceiro, ermita)* have been retained in the original since translation of such vocabulary is cumbersome and an English word does not always convey the exact equivalent.

In Galicia spellings of place names may vary: Galician spellings may be used on signposts, for example, and/or Castilian on maps. If versions given in this guide appear inconsistent at times, this is because they are based on those seen on street and place name boards and signposts encountered along the way, not on those found on maps or in other guidebooks (and for this reason the Galician term is often the one provided).

Abbreviations

These have been kept to a minimum. L indicates that you should turn/fork left, R that you should turn/fork right, (L) and (R) mean that something you pass is to your left or right, LH = left hand, RH = right hand, KSO = keep straight on, > = becomes, becoming, rte = restaurant, CD = cash dispenser, HT = high tension, // = parallel, km = kilometre, KM = kilometre marker (found on the sides of all main roads), FB = footbridge, FP = footpath. N followed by a number (such as N630) refers to the number of a main road, C (or the first two initials of the province you are in, such as ZA = Zamora) to a local road, RENFE is the abbreviation for the Spanish national railway network, s/n after a street name in an address means *sin número* (the establishment in question does not have a number, either because the street is

very short or because the building – bank, museum, big hotel, for example – is extremely large).

Appendices

For those who feel that their pilgrimage would be incomplete unless they continued to Finisterre/Muxía a description of this route is given in Appendix A. Other appendices contain a summary of Santiago and pilgrim references in places along the way (B), a bibliography with a list of suggestions for further reading (C), useful addresses (D, both web and postal), a glossary of geographical and other frequently encountered terms (E) and an index of principal place names (F).

Finally...

Unlike pilgrimages to Lourdes, Fatima or other locations where miracles are sought and help for specific problems requested and where being in the pilgrim destination itself is the most important factor, on the Vía de la Plata/Camino Mozárabe it is the making of the journey itself that is the pilgrim's principal concern, the arrival in Santiago being only a conclusion to the rest of the undertaking. The route is practicable, though not necessarily recommended, all through the year (and definitely NOT in July and August if you are starting in Seville or Granada, when the temperatures will be at least 40 degrees Centigrade and frequently exceed 50 degrees in Córdoba and Cáceres). It is also suggested that you avoid the *Semana Santa* (the week leading up to

Seville Cathedral, north façade

Easter) as accommodation will be extremely difficult at that time. In winter the days are short, it is often very windy on the southern part of the route and it rains a lot in Galicia. The weather may be dry over much of the route through Extremadura and Castilla-León but as a lot of it is quite high up (Salamanca, for instance, is at over 760m though the area around it is more or less flat) it gets very cold, with a biting wind. If you are not restricted to a particular time of year the end of March to the middle of June or the autumn are best – dry, but not as hot as in summer, and accommodation is also much less crowded. Traditionally, of course, as many people as possible aimed to arrive in Santiago for the festivities on July 25th, St James's day, particularly in Holy Years. Many still do.

¡Ultreya!

Seville 12m, 650,000 (0/1000)
The fourth-largest city in Spain, the Híspalis of Roman times, situated on the Río Guadalquivir. All facilities; international airport, RENFE, buses to all parts of Spain. Accommodation in all price brackets but no *refugio* or other specifically pilgrim facilities (note that the nuns in the Hospedeía Santa Rosalia, Calle Cardenal Spinola, no longer accept pilgrims). Tourist office at Avenida de la Constitución 21.

  The Asociación de Amigos del Camino de Santiago, who issue the special Vía de la Plata credenciales ('pilgrim passports' – their address and contact details can be found in Appendix D) have information sessions where you can obtain either this credencial or other up-to-date information about the route. Alternatively you can get this 'passport' (and/or the first stamp in it) from the cathedral office, entering by the Puerta de las Campanillas (M–F only, 11.00–14.00 and 16.00–19.00).

Virgen de Macarena in Basilica, Seville

Santiago statue on west façade of **Seville Cathedral**

Try to spend at least one whole day here. The major monuments include the cathedral, the Giralda, the Alcázar and gardens, Pilate's House, the Santa Cruz quarter. The best way to see Seville is on foot (ask at tourist office for map with walking tour and for details of combined ticket giving entry to principal monuments). Santiago and pilgrim references include a painting of St James (Juan de Roelas) in Capilla de Santiago in Cathedral Santa María de la Sede (north aisle), statue of San Roque in chapel of Hospital de la Caridad and statue of St James the Pilgrim in the frame of the cathedral's west portal (opposite which you will find your first waymark on a lamp post).

A word of warning: Seville is notorious for its thieves and pickpockets.

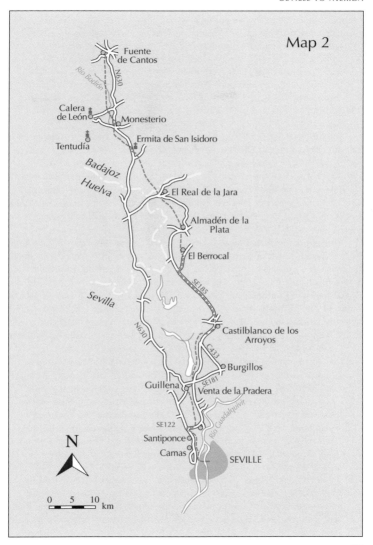

Map 2

Fuente
de Cantos

Río Bodión

N630

Calera
de León

Monesterio

Ermita de San Isidoro

Tentudía

Badajoz

Huelva

El Real de la Jara

Almadén de la
Plata

El Berrocal

SE185

Sevilla

N630

Castilblanco de los
Arroyos

C433

Burgillos

Guillena

SE181

Venta de la Pradera

Río Guadalquivir

SE122

Santiponce

Camas

SEVILLE

N

0   5   10 km

On your first day there are **two possibilities**:

  a) you can walk from Seville to Santiponce (10km) in the late afternoon/early evening, with time to visit the Roman city of Italica (closed on Mondays) without your rucksack and then return by bus (frequent service) to Seville (Plaza de Armas bus station, by river) to sleep. This section is very industrial, not very scenic, and this option would enable you to walk on to Castilblanco de los Arroyos (42km from Seville) the following day.

  b) you can leave Seville in the morning and walk to Guillena (23km), a short day with time to visit Italica en route.

Starting from the cathedral and with your back to it, cross the **Avenida de la Constitución**, go down **Calle García Vinuesa**, *marked with the first of many plaques with a stylised star: follow the direction of the head (they are angled accordingly) of the star and not the spread out 'fingers'.* Turn first R into **Calle Jimios**, forking L. Continue ahead on **Calle Zaragoza** (veering slightly L) to the end (well waymarked). Turn L into the **Avenida de los Reyes Católicos** to the end. Cross the **Paseo de Cristóbal Colón** and continue over **Puente Isabel II**, crossing the **Río Guadalquivir** into the Triana district (note *azulejos* – blue ceramic tiles – on buildings).

Continue to the **Plaza Altozano** and then turn R on the other side into **Calle Jorge**, R into **Plaza del Callao** and L into **Calle Castilla**, a very long street, crossing the **Ronda de Triana** and passing to the L of the church of the **Virgen del Patrocinio** *(visits 10.30–13.30 and 18.00–21.30)*. At the end, before a LH bend, cross a slabbed area (**Plaza Hermanos Cruz Solis**) and turn R up a flight of steps. Cross both sides of **Avenida Carlos III**, turn L on the other side and then turn R. 100m later turn L to a car park office and continue diagonally R towards an electricity pylon and then past floodlights in order to turn L onto a minor road and cross a bridge over the other half of the **Río Guadalquivir**.

On the other side **you have two options** (both waymarked):

  a) The original *camino* went through **Camas**, now a suburb of Seville, 5km away (but apart from the Hostal Cruce on the N630 and despite its name it has nowhere to sleep). If you want to go there (*shops, bars, banks*) continue ahead along a track, go under the E803 and KSO(L) on a bike/pedestrian track which leads you directly to its centre. Turn R (**Calle José Payan**) and KSO past a supermarket. Fork L at the church of **Santa María de Gracia** (opposite the *ayuntamiento*). Continue on the road to Santiponce and then proceed as in b) below. *(Hostal El Madera is midway between Camas and Santiponce, on LH side of road.)*

  b) The other (main) option is much quieter but neither more scenic nor any shorter, taking you away from the road and nearer to the river. In winter, however, this alternative is likely to be flooded as the area near the river is very low-lying. For this option fork R down the slope, immediately after crossing the bridge, past a building marked 'Aljarafesa Ebar Camas', go over a bridge over a canal and continue on a wide earth track // to the river. *No shade at all in this section. Former wasteland now planted with cotton fields.*

Continue // to the river for 1km and then turn L and then diagonally R to pass to RH side of a *finca* and then turn L *(lots of dogs!)* on to an untarred road. Continue on it *(suburb of Camas ahead to L)*. Go under the motorway and KSO ahead, veering slightly R, passing a *campo de tiro* (rifle range) and go under a railway bridge. KSO on other side (road now tarmacked) – *more cotton fields on either side* – towards the **Monasterio de San Isidro** *(now visible ahead, 1km)*.

Note: large-scale roadworks have been underway recently, resulting in possible minor changes to the camino.

Continue for 1km, pass a house on L called 'Mi Ranchito' and reach a junction with the N630. Turn L, go under the N630 (signposted 'Italica') and cross a slip road to the N630. KSO ahead to a roundabout and petrol station (at entrance to Santiponce). Turn R (signposted 'Italica' – monastery is now on your R) and enter

10km Santiponce 16m (10/990)
Shops, bars, bank (+CD), Hotel Ventorillo Canario opposite entrance to Italica. Site of Roman city of Italica, founded in AD 206, with Roman theatre on outskirts (city buses from Seville terminate here, half-hourly or more frequent service in the week, hourly on Sundays). Monasterio de San Isidoro has now been restored and visits possible.

Continue past the monastery (R) and public garden (**Avenida de Extremadura**). Turn R at a T-junction and continue ahead, passing the ruins of **Italica** on L. KSO to the junction (800m) with the N630, veering R. Cross it (carefully) and continue ahead on the other side on the SE 182 in the direction of 'La Algaba, 3'. Go under the motorway bridge, cross the slip road on the other side, fork L immediately onto a track by a group of some 15–20 tall trees and then turn L, just before a disued bridge, onto a *camino de tierra* through fields.

Here you have a choice, though neither of the options offer any shade:
a) *Walkers (only):* Fork R by gateposts and KSO on track, // to but not next to river to your R to start with. *This is a quieter option but may be boggy after rain.* Continue and after 500m reach a ravine with a broken concrete bridge *(may be boggy here)*. KSO ahead on other side, picking up a FP alongside field to your L. 300m later KSO ahead across track (agricultural buildings to L). KSO for 2km more, sometimes closer to the river, sometimes farther away from it, then veering L to walk between fields on both sides. *(Note: the village over to the R ahead is NOT Guillena.)*

When you get to a T-junction at end of very long fenced-in field turn L onto slightly bigger track. 1km later reach another T-junction by a small bridge and turn R: this is where you join the cyclists' option, after which the two continue as a single route.

b) **Cyclists** *(and also walkers in wet weather)*: KSO (literally) at gate posts along a wide track between fields, undulating slightly, passing a large concrete tower/chimney after 3km, just after crossing a river *(the walkers' route joins from R at the previous crossing)*. **Note:** if it has rained heavily the ford across the river may be completely waterlogged and too deep to cross. If so, turn L alongside field by river, which gets gradually narrower, until you can find a suitable crossing place, after which you will have to retrace your steps to the concrete tower/chimney.

3km after that reach a T-junction and turn R *(Guillena visible ahead)*. 400m later turn L alongside a fenced-in plantation of orange trees on a track leading to a (usually) nearly dried-up river. Cross it via stepping stones (**cyclists** dismount). *After heavy rain, however, this river may also be too wide to cross. If so, turn L alongside the field by the river until you reach the main road and turn R along it into Guillena.* Turn L on the other side and continue on a wide track between plantations of trees and under electric cables, leading past a cemetery (R) and along **Calle Portugalete** into

> ### 13km Guillena 22m (23/977)
> All facilities, banks (+CD), hotel. Hostal-Bar Francés (955.78.51.77) on main road to west side of town has rooms. R&F in sports centre (ask Policía local for key). Fifteenth-century church of Nuestra Señora de la Granada.

Continue ahead (**Calle Real**), passing **Plaza de España** and the *ayuntamiento*, to a church. Continue ahead to its RH side (**Calle Echegary**). Continue ahead again, passing a sports centre and after a new sports hall turn R to a river (**Río Rivera de Huelva** – *the original crossing place for the Camino de Santiago*).

Cross the river via a causeway and then veer R and then L on a wide track leading you to the road just before the **Venta de la Pradera** (3km). *(Note: The road bridge was closed for repairs at the time this edition was prepared and the waymarked route missing; normally you can continue on LH bank of river and turn R over it and continue on road to roundabout by the Venta de la Pradera.)*

> ### 3km Venta la Casa de Pradera (26/974)
> Bar/mesón (open early).

From here to Castilblanco **cyclists** *will need to dismount in some sections. Otherwise they should continue on SE181 to Burgillos then turn L there onto C433.*

If you forded the river, cross the SE181 (road to Burgillos) and then turn L into the **Poligono Industrial El Cerro**, along the **Calle Diprasa**. Veer R at the end and then turn L to cross bridge over stream, continuing on earth track, with orange plantations to R and olive groves to L. *This is the start of the Vía Pecuria Cañada Real de las Islas, 16km long, and which goes to Castilblanco de los Arroyos, with undulating countryside but little shade.*

After 5km reach a *cledo* with a cattlegrid and a notice board telling you about the *cañada*. KSO ahead on a clear track and KSO 1km later when track joins from R. 1km after that KSO(R) at fork and then KSO(L) 500m later at another (fork). 500m after that KSO(R) at fork. *After the gate you walk through encina plantations but then through cistus bushes and increasingly rocky terrain.* 500m later track joins from back L. KSO ahead, forking R (*not steeply left ahead, uphill*) and 500m after that KSO(R) at fork.

4–5km after the first *cledo* go through a second one (also with a cattle grid) then 1.5km after that go through two more *cledos* and KSO. 1.5km later reach gravel road coming from L. Turn R along it for 1km to the Burgillos–Castilblanco road and turn L along this for 4km. *(A FP is waymarked on the RH side for most of the way, apart from where the verge is too narrow.)* Emerge near a small roundabout just before the **Hotel Castilblanco**.

After passing the hotel (on your R), reach another roundabout where you can **a)** turn L into the town itself, veering R into its centre, along **Avenida de España**, or **b)** KSO(R) to petrol station (on R) which has the *refugio* behind it.

Pastureland in the springtime, near Castilblanco de los Arroyos

Note: if you sleep in the *refugio* you do not need to enter the town to continue the following morning. Instead you can KSO down the road (**Avenida Antonio Machado**), veering L at the bottom to continue on the SE 185, the **Carretera de Almadén**.

16km Castilblanco de los Arroyos 329m (42/958)

Small town with all facilities. Hotel Castilblanco, Pensión Salvadora (unmarked, 43 Avenida España). Bar Isidoro, Avenida de la Paz, does food, as does Bar Reina on main road. *Refugio* located behind petrol station on main road at entrance to village (ask there for key and pilgrim stamp). Sixteenth-century Iglesia del Divino Salvador. Castilblanco formerly had a pilgrim hospital and a Cofradía (a religious congregation devoted to the welfare of pilgrims).

If you have gone into the town, continue down **Avenida de España** then along **Calle Costanillas** and **Calle Pilar Nuevo** and reach **Carretera de Almadén de la Plata**, opposite a large water trough marked 'Agua non potable'. Turn L onto the SE185, the **Carretera de Almadén**, and KSO for 16km(!), undulating, but more up than down until you reach a TV transmitter on L, just after road KM14; *little shade to walk in and few places to sit down. Cortijos to either side, often with elaborate entrance gates, so no other FPs or alternative paths.* After 16km reach the entrance to

---

16km El Berrocal (58/942)

A provincial nature reserve, dedicated to replanting of trees. The hexagonal 'sentry box' by gates, with seats, is a shady place to rest.) The *camino* (waymarked with usual yellow arrows) takes you through 13km of undulating woods, with no prominent features apart from three ruined houses, though several herds of deer are visible if you are attentive. However, the reward comes at the end when, after climbing a very steep hill, you suddenly arrive at two *miradores* (viewpoints) with splendid views in all directions. It is then only 1.5km down into Almadén de la Plata.

Cyclists, however, may prefer to continue on the road to Almadén de la Plata, though before making up their minds they should read through the next section carefully. The ride through El Berrocal is very quiet and pleasant, most of it on easily rideable tracks, but for the last kilometre up to the two *miradores* you will have to get off and push your bike up a VERY steep hill. The view from the top is probably worth it, though the descent the other side (1.5km) is also steep and you will need to walk

Entrance gates to El Berocal (photo: author)

part of the way down too. Alternatively, if you feel like walking up to see the view, you can do so from Almadén – the path is signposted from the town.

Turn R through the entrance gates and continue ahead on a small road. Pass a watch tower (L) and the turn-off to El Berrocal III (on R) and continue ahead, downhill, through cork plantations. 1km later go through the gates of the **Casa Forestal** and veer L towards large modern farm buildings. Pass to LH side of them, stay on the tarmac road and go through some gates.

Continue on the road, ignoring turns, for 2.5km to the valley bottom. Cross a causeway with concrete bollards, after which you start to climb again slightly and tarmac path gives way to gravel road 500m later turn L onto another causeway towards a deserted white concrete house on the hillside. Veer round to R, passing behind animal enclosures and continue ahead on a wide earth road, climbing steadily. 1km later the spruce plantations on the L give way to eucalyptus trees and you begin to descend again (gradually). 1km after that go through some very tall gates (kept open) onto open heathland with cistus bushes *(the ones that smell like church incense)*.

Continue ahead, climbing gradually, ignoring the first LH and RH forks. 1km later, at a fork of two equal paths, fork R ahead (the L one leads downhill). 400m later reach a junction with several paths and a tall gate; go through (use ladder at side if locked) and take the LH (grassy) path ahead. KSO, following the line of fence to your R all the time, climbing gradually *(**cyclists** may find this part a bit bumpy)*. Continue for 2km, after which the track climbs very steeply (cyclists dismount here), still following the line of the fence *(good views to rear)* Veer L, uphill all the time, away from the fence.

61

Do NOT take the clear track to L when you reach a crossing of tracks but continue ahead on a rocky path, more and more steeply, gradually veering L, diagonally uphill along the side of the hill all the time. When you reach a track coming up from the L turn hard R onto it, uphill, and 100m later reach the two

---

11km Miradores del Cerro del Calvario 550m (69/931)

Two viewpoints, like brick pulpits, with plunging view of Almadén de la Plata and the blue marble quarries (of Roman origin) to the north and the Sierra del Norte de Sevilla, that you have just come through, to the south. Splendid views in all directions. Cerro del Calvario was also, formerly, a place of religious cult.

Continue straight ahead, downhill on the other side, veering L. Follow the track down, go through *cledos* and turn R down a concrete lane continuing as a *camino de tierra*. Turn R at the bottom then immediately L along **Calle Olmo** then turn R at the end to **Plaza del Pilar** in

---

1.5km Almadén de la Plata 449m (70.5/929.5)

Small town with all facilities. Bar Casa Concha has rooms (954.73.50.43), as does Bar Las Macias (954.73.54.61). Albergue de Peregrinos on way out of town on in the direction of the cortijo Arroyo Mateos option (see below; key from tourist office, *ayuntamiento* or phone 954.73.50.25 or 625.41.00.00). Church of Nuestra Señora de Gracia; the *ayuntamiento*, with its clocktower, was built in early twentieth century behind façade of the former Ermita de Nuestra Señora de los Angeles. Here, as in many other small towns in the south, (bitter) orange trees line the streets, much as plane trees do in Britain. Almadén formerly had a church dedicated to Santiago.

From Almadén to El Real de la Jara you have two options. You can either continue all the way to El Real de la Jara on a quiet, undulating and fairly shady road with little traffic (**cyclists** should take this option) or go on paths, very hilly but quiet, through the **Dehesa Arroyo Mateos**, a cortijo (private estate), where the route is well waymarked. (It is no longer necessary to telephone the estate office the evening before as the gates are now opened each morning so that you can now both enter and leave the *cortijo* without any problem.)

---

a) *Road option*. Turn R in the centre of Almadén past **Plaza del Pilar** and KSO to end of town, passing a cemetery (on R). KSO on SE177 (= A463). After

10km KSO past a turn-off (on R) to Cazalla de la Sierra and enter **El Real de la Jara** via **Calle La Paz**.

b) *Dehesa Arroyo Mateos*. From the **Plaza del Pilar** continue ahead past the **Casa de la Cultura** and the **Policía local** (on R) and turn L along side of church *(Oficina Municipal de Turismo opposite its front door)* to square with the *ayuntamiento*. Continue up RH side of square and at next fork **a)** KSO(R) to continue or **b)** fork L into **Plaza de los Palmeros** to go to *refugio,* forking R at end (marked 'Santa Olalla') along **Calle Cervantes** (a very long street) and turn R after house no. 57 to the *refugio*.

To continue (i.e. having KSO(R) at fork) turn first R uphill out of town and pass to LH side of **Plaza de Toros** (bullring) on a walled lane. KSO(L) at fork, gradually downhill. At next crossing KSO ahead through some metal gates, veering R. KSO(L) by pond, go through another gate, pass to RH side of large orange house and turn R over new stone bridge. 200m later, by drain, with bollards on either side, turn L uphill through trees, veering R and then L, up and down. Go through another gate and KSO ahead, // to road that is now over to your R. *Shady section.* 200m later veer R in order to turn L along a very minor road that has just branched off (to the L) from the bigger one above. KSO, passing one of the by now familiar Camino de Santiago stone columns. Road > a *camino de tierra*.

1km later reach a junction with the **Colada de los Bonales** (a Vía Pecuaria) forks L. KSO(R) here, uphill, and 1km after that reach the

6.5km Dehesa Mateo Arroyo (77/923)

KSO ahead inside the estate, downhill, then turn hard R at junction downhill again, passing a long water trough (on your R) and then passing to the RH side of a white house. Continue very steeply down to stream in valley bottom (probably dry), veering L and then R uphill again, to junction of tracks by gates. Turn L through the small gates downhill.

Turn L shortly afterwards to cross another stream (bed) and continue ahead up rocky track uphill, leading its way along the side of the hill. 600m later, under line of electric cables and just before a perimeter fence, turn R uphill. KSO, go through gate(way) and continue ahead, veering L and levelling out before undulating, more up than down, around side of hill until you reach the electric pylon at the top *(and the same cables you went under below – the original course of this* camino *went vertically uphill there, when it was first waymarked, along the perimeter fence!).*

Go through the gates ahead of you. Continue ahead, slightly uphill then down, in the general direction of a farm way ahead of you in the distance, then, when you reach

Town with castle, El Real de la Jara

a track coming from the L (just before you reach a perimeter fence) turn R along it. Continue alongside perimeter fence to gateway, go through it and KSO ahead on a ridge with splendid views all round.

Reach another gateway shortly afterwards but do NOT go through it. Turn L instead alongside fence, go through a gate, go through another gate and KSO, still high up, until you come to the estate's exit gate. KSO ahead on other side, go through small gate, turn R onto gravel road, go through another gate immediately and KSO gently downhill, through another gate and then another.

KSO for an easy 4km walk to **El Real de la Jara**. *At KM1 look out for a memorial to the late José Luis Salvador Salvador. He was one of the two people to really revive the use of the Vía de la Plata as a viable pilgrim route in the late twentieth century and some of his ashes are buried here; the rest are in the outside wall of the refugio in Fuenterroble de Salvatierra (Salamanca).*

The walled lane you are on > a street (the **Calle Pablo Picasso**) as you enter the town. Turn R at the bottom into **Calle Murillo** and then L to the **Plaza de España** in the centre of

---

16.5km/10km El Real de la Jara 460m (87/913)
Small town with all facilities (bank + CD). Unmarked Pensión Molina at no.70 Calle Real (inexpensive, but note that not all rooms have windows). No *refugio* as such at present though pilgrims can sleep in the changing rooms (*vestuarios*) in the Campo de Futbol on the way out of town on the main road – ask in tourist office (on first floor of *ayuntamiento*) to arrange for key.

Continue along the street to the centre of town by the *ayuntamiento*. *(Turn L at the end for the church of San Bartolomé: Meson Cochero opposite does meals)*. Continue ahead along **Calle José María Pedrero** to the end, where it becomes a *camino de tierra* (the Vía Pecuaria Cordel del Monesterio). Alternatively, from the church, take **Calle San Bartolomé** then turn L to **Calle José-María Pedrero**. *(If you want to visit the Castillo Real, with a* mirador *(viewpoint), up on the hill 300m to the east of the town you can do so via a FP.)*

KSO along a walled lane. Pass the remains of another *castillo* (to R), 1km later. *This is where you leave the province of Sevilla and the autonomous region of Andalucía and enter the province of Badajoz, in the autonomous region of Extramadura. The route from here to the Ermita San Isidoro is very straightforward, through undulating countryside with cork trees, encinas and dark brown pigs grazing underneath them.* KSO.

7km later pass the entrance gates to **Dehesa Romeral** (a *cortijo*) and KSO. 2km after that pass the entrance gates to **Dehesa La Mimbre** and KSO. 3km later, when you reach a couple of white buildings (a *riding school*), one of which looks like a small chapel, go up the bank ahead of you, cross a minor road and KSO ahead along a *cañada*. KSO for 400m to the N630 and turn R alongside it for 100m to the

12km Ermita de San Isidoro (99/901)

Chapel on site where the retinue transporting the body of Saint Isidore up the Vía de la Plata from Seville to León stopped en route to his final resting place in the Basilica de San Isidro in León. After this, the landscape begins to change, the *cortijos* disappear and there are a lot of walled lanes. You will also see many donkeys and mules in this area, still used to work the land.

Ermita de San Isidoro

Continue on clear sandy track through eucalyptus woods, // to but not next to the main road (N630). KSO for 2km until you reach a section of the *old* main road (on your R). Cross over to LH side and continue on small FP below the hard shoulder. 500m later, at junction, turn second left *(the first turn to the L is signposted to a campsite)*, veering R, on section of old road. Return to the N630 opposite gates to a *finca* called **Las Navas** and continue on a FP and then track to LH side of the N630.

Note: *in this area there are also other waymarked long-distance walks (with yellow AND WHITE markers): be careful not to follow these as only in places (not all the time) do they coincide with those of the Vía de la Plata. Similarly 'VP' on marker stones refers (confusingly) not to the Vía de la Plata but to a 'Vía Pecuaria' (see introduction), this one waymarked in white between Almadén and Monesterio.*

Pass a second set of gates marked 'Las Navas' (on LH side this time) and continue uphill on a *camino de tierra* // to the road, passing a large, shiny corrugated-iron building (L). Continue uphill to the top at the

---

8km Cruz del Puerto 753m (107/893)
Large picnic area, wayside shrine, fountain (not usually working). KSO on road for 1km down to

---

1km Monesterio 752m (108/892)
Small town with all facilities (bank + CD) and plenty of accommodation of all types, including Hostal D.P. El Pilar on main road (941.51.67.56). Small *refugio* for those with *credencial* in former Cruz Roja (Red Cross) building on LH side of main road at entry to town (key from Hotel Moya next door).

7km west of here, at **Calera de León**, there is the medieval monastery of the Order of Santiago, with Gothic church and two-storied cloister (worth visiting): you can walk there by deviating from the camino – see *** below.

Another side trip (8km) to the monastery of **Tentudía** is also recommended. (The name is a corruption of 'hold the day', as the Virgin Mary extended the daylight so that the Christians could complete their defeat of the Moors here.) It contains the courtyard of a mosque, Mozárabic, Mudéjar, late Romanesque and Classical elements, a Capilla de Santiago and fine Italian tile-work, including a splendid tile Santiago Matamoros in the chapel. Open 10.15–17.25, free, closed Mondays. To walk there from Monesterio follow the signs to Calera de León and Tentudía west off the N630 up *Calle Primero de Mayo* and *Avenida Ramón y*

Tiled Santiago Matamoros in Capilla de
Santiago, Monasterio de Tentudía

Cajal. 500m beyond the modern *Ermita de Nuestra Señora de Tentudía* turn R along waymarked path (yellow and white flashes) for 8km to monastery. Retrace your steps for the return journey.

Note: there is hardly any shade, no water and no villages between Monesterio and Fuente de Cantos, 22km away.

To leave Monesterio: *continue along the main road (**Paseo de Extremadura**) to the very end of the town (1.5km), turning L after the football ground (by town exit boards) onto a camino de tierra downhill alongside **Arroyo de la Dehesa**. Pass a concrete bridge on L and KSO. After 1km you reach a place to ford the river (stepping stones) and a large water trough on the other side. Do NOT cross here: the walled lane on the other side (marked with yellow AND WHITE flashes) from here leads to Calera de León (the camino to Fuente de Cantos is marked with yellow arrows).*

***However, if you *do* want to go to Calera de León cross over the river here and follow the yellow and white flashes but once you arrive in the town *(shops, bars)* they stop. If you are not retracing your steps to Monesterio you can return to the Vía de la Plata by taking the local road signposted 'N630 6km' for 3km. At the top of the hill turn L at the THIRD white gate post with cattle grid* (wide track with no gates on RH side of road here).

Otherwise, KSO alongside the river for 300m to a proper, solid concrete bridge (suitable for vehicles, nearly 2km from where you left the main road). Cross over, turn R and then L up a wide walled lane, veering L at the top then R at junction of tracks, passing (on L) a brick building with two round rooms and no windows. KSO for 2km until you reach a minor road, 5.5km from Monesterio. *Calera de León visible on hill top to L.*

Cross over and go through gates (cattle grid*). Continue ahead, veering L and following the line of the wall. 1.5km later go through another gate and continue on a walled lane ahead. KSO(R) at a fork along the line of the wall and 800m later reach two gates in the corner of a field. Go through LH (double) set and continue ahead on a grassy track gently downhill, through an area planted with scrubby broom trees, veering R alongside the line of a wire fence. *Watch out carefully for waymarks in this section as there are not many places to put them.*

At the bottom veer L alongside a fence, keeping close to it and following it round to the R uphill when it curves round. 500m later go through some gates and continue alongside a fence, through another (double) gate and KSO in a straight line ahead on a clear track when the fence stops. *This area is a paradise of wild flowers in the spring-time, 'wall-to-wall' to the horizon, with wild orchids later in the year, on the track and elsewhere. Fuente de Cantos is suddenly visible, though still a long way away, when you get over the brow of the hill.* Continue gently downhill, the track veering R, L, R and L again to the valley bottom. Cross the river via stepping stones, turn R towards a wall, L in front of it and continue on the track veering L, R, L and R. KSO(R) ahead at a fork (leading to a semi-ruined farm on L).

When a track joins from back L do NOT go ahead over a cattle grid but fork L between fields. KSO, following the road round. Approximately 1km before you reach the main road veer R over a bridge over the (probably dry) river. KSO. When you see the road ahead and a factory marked 'Fábrica de Material ganadero' fork L, // to the road, and KSO. This brings you out at the end of the town, by the road. Cross over and enter

22km Fuente de Cantos 583m (130/870)

Small town with all facilities. Casa Vicente on main road has rooms (924.50.02.77). Hotel la Fábrica in converted flour mill at end of town close to main road (924.50.00.42). New Albergue de Turismo (ask for 'Casa Rural'), very quiet and calm, in converted convent on outskirts of town, Calle Frailes s/n, (924.58.00.35 & 660.45.12.56, pilgrim price 12 Euros incl. bkft). No R&F at present.

One of the town's two churches is another Iglesia de Nuestra Señora de la Granada, containing a) statue of Santiago Apóstol on main altar (with shells on each lapel) and b) statue of San Roque on RH side of church (when facing altar). Fuente de Cantos was also the birthplace of the painter Zurbarán (the *casa* can be visited).

Note: There is no shade at all between here and Zafra.

Continue ahead up **Calle Julián** to the end (a very long street), turn R into **Calle Prim/San Quintin**, veering L and then turn R to go to the **Plaza de la Constitución** (church and *ayuntamiento*).

If you want to sleep in the *Casa Rural* (and with your back to the *ayuntamiento*) pass to L of church and turn first L down **Calle Arias Montano** to bottom and then continue on **Calle de los Frailes**.

Otherwise: continue (out of the square) along **Calle Pizarro**, **Calle Olmo** (not marked at start) and KSO down **Calle San Juan** to **Ermita de San Juan** *(1515 but restored in 1999).* Cross the main road and continue ahead up an earth road between walls; this is the old road leading out of town, with the original *calzada romana* underneath it. KSO, ignoring turns, for 6km.

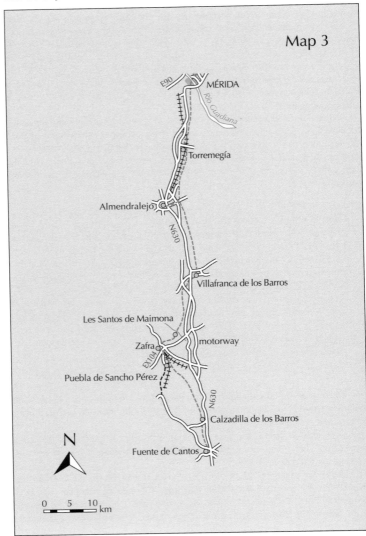

Map 3

MÉRIDA

E90

Río Guadiana

Torremegía

Almendralejo

N630

Villafranca de los Barros

Les Santos de Maimona

Zafra

motorway

EX104

Puebla de Sancho Pérez

N630

Calzadilla de los Barros

Fuente de Cantos

N

0   5   10 km

Cross a minor road and enter the village of

6.5km Calzadilla de los Barros 556m (136.5/863.5)
Shops, bars, farmácia, bank. YH, Hostal Rodríguez (on N630, 924.58.47.01).
   Large ceramic tile plaque on wall at entry, with map and indication of the town's monuments. These include the sixteenth-century Ermita de Nuestra Señora de la Encarnación, the Ermita de San Isidro and the fortress-style parish church of the Divino Salvador (fourteenth–sixteenth centuries); this is a National Monument, as is also its main altarpiece (fifteenth–sixteenth centuries) by Antón de Madrid, with 23 sections depicting scenes from the life of Christ. Town coat of arms contains scallop shell and sword of Santiago.

   Cross the village from S to N by going down the main street (**Calle Fuente de Cantos**), turn first R, first L and then KSO (behind the *ayuntamiento* arch) into **Calle Zafra**, out into open country, and KSO. Fork L near two pig farms (one on each side) and KSO, ignoring turns until you reach the N630 at road KM693, behind the crash barrier at a sharp bend. *(3km from Calzadilla; stork's nest on telegraph pole at side of road, formerly useful to orient yourself, is no longer there so watch out carefully in this section as waymarking is poor).* Continue ahead, on a section of old road, cross a bridge over **Río Atarje** and 100m later turn L onto an earth track between fields, running // to the river.

   After 1km veer R, cross a small river via stepping stones and KSO(R) uphill with fences to either side. 1.5km later KSO at a crossing by a large pig farm (over to L) and KSO, the track becoming grassy along the shallow valley bottom. At an unmarked junction 400m later (no waymark) KSO(L) ahead.

   3km later reach a junction with pink tarmac. KSO, ignoring turns until you reach a level crossing (2km before Puebla de Sancho Pérez). Cross the railway line, KSO ahead and enter the main street (**Calle Sancho Pérez**), continue along **Calle Belén** and follow it down to the **Plaza de España** and **Iglesia de Santa Lucía** in

---

15km Puebla de Sancho Pérez 522m (151.5/848.5)
Three shops (one at entry on L), bars (though all seem to shut down in the afternoons except Bar Galea on main road at end of village). Iglesia de Santa Lucía, Ermita de Nuestra Señora de Belén.
   Note: this section (as far as Zafra) was not well-waymarked at the time this edition was prepared.

Town coat of arms, Calzadilla de los Barros

Cross the **Plaza de España**, go down **Paseo de Extremadura** and then the **Calle Obispo Soto** to the end. Cross the road (to Zafra) and go along a track to RH side of a dried-up river, veering round to R onto a minor road. Cross a bridge over a railway line and 500m later reach a level crossing. Do NOT cross the tracks but turn L alongside them to Zafra railway station (*the town is over to your left here, not ahead*). Go past an old station building and turn L along **Avenida de la Estación** for a further 2km into the town centre. (*Bike repairs: in Calle Juan Ramón Jiménez, off Avenida de la Estación to L.*)

4.5km Zafra 509m pop. 15,900 (156/844)
All facilities, RENFE, buses to Madrid, Seville, Mérida, Salamanca and other parts of Spain. Tourist office in the Plaza de España. Hostal Carmen, Avenida de la Estación 9, has two restaurants (Rogelio and Nuevo Rogelio) and rooms (924.55.14.39). Hostal Arias (924.55.48.55) by petrol station on the Badajoz road (200m off camino) plus several others. For pilgrim stamp and spartan *refugio* facility organised by the Amigos in Zafra (not available during September or early October and closed for building work at the time this guide was prepared): ask at Policía Local in centre of town.

Warning: as indicated in the Introduction, during the Feria de Zafra (agricultural fair), which takes place during the whole of September and the first week in October, it will be IMPOSSIBLE to find anywhere to stay, either in Zafra or in the *pensión* in Los Santos de Maimona. During this period it is suggested (pilgrims with credencial only, however) that you continue to Los Santos and sleep in the *albergue* there (access via Policía Local in Casas Consistoriales).

Zafra is a historic town (often described as a 'mini Seville') with castle of the Dukes of Feria (now a parador), Colegiata de Nuestra Señora de la Candelaria (contains an altarpiece with painted panels by Zurbarán in a south lateral chapel and a Santiago Apóstol on main Baroque altarpiece; church is kept locked except at service times so best time to visit is just before evening mass). Former Hospital de Santiago still standing.

In the city centre turn L opposite Parque de la Paz and then turn R down **Glorieta Comercial** to the **Plaza de España** (*tourist office in building on corner*), cross it diagonally and then turn R down the **Calle Sevilla**. At the end turn L into the **Plaza**

Grande and KSO into the **Calle Tetuán**, R up the side of the church of the **Candelaria**, along the **Calle Conde de la Corte** and into the square in front of the *ayuntamiento*. KSO along **Plaza del Pilar Redondo**, cross a street and go up a very wide tree-lined avenue (the **Calle Ancha**, but no name at start), straight across the **Plazuela San Benito** at the end and up **Calle San Francisco** to the top. Cross the main road and KSO past a group of eight blocks of modern flats on R with a medieval church tower 'growing' in the middle of them, up a minor road into open country. *This is the route (waymarked) which takes you on a tour of the town and past all the main 'sights' in Zafra.*

However, for a simpler route to leave (not waymarked but easy to follow) go through the park when you reach the town centre and turn R at the end, past **Biblioteca Municipal** (on L) with fountain behind it. Turn L into the main road to Badajoz, pass bus station and then you will see the blocks of flats on R surrounding the medieval church tower. Turn R up this old road and continue ahead.

Shortly before you reach it you will have a splendid 'balcony' view over the small town of

---

5km Los Santos de Maimona 528m, pop. 8100 (161/839)
Shops, bars, banks. Pensión Sanse II (924.54.42.10) near main road at other end of town. Albergue (like a youth hostel, with bunks, kitchen) accessible via local police in *Casas Consistoriales* (924.54.42.94 if closed).

Maimona was a Moorish king and the 'Santos' not saints but merely 'altos', high-placed, important people, and there are several large historic houses in the town. The building which is now the town hall (Casas Consistoriales) was once the Palacio de la Encomienda (Command HQ) of the Order of the Knights of Santiago, and Los Santos formerly had a pilgrim hospital as well. Municipal coat of arms has cross of Santiago and two scallop shells and church has a Puerta del Perdón (where pilgrims who were too weak or ill to continue were granted the same remission of their sins and the same indulgences as those who completed the journey to Santiago; lion with sword of Santiago above door).

Go down the main street to the square in front of the church, pass to L of it, KSO down the street *(bar on R, no name but with a lot of old photos on walls, has pilgrim stamp)* and cross the **Calle Sevilla**. Continue ahead down **Calle Teniente Blanco Marín** and **Calle Obispo Luna**, turn L and then R and cross the local road by house no. 38. Continue down **Calle Valmoreno** and then turn L, diagonally, into **Calle Maestrazgo**. Turn R then L then R again *(Calle Santísima)* down to cross **Río Robledillo**.

Continue ahead on a road lined with recently planted trees. 100m later turn R onto a *camino de tierra* and then turn L at a fork onto a walled lane, veering L when it levels out. KSO ahead at a crossing alongside a farm wall and then continue on an untarred road joining from back L.

KSO(L) at a fork 500m later (N630 is over to your R) and KSO on a clear *camino de tierra* with vines to either side and olive trees. At the next fork, 1.5km later, KSO(R) ahead. 1km later KSO at a crossing on a track between fences.

When the fencing ends some 2km later *(view of Villafranca de los Barros ahead here)* KSO(L) through olive plantations towards an industrial metal tower ahead (7km from Los Santos). Pass the ruined Ermita San Isidro (on R), with a very large fig tree beside it – *shady place to sit down* – and KSO through more olive groves.

At a crossing with a well and a pump house on RH side (motorway nearby ahead) turn R. When you reach a railway line go over the level crossing and KSO(R) for 300m to the N630. Turn L along it for 200m then cross over to other side at end of crash barriers. Go under a fence to continue ahead (i.e. R from the N630, shortly after road KM669) on gravel road coming from your R. Turn 3rd L (a junction with tree in the middle) and KSO uphill for 2km until you enter the town by the **Calle Caballeras** *(sic)*.

15.5km Villafranca de los Barros 450m (176.5/823.5)

Town with all facilities. Hostal Horizonte (924.52.56.99, not open all year), Pensión Mancera Lara, Bar/Rte La Marina (corner of Avenida F. Aranguén and N630) has rooms, also Casa Perín (Calle Caillo Arias 40), Hotel Diana**. Hotel Romero 1km away on main road. New *albergue turístico* La Almazara on N630 at KM670, in a former oil mill (686.89.88.41, pilgrim price 12 Euros incl. bkft). Pilgrim stamp in *ayuntamiento*.

Church of Santa María (much shell decoration inside, San Roque in south porch and Santiago Apóstol with book and shell in main altarpiece) and a number of interesting old houses.

Turn R into **Calle Zurburán** downhill. Cross the 'river,' continue ahead and turn L into **Calle Larga** and the **Plaza de España** (church and *ayuntamiento*). Cross it diagonally and take the top LH street (**Calle Santa Joaquina de Vedrona**) into a triangular 'square' (a *plaza*) with trees. Fork L up **Calle Calvario**, cross **Plaza de la Coronada** diagonally (second church – *San Francisco* – on L) and turn L along **Calle San Ignacio** past *Colegio de los Jesuitas*** out into open country (**ask for this as a landmark if you get lost). Arrows start again here.*

500m later reach a local road. Cross over and KSO ahead on a wide *camino de tierra* between vines (building to R marked 'Viveros San Isidro' and *camino* is marked as 'Camino Público el Vizcaíno, 10.7km'. *No shade at all from here to Torremegía.*

Yellow gas posts appear at frequent intervals along the way but waymarking with yellow arrows is spasmodic.

KSO for 4.5km, after which the track begins to veer R (*small white farm over to R*). Fork L here onto smaller *camino de tierra* and KSO for 4.5km more, until you reach a junction with a much wider track coming from the R. Turn L here along it. 700–800m later a track joins from back L that looks, from the style/angling of the waymarking, as if an alternative or variant *camino* has come that way *(it has a noticeboard indicating that it is the 'Camino Público de las Vegas, 8.1km').*

KSO ahead here and 500m later cross stream via a bridge with concrete bollards. 200m later the track bends sharp R, along the line of HT pylons. 350m after a group of buildings on R (2km from bend) the *Camino* crosses a minor road and the junction is marked not only with a granite cube but also with a Vía de la Plata plinth. **Here you can either**:

a) cross over and continue ahead to Torremegía, or

b) to sleep in Almendralejo (a deviation of 4km in each direction), turn L here. *Town is now visible ahead.* Continue on this minor road (used as a popular local *paseo*, both morning and evening) and after 2km cross the motorway. KSO on other side, entering the town via the **Calle del Molino** (big distilleries on R). Turn L at the end, veering R over the level crossing (railway station to R) to reach the main road (N630) on the outskirts of

---

17.5km Almendralejo 337m, pop. 23,600 (194/806)

Medium-sized town with all facilities, wine production centre. Bar Hotel Los Angeles* on main road (924.67.03.19), Hotel España** (San Antonio 77, turn R on reaching main road in town), 924.67.01.20 and several more (modern expensive) hotels on main road to L on entering town. The town itself is not on the Vía de la Plata as it dates only from 1536 and was therefore not on the *calzada romana* and its centre is nearly 2km away to the west. Ermita de Santiago (in outer suburb, 2km to west).

If you stay in Almendralejo you can either return to detour point before continuing (i.e. turn R over level crossing), veering L and turn R on road past big distillery cylinders, then continue over motorway to junction with Vía de la Plata plinth (4km) and turn L, or rejoin the camino (turning L onto it) 3km to north by taking road to Alange, marked 'Don Benito' at crossing on leaving town, and KSO ahead over the motorway (via the next bridge to the north) before you reach the camino again. This is not only well-waymarked but also easy to spot as it is a very wide, sandy *camino de tierra* that runs underneath a line of HT pylons.

From the turn-off to Almendralejo continue ahead through more vines and KSO for 2km. Cross the road to Alange and KSO ahead through more vines and olive trees, ignoring turnings, for 6.5km. *Torremegía visible in the distance ahead.* 500m after passing a large fenced-in *cortijo* on R (painted yellow), cross bridge over stream *(old bridge to R with large tree is a good place for rest)* and reach a junction where the track you are on bends sharp R. KSO ahead here on *camino de tierra* through fields, getting gradually closer to the railway line, which you reach by a bridge taking it over a stream. Do NOT go under the railway here (despite old arrows indicating that you should) but cross stream as best you can and KSO ahead instead. 400m later reach a large concrete bridge over the railway line. Either go up the bank and turn L onto it or (bikes) veer R and then turn L onto the wide gravel track that leads over the bridge into the village.

> **10.5km Torremegía 302m (204.5/795.5)**
> Shops, bars, rte, *alberque turístico*, but no other accommodation. Iglesia de la Concepción, Palacio de los Megía (with shells in the door).

KSO (the tarmac starts and the road you are on > the **Calle Gabriel y Galán**) and if you want to eat or go shopping continue ahead to the N630, where all the shops, bars, etc. are located. Otherwise, to continue directly, turn first R (onto the **Calle de la Calzada Romana**, unnamed at start), cross the **Calle Almendralejo** and the **Calle El Castuo** and KSO ahead to very end of the village *(last part of street has tall trees and seats, good for a sit-down)* then continue ahead on a *camino de tierra* into open countryside, forking L in the direction of a cemetery and brick water tower, both on the other (LH) side of the N630.

Continue alongside but below the main road on a *camino de tierra*, passing Viveros Castaño *(supplier of swimming pools and garden ornaments)* and the *bascula pública (small building marked 'control y pesaje de camiones')*. Continue for 2km more. Cross a small river and another local road to Alange and Don Benito and reach a section of the old N630, 3km from Torremegía. Fork slightly R here, passing a group of very tall eucalyptus trees *(shady but very dirty)*.

Continue ahead on an old road until you reach a black and white bar (a barrier) in front of the railway line. Continue ahead, crossing the line carefully (trains still use it) and then KSO ahead on an old tarred road until it rejoins the N630. Continue along its RH side (or in field if mown) and at the top of the hill, 3.5km later, when the N630 bends L, pass to RH side of the crash barrier just before the bend and continue on a section of old road, veering L *(farm over to R; you are now right next to the motorway.)* At another group of eucalyptus trees (just below road) – *shady, view of Mérida ahead*

Roman bridge over Río Guadiana, Mérida

– turn R down the FP through fields, leading in a more or less straight line towards the town, gently downhill with open fields to either side.

When track joins from back R KSO ahead then KSO(R) ahead 250m later at junction. 500m later reach a concrete structure that looks like a wayside cross with the top missing and KSO ahead here. When another track joins from back R KSO ahead. KSO(R) at fork 300–400m after that and KSO ahead 100m later at crossing. KSO(L) at next fork, after which track veers L downhill near trees towards farm then veers R in front of it. Continue ahead through fields, with large ditch to your LH side then between fencing, until you reach a T-junction with a *camino de tierra* and HT cables overhead. Turn R and continue until you reach the end, between two factories near the river. Turn L, go under the road bridge and continue on an unpaved road // to the river (the **Avenida de Vicente Sos Baynat**) until you reach the **Roman bridge** (pedestrianised). Turn R over it and cross the **Río Guadiana** into

16km Mérida 218m, pop. 51,600 (220.5/779.5)

Turn to page 125 to continue.

Granada 682m, pop. 243,341 (0/403)

Large city with all facilities. Worth spending two days here (one to visit the Alhambra). RENFE, buses to Seville, Málaga, Madrid, etc. (Bus station is on western outskirts of town – take bus no. 3 to city centre). Plenty of accommodation in all price brackets, much of it in the Gran Vía and Calle San Juan de Dios area and side streets. Youth hostel. It is suggested that you obtain a street plan from the tourist office (in the Corral del Carbón) to help you leave Granada.

Alhambra: tickets for the same day are only available from the Alhambra itself. There are two *turnos* (sessions) each day, 8.30–14.00 and 14.00–20.00. You can buy tickets in advance by telephone, on the internet or at any branch of the BBVA (one of the big Spanish banks). Make sure you check whether your ticket is for the morning or the afternoon session.

Other main sights include the Renaissance cathedral, the Gothic Royal Chapel, the monastery of San Jeronimo, the Baroque churches of San Juan de Dios and San Justo y Pastor, the Albaicín and Sacromonte areas of the town, the Arabic baths and several museums.

Alhambra, Granada (photo: author)

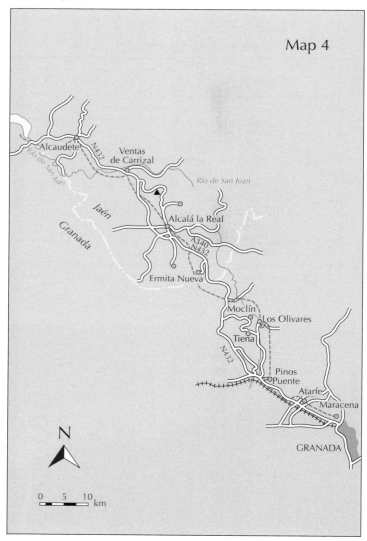

Map 4

*Santiago Peregrino, Iglesia de
Santiago, Granada (photo: author)*

Iglesia de Santiago (sixteenth century) in the Calle Marques de Falces (off the Gran Vía). Statue of 'hybrid' St James over entrance door. Hat, with shell at front, stick missing, book, but no St James references inside the church, which has a Moorish wooden ceiling and balcony all around front of nave – narrow, like banisters on a landing.

Sello: you can get your first pilgrim stamp from the nuns at the Comendadores (see below: best time early evening) Otherwise you can get one in the tourist office or one of the other churches (ask in the sacristy after mass). Note, however, that the Iglesia de Santiago is not a parish church and does not, therefore, have its own stamp but one for the parish of San Andrés, to which it is affiliated.

The Asociación de Amigos del Camino de Santiago de Granada has information sessions every Tuesday (apart from public holidays) in the Bar de la Hermandad Ferroviaria (second floor), Calle Lavadero de las Tablas 1, from 20.00 (off the Avenida Gran Capitán in the town centre). They also issue their own *credencial*.

The walk out of Granada is reasonably shady as many of the streets are lined with trees. Once you leave the city boundary, though, and go under the motorway, there is very little shade at all. From Granada to Pinos Puente the *camino* is more or less level.

Note: *if you would like to walk the first 11km through the town and out of it without your rucksack you can go as far as* **Atarfe** *and then return to the centre of Granada by bus #23 (roughly every half hour). You can then return to Atarfe by bus the following morning and thus shorten the 31km (hilly) walk to Moclín.*

Alternatively you can walk as far as **Pinos Puente** (17km) and, if you are not staying there, return to Granada by bus (regular service but check the times in the bus station first).

The *camino* starts at the **Real Monasterio de las Madres Comendadores de Santiago** *(get your first pilgrim stamp here)* on the corner of the **Calle Santiago** and the **Calle Comendadores de Santiago** in the northeast part of the town (in the old Realejo district). *(Notice on wall in Calle Santiago re. Convent: '1er convento fundado en Granada "Madre de Dios" Comendadores de Santiago S. XVI.')* The first waymark is high up on the wall, opposite you as you come of out the convent gateway, with a pilgrim plaque on the wall:

> Text on plaque outside Real Monasterio de las Comendadores de Santiago:
>
> Tú, peregrino, que inicias el Camino de Santiago acquí, estás en el punto de partida del 'Camino Mozárabe' que nos introduce en la devoción jacobeo medieval.
> Que la bendición de Dios y la protección de Santiago te acompañen en tu peregrinación a la tumba del Apóstol, y cuenta con el cariño y las oraciones de los Amigos del Camino de Santiago y la Comunidad de Comendadores de este Monasterio.
> Granada Festividad de Santiago Apóstol
> Año MM Año Jubilar
>
> *Pilgrim, you who are beginning the Camino de Santiago here, are at the starting point of the Mozárabic Way, which introduces us to the medieval cult of St James. May God's blessing and the protection of St James accompany you on your journey to the apostle's tomb. You can be assured of the love and prayers of the friends of the Camino de Santiago and of the community of the Comendadores in this monastery.*
> *Granada, Feast of St James the Apostle*
> *2002 AD, Jubilee Year.*

Turn L out of the convent along the **Calle Comendadores de Santiago**, which then bends R. Turn R at end then immediately L into **Calle Cobertizo Santo Domingo** and go under tunnel to Plaza and **church of Santo Domingo** *(sixteenth and eighteenth centuries, frescoes on front of building)*. Continue ahead opposite the church door

Pilgrim plaque outside Convento de las Comendadoras, Granada (photo: author)

down **Calle Ancha de Santo Domingo** *(not named at start)*, passing **Casa Arabe de los Girones** *(thirteenth to sixteenth centuries)* on R street – **Calle Jesús y María**. Continue to very end, turn R into **Calle San Matías** and then immediately L into tiny **Placeta de los Peregrinos**. Continue ahead to very small, unmarked square then turn R into **Calle Lepanto**. Turn R at end to the **Corral del Carbón**, a fourteenth-century building that was formerly the market, with galleried patio and the tourist office inside *(collect street plan here if you haven't already done so)*. Turn L opposite entrance to the *Corral* into the **Calle Puente del Carbón**, cross the **Calle Reyes Católicos** and continue ahead on **Calle López Rubio**. Cross **Calle Zacatín** and go down **Calle Alcaicería**, a narrow arcaded street with craft and jewelry shops to either side, part of a network of old Moorish-style souk-like streets. Reach the **Plaza de Alonso Cano** at end, pass eighteenth-century **Iglesia del Sagrado** *(on your R)*, the **Plaza de las Pasiegas** *(on your L)* and continue along the **Calle Pie de la Torre** along the side of the cathedral. Turn R into the **Calle Cárcel Baja** then L into the **Calle San Jeronimo**. Pass the **Plaza de la Universidad** *(on L)* with the **church of San Justo y Pastor** *(seventeenth–eighteenth centuries)* and continue to the end. Turn R into the **Calle San Juan de Dios** and at the end (a big junction) turn L into the **Avenida de la Constitución**, crossing over to the other side to the pavement that passes between the Jardines del Triúnfo (a public garden).

Continue along the **Avenida de la Constitución**, passing *(on L)* the Parque Fuente Nueva (a large public garden) until you reach the **Plaza de la Caleta** *(on R, a large modern square)*. KSO(R) ahead here at fork, along the **Avenida de Andalucía** *(yellow arrow on 3rd street lamp)* and KSO for 2km until you reach the *(modern)* **Parque Almunia**. (N.B: if you walk along the LH side of the avenue to avoid the sun cross back to the RH side after crossing the *Calle Sagrada Familia*.)

Turn R into the park *(shady seats)* just after the junction, go up steps then turn R at top. Cross wide avenue, go up more steps and turn L along a tree-lined walkway with seats and a small water channel down its LH side. Leave the park by the last gate on the R, turn L, cross a two-lane avenue and KSO ahead on dual carriageway with palm trees in its central reservation (**Calle Periodista Miguel González Pareja** – you are now in the **Barrio de los Periodistas** or 'journalists' district' – a modern residential area). Turn L at end by a roundabout with a hedge round it and bushes in the middle and continue down the **Calle Eduardo Molina Fajardo**. Turn 3rd R by children's play area down **Calle Periodista Juan López del Charco**, continue past sports ground (on R) and KSO ahead, gently downhill on **Calle Periodista Miguel Martínez Sanchez** to a small square and go under the tunnel under the motorway.

On the other side is a large expanse of waste land with industrial buildings over to your L. Veer slightly L then continue straight ahead (// to the factory to your L) and when you reach a sitting area (on your R) at the first houses in **Maracena** (just past a large isolated tree on your L) turn L under the electric cables and continue along the LH bank of the **Arroyo del Baranquillo** (a stream), on the outskirts of

5km Maracena (5/398)
All facilities, shops, etc.

The camino doesn't go into the village (now a suburban overflow from Granada) but skirts it on its L.

KSO and 300m later reach road by bridge and KSO ahead on other side, still on LH bank of stream. *Large supermarket to R.* KSO and 500m later reach a minor road. KSO(L) along it. Waste land stops and fields begin on either side. After a while the tarmac stops and the road > the **Camino de los Cereales**. The Ermita (small chapel) de las Tres Juanas and an *atalaya arabe* (watchtower) are on the hilltop over to the R ahead.

KSO, ignoring turns to L and R. Tarmac starts again by the beech plantations. Continue until you reach a road (and a roundabout) at the entrance to **Atarfe** *(Hotel/Rte** El Doncel on L, open 24 hours.)* Cross over, continue ahead, take RH fork, cross road and continue on **Calle Alfonso Bailon Verdejo**, veering R to **Plaza España** in

6km Atarfe 598m, pop. 10,045 (11/392)
Small town with shops, bars, banks (+CD) etc.

From the **Plaza de España** (*ayuntamiento* on L, pass in front of it) turn L along **Avenida de Andalucía** and then the **Avenida de la Estación** to a shady square by a roundabout with a large sculpture in the middle. Turn R here along the **Calle Aragón** (not marked at start). KSO, passing electricity sub-station (on R) and a curious Gaudi-like construction (to the L).

Go under tunnel under motorway and KSO on other side for 1km, ignoring turns to L and R. At T-junction by large complex of ruined industrial buildings (at foot of steep hill in front of you) turn L. 300m later reach a 'stop' sign. Cross the N432 (Granada–Córdoba main road) very carefully; continue for a few metres on other side (marked 'Fuente Vaqueros' and 'Valderrubio'), cross railway line almost immediately afterwards and turn R alongside it.

KSO for 2km then cross railway line at a small level crossing (by track marker 109–9) and continue ahead on RH side of track. 1km later, just before a road bridge over the railway line, turn R onto a stony track. Turn R onto gravel road coming from road bridge (on your L), veering L and then R back to the N432 at a bend in

6km Pinos Puente (17/386)
Shops, bars, post office, banks (+CD), bar/rte at bend in main road; hotel*** opposite. Regular buses to Granada. [R&F: Esclavos de María y los Pobres, Casa Parroquial.]

Cross road at bend and junction and turn L (street not named at start), passing public garden (on L) and then turn L at end *(more bars)* under large archway leading to bridge over river below. Turn L at end into street *(with shops etc.)* to church.

Cross square in front of church (diagonally) and turn R up **Calle Ancha**, uphill all the time. KSO(R) at fork by mini-roundabout, to the very top. Continue ahead on road which levels out now. 200m later fork L on gravel road through olive plantations. KSO, gently uphill all the time, ignoring turnings to L and R. After 6-7km the track levels out and begins to descend gently.

After 8–9 km (from Pinos Puente) reach a crossing with a wider track and turn L along it. 1km later KSO(L) at fork. 1.5km after that reach a minor road and turn L along it (not much traffic). KSO for 2km, ignoring turns, until you reach the outskirts of

12km Los Olivares 1022m (29/374)
Small hilltop village with two bars, shops, bank. Hotel El Dueño.

Turn second R after village name board, downhill, then, when street bends R, KSO ahead down concrete lane that > a gravel track, downhill, through waste land. Veer R to continue behind houses (// to road below) then continue downhill to reach area with seats, trees and a fountain.

Continue straight ahead *(bar on L)*, cross bridge over river way below you *(another bar on other side of bridge; ahead)* and turn R on other side (**Calle Raphael Alberti**), veering L and then R to cross a minor road. Go steeply uphill on rough track (a *vereda*) to R of property (on L) with fencing and with olive plantations to your L. (**Cyclists**: *OK thus far, but you will have to get off and push now – the alternative is to take the road to Tiena and then to Moclín, but this is some 8km instead of only 2km). Look out for eagles around here but also watch out carefully for the waymarks as there are a lot of different tracks in this area and you are likely to be tired at the end of the day and lose concentration by the time you get here.*

The route you want – straight uphill to Moclín *(a village perched behind the gap in the skyline to your right)* – is barely 2km away, straight uphill in front of you (the *ermita* in Moclín is behind the big rock in front of you). Be careful to pass to the right of it: if you go to the left you will end up in Tiena (another village, with 6km of road walking up to Moclín).

When you arrive at the *ermita*, KSO to the *ayuntamiento (with a bar in its plaza)* in

---

2km Moclín 1301m, pop. 4917, (31/372)
Small village with bar, shop and bank (+CD). [R&F: ayuntamiento].

Important town in the fourteenth and fifteenth centuries, conquered in 1486 by the Reyes Católicos. Castillo at the very top of the village, with two walled enclaves – the inside one with the church of Cristo del Pano (*romería* – local pilgrimage – 5th October). Upper enclave has remains of an *alcazaba* (citadel), with a huge *aljibe* (cistern) and the Renaissance Casa del Pósito, with coat of arms of Felipe II. Fantastic views on a clear day.

Facing bar and with your back to the *ayuntamiento*, turn L uphill (street unmarked at start) towards top of town. Reach road *(former Guardia Civil barracks to L)* with large wayside cross. Continue on road for 200m then fork R downhill, opposite sitting area, steeply, on gravel track. Pass industrial building on R and continue downhill to road at bend. Fork R off it a few metres later, down a similar track with a wall to the L and KSO(L) downhill when it divides, a few metres later. Reach road again and turn R along it, with Arab forts/lookout posts perched on hilltops to L and R. *(The descent from Moclín coincides – in part – with a section of the Ruta del Califato.)*

500m later reach sign for the *Fuente de Malalmuerzo*. Turn L slightly uphill at fork to fountain itself (on L) then KSO(R) ahead in front of it.

> **2km Fuente del Malalmuerzo (33/370)**
> The 'bad lunch fountain', near to site of neolithic cave, with sitting area, trees, roof and lavadero.

KSO(R) at fork 200m later, gently downhill. Cross FB over stream at bottom and reach minor tarred road. Turn L and KSO for 2km until you reach the N432. Turn R then 250m later turn L uphill by small round house – this is the beginning of the

> **5.5km Cordel de las Gallinas (38.5/364.5)**

500m later fork R then turn L and continue uphill beside the fence on your L and with olive plantations to your R (slippery after rain). *The original cordel, on your L on the other side of the fence, is now very overgrown and difficult to use, as you can see, and is more like a ditch than a roadway.* Reach top of the hill 800m 1km later by electric pylon and turn R down semi-shaded lane – downhill again! – then levelling out. 1km later a gravel road joins from back L. KSO(R) along it for 1.5km until you reach the N432 again, opposite a large olive oil cooperative.

Turn L along the N432 for 1.5km (i.e. on its LH hard shoulder) then shortly before road KM marker no. 338 turn L off the road by a ruined building and continue ahead on a track between fields leading to a small village on hilltop. Then, part way up, fork R onto a clear track that winds its way around the side of the hill for 2km more, to the outskirts of **Ermita Nueva.** At junction with bigger road by wayside, cross at entrance to village KSO ahead.

> **7.5km Ermita Nueva (46/357)**
> Very spread-out village with 3 bars, (shop?), water fountain.

At next junction, more or less in the centre of the village, the arrows lead you forward ahead, past the bus shelter (on your R). *However, if you want to visit the bar(s) turn L here, up* **Calle Pilillas** *(not marked until part way up) for 300–400m (and then retrace your steps to continue). There is a fountain (and lavadero) by the first bar, which also does sandwiches. You are now in the province of Jaén.*

Continue ahead on street with bus shelter on RH corner, gradually downhill *(handy seat on your L, 500–600m later)*. KSO and 1.5km from Ermita Nueva cross the **Arroyo Palancares** and shortly afterwards continue along the **Paseo de los Almendales** *(almond trees, partly shaded)* until you reach the N432 again. Turn L along it for 100m then cross over to other side and turn R over stream onto clear track leading out into open country.

Pass an isolated building (on R) and then veer L. 400m later KSO(R) at fork, between trees. Continue to large *cortijo* (farm) and turn L in front of it *(fountain over to L)*

150m after passing a tall ruined house, fork L off track onto small FP alongside irrigation channel, veering L to go alongside field with a line of (dead?) trees to L. When irrigation channel turns R *(Roman fountain on L; very clear water but uncertain if it is OK to drink)* cross it (channel) and veer R and then L to pass white cross *(large tree to R just before is a good place for a rest)*. KSO, ignoring turns, gradually uphill all the time.

3km after the white cross reach the main road (N432) again, with another similar white cross. Do *not* turn L onto the road but go up the bank (to the L) just before it and walk alongside an olive plantation, // to the road on your R. At the end of the field turn R to enter a walled lane and continue down it until you reach the first houses on the outskirts of the town. Continue downhill, veering L, turn R at the bottom, then L and then R, opposite the bus station, into the **Avenida de Andalucía** in

---

10km Alcalá la Real (56/347)
Small/medium sized town with all facilities. Hostal/Pensión Rio de Oro** (Calle Abad Moya 2, 953.58.03.37, 953.58.41.74/680.57.82.84?), Hospedaría Zacatín, Calle Pradillo 2, 953.58.05.68), both in the old part of the town; Hotel Torrepalme (Conde de Torrepalme 2, 953.58.05.68, not far from bus station). Buses Alcalá – Granada (and vice versa) up to eight times a day, M–F. (Note: if you want to set off early in the morning the bus station café opens at 5.30am.) [R&F: Casa Parroquial, Santa María la Mayor.]

Alcalá's main sight is the Fortaleza de la Mota, at 1033m, not merely an Arab fortress but the site of the town of Alcalá itself until the beginning of the nineteenth century. Worth a visit for its spectacular views alone (360°) but also as an insight as to what the former town was like. It contains nine of its original 13 watchtowers and three of its gates, one of which is a Puerta de Santiago.

The complex also includes the hilltop abbey church of the Iglesia Mayor Abatial. The LH door to side room on upper level (when facing altar) has 15 convex conchas round its frame. RH door (to stairs) has 19 plateresque/early Renaissance design motifs (like roses). Capilla la Peregrina has large (concave) scallop shell in wall (where an altar would be), to L of door on entering church) plus 14 (concave) scallops on arch at entrance.

The (lower) town's other sights include the churches of San Antón, San Juan Bautista, las Angustias, Encarnación (Dominican convent) and Trinidad, all of them from the sixteenth to the eighteenth centuries. Like other places in this region Alcalá is renowned for its olive oil production.

Continue up the *Avenida de Andalucía* and then along the **Carrera de las Mercedes** to the **Fuente de la Mena** *(both decorative and drinking fountains)* and the church of the *Consolación* (on R). *If you want to visit the Fortaleza de la Mota turn L here, up the Calle Real.*

Otherwise: continue ahead down unnamed street downhill then turn (not fork) L at junction 100m later into **Calle Mesa**, veering R into the **Avenida de Portugal**. Turn R steeply downhill at first junction then L at the bottom, passing a day centre for handicapped people (on L).***

[However, as a short-cut you can fork first L (to the L of the telephone box) down **Camino Nuevo**, which then > the **Camino de Guadalcotón**, which will take you directly to *** above.]

In either case, KSO(R) at fork after that, downhill, past new blocks of flats under construction, on a *camino* that leads you into open country (stream // to R, below).

Continue downhill, KSO(R) at fork, KSO(R) by white cross and fork L shortly afterwards and then cross single-arch Roman bridge over a stream. This track is on the line of a *calzada romana* (is paving the original?) so you (quite literally!) KSO, undulating from time to time. Pass another white cross and KSO.

6km from Alcalá (3km from Roman bridge) reach a local road and turn L along it. KSO for 300m to a junction and then KSO(R) ahead, downhill, into hamlet of **Puertollano**, veering R by fountain *(and lavadero with roof)* and then fork R (marked 'La Pasailla') down gravel road that is // to main road (N432) over to your L (but not next to it). *This section is nice and shady in the mornings, with olive groves to either side.* Continue gently downhill all the time.

KSO(L) at junction 2km later (marked 'La Pasailla' again) then KSO(R) ahead 200m later (when the LH option is marked 'La Pasailla'). KSO(L) at next two forks and then KSO(R) at third. KSO(R) at fork 1km later (when you are getting close to the road) then go steeply downhill (this section has been concreted) to go under the tunnel under the N432 (may be very muddy).

On the other side it is not clearly waymarked to indicate what you should do, but continue up the rough track ahead. You should then come to a junction where you turn R and at a second junction you turn L uphill. KSO along this track until you get to the top of the hill (with fence posts on your L). Descend steeply to cross stream (probably dry) then climb up again and KSO ahead when track joins from back L. At top of next hill fork R and then KSO(R) down gravel road downhill.

KSO(L) when minor tarred road joins from back R. Reach the N432 at road KM372, cross over and continue on gravel track on the RH side of the crash barrier. 250m later look out for arrows leading you hard R downhill then turn hard L very shortly afterwards. KSO, ignoring turns, to main street and turn L along it to the centre of

14km Ventas de Carrizal (70/333)
Small village with Bar El Parque (does sandwiches).

Reach main street through village (turn L for bar) and to continue cross main street. KSO ahead on other side then turn R down **Calle de la Plaza**, *veering L down towards river. Continue ahead, cross river and 100m later turn L up gravel road, // to river and above it to begin with. KSO, past more olive groves.*

Cross stream and KSO(R) uphill on other side then KSO(L) at next fork. KSO, gradually uphill all the time, for 2km. After track levels out KSO(L) at fork. KSO for 1.5km more, ignoring turns, and at top of hill gravel road joins from back R. KSO. Pass large factory below to L and KSO, gradually uphill or level all the time.

2–3km after the factory reach a tarmac road on the outskirts of Alcaudete, with public garden to L and fountain to R (*potable* and marked both as 'Fuente de la Vitoria' and 'Fuente Amuña'). Continue down tarmac road and 300–400m later turn L down street to **Ermita de la Fuensanta**. (*Santuario de Nuestra Señora de la Fuen Santa, a very large church with a garden opposite – trees, benches etc. and a better place for a rest than the public garden higher up.*)

Turn R diagonally through garden and continue ahead down tree- and seat-lined street through the town park (*café/bar at end on L*).

10km Alcaudete (80/323)
Small town with all facilities. Hostal/Rte Hidalgo**, Avenida de Córdoba (953.56.10.78). Tenth-century fortress, with several of its towers intact. Neogothic cemetery has cover of sarcophagus from time of Constantine. [R&F: Casa Parroquial, Párroco del Carmen.]

On leaving the park new construction has covered up/destroyed the yellow arrows. **You can either:**

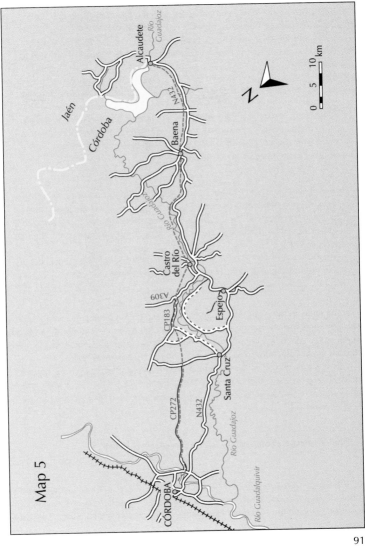

Map 5

a) turn L ahead, downhill, to roundabout with modern statue and then turn R down **Avenida de Córdoba**. After that fork/turn R (marked 'centro') up narrow street with several interesting old houses and which leads directly to the *ayuntamiento*, passing the Iglesia del Carmen on the way. (After that proceed as from ** below.)

Or

b) turn R on leaving park then turn first L (**Calle Peñuelas**) the KSO(L) at fork (unnamed) then turn R and immediately take LH fork (first house on R is no. 77). This is, in fact, the **Calle Alta** (name appears later). Continue to the top and continue ahead (on narrow street – not named) to descend to bottom *(wayside cross on L)*. Turn L (upper of two streets) onto **Calle Llana**, which brings you out opposite the *ayuntamiento*.**

Note: Repainting of the exterior of several of the houses on this route has also obscured some of the arrows. However, the purpose of this alternative seems to be to take you on a tour of the town. It is therefore suggested that you do this 'sightseeing option' in the evening and leave by the more direct route the following morning.

If you want to visit the fortress and/or church of Santa María (high up) go uphill through the arch to the LH side of the *ayuntamiento*.

To continue (the 'sightseeing' option): go down **Calle Campina** (to the RH side of the *ayuntamiento*). At the very bottom (a long street) reach the **church of San Pedro**. Turn L and L again then R immediately, diagonally along an unmarked street then fork R again down **Calle Silos**, passing a white wayside cross halfway down.

Reach a local road at the bottom, cross over and go through olive grove with a ruined house on L and a lot of rubbish. Veer L here and reach the N432 (the *Carretera de Córdoba*). Cross over (carefully) and turn R along it for 70–80m to the turning (on L) of a local road.

Read the next section carefully before you walk any further.

The arrows lead you down this road for 1.5km, after which you are supposed to fork R down a *pista de tierra* through olive groves but recently huge excavation work has been going on for what looks like a motorway, with all the land to both sides bulldozed up and no arrows in sight (or anywhere to put them either). After that you should be able to walk through more olive groves, pass the **Cortijo de la Paloma** *(the last opportunity for any water before Baena, more than 20km away)* and then return to the N432 in order to cross the **Río Guadajoz** by the road bridge (at road KM 352). For the time being, however, you will have to continue along the N432 from Alcaudete to the bridge, mostly downhill *(there is a bar/rte at the petrol station at the junction with the road to Jaén near KM356)*.

Between road KM 353 and 352 you will see yellow arrows bringing the *camino* up a track from back L and leading you along the N432 until you have crossed the bridge (KM352). *The Río Guadajoz forms the boundary between the provinces of Jaén (that you are leaving) and Córdoba (that you are entering).* On the other side of the bridge fork R onto an earth track marked 'Carril Particular' (i.e. 'private lane', though in fact it isn't), // to the road (below it) to start with, then veering R and then L to pass in front of a *swimming pool* (near electric pylons). Fork L uphill here, through (yet more) olive plantations, to a section of the old main road coming from back L. KSO on it for 100m then fork R up earth track that veers R uphill towards a white building used for storing farm machinery and pass to R of it. *This is usually a good place for a rest as one side or the other will normally be in the shade.*

KSO here (i.e. having passed round the building with it on your L) and continue, ignoring turns and heading slightly uphill for 1km. After track begins to descend reach a junction with another track coming from R and fork L here, heading for the *silo de aceite (*a large breeze-block construction ahead of you). *One of the problems with route-finding in this area is that the landowners have ploughed up all the land, including the tracks, so that in places all you have to follow are the tractor marks.*

Turn R here on a gravel track coming from L. KSO for 1km (level now) and then at fork KSO(R). After you pass level with a line of abandoned houses 200m over to your L the track descends gently to the

---

13km (from road turn-off to R) Laguna de Salobral (Laguna del Conde) (18km from Alcaudete) (98/305)
This area is a nature reserve. The lake itself – only 1m deep – may be dry at some times of the year.

Pass to RH side of the lake and KSO. After 1km track joins from back L – KSO(R) ahead until you reach a minor tarred road and the course of the former *tren de aceite* (olive oil train), now converted into a cycle track. Cross the former railway line (*building on R was former railway halt*) and turn R onto road behind the house. Then almost immediately afterwards fork R off it, downhill to a stream at the bottom.

Laguna de Salobral, between Alcaudete and Baena (photo: author)

Cross it as best you can (arrow on large rock on other side indicates that you should turn R). Turn R on other side but then a few metres later turn L steeply uphill (to RH side of fence posts). At top reach a minor tarred road and turn R along it (CP104). Then, when it bends sharp R, just after road KM4, turn L onto track through olive plantations, which continues as a banked-up lane after a while.

Some 1.5km later pass a *cortijo* (to R) with horses and KSO, mainly uphill. 2km after that reach a tarred road, cross over (arrow on 1st tree on L) and KSO again, in a straight line all the time. 3–4km later reach crossing of similar tracks and KSO ahead. 1km later pass a large factory on R *(view of Baena ahead below)*. Continue for another 2km, down to stream at bottom of hill on outskirts of town. Turn R over bridge and KSO ahead, steeply uphill, and road > **Calle Natalio Rivas** when the houses start. Cross **Calle Fernandez de Córdoba** and KSO on other side. Continue until you reach a junction with a public garden opposite then turn L downhill on **Calle Vivrey Don Joaquin del Pino**. Pass the **Santuario de Guadalupe** (on L) and reach the square with the Hostal Rincón in the centre of

9km Baena 407m, pop. 16,599 (107/296)

Town with shops, bars, rtes, banks (+CD) etc. Hostal Rincón (Callle Llano del Rincón 13, 957.67.02.23, inexpensive), Pensión Los Claveles (Juan Valera 15, 957.67.01.74), Albergue Ruta del Califato (Calle Coro 7 & 9, 957.66.50.73), plus 2 hotels. [R&F: Casa Parroquial, Santuario de Guadalupe.]

Baena is renowned for its virgin olive oil and has a museum devoted to this activity. Remains of ninth-century castle and Almedina (old quarter of town). Sixteenth-century Iglesia de Santa María la Mayor, fifteenth- and sixteenth-century Iglesia de San Bartolomé, seventeenth-century Iglesia de San Francisco, sixteenth-century Convento de Madre de Dios, Santuario de Guadeloupe is also sixteenth-century. Mudejar has a coffered ceiling. Oficina de Turismo. Calle de Domingo Henares, s/n.

To continue: veer R and then L (past Hostal Rincón) to a five-point junction with some traffic lights. Take second RH turn (signposted 'Cañete de las Torres') – the **Avenida Cañete de las Torres**. 1km later KSO(L) at a junction (i.e. on same road) then 700–800m later turn R up gravel road with white agricultural buildings to either side and continue uphill through olive groves. KSO, undulating, for 3.5km until you come to a junction at the bottom of a hill and with a small concrete 'bridge' in front and with yellow waymarks telling you NOT to continue that way (i.e. an 'X'). Turn hard L here (arrow is on tree to your L but may be hidden by branches) on track leading you to a road 100m later. Turn R along it, veering L and then R and 1km later, when you see the road bridge in front of you *(cantina (simple bar) in house on RH side but only open evenings/weekends?)* go down a track to the LH side of the road and cross the **Río Guadajoz** by the old bridge. Turn L along what is now a minor tarred road but which was originally a *cañada* and KSO along it, with the river to your L all the time, for 10km *(little shade)* until you reach the outskirts of

20km Castro del Río (127/276)
Small town with bars, shops, banks (+CD) etc. Pensión Casa Antonio (pilgrim-friendly and very close to camino on leaving town), Calle Olivo 13 (nearly 1km behind Iglesia Madre de Dios), 957.37.28.06/37.23.45 and 627.63.49.87; Pensión Sacri, Carretera de Baena, but no other accommodation. Oficina de Turismo: Colegio 31. [R&F: Casa Parroquial.]

Pre-Roman town in important strategic position as a defence on the route from Córdoba to Granada under the Caliphate.

Continue on the road that > the **Avenida de Jaén Baja** and then **either** a) turn R uphill at a junction **to continue** or b) **to visit the town** turn L downhill at junction to a *glorieta* (roundabout) and then turn R uphill to square with *ayuntamiento*. *Map of town outside shows best route for visiting town's main monuments.*

After Castro del Rió the landscape begins to change a little and you will see fields of corn and other cereals, as well as olive groves.

The yellow arrows indicate that you should turn R uphill at the end of **Avenida de Jaén Baja**. At the top veer L and take second (bigger) road (**not** Calle Pozo), a sort of ring road, passing church (on L), veering L downhill all the time. Reach junction with road marked R to 'Bujalance' *(Bar Córdoba and Pensión Antonio are only 100m before that)*.

However, if you continue as described to the *ayuntamiento*, KSO(R) ahead to the **Iglesia Madre de Dios** *(with a clock on it)* and then continue down a very long street to L of church you will reach the square with the Bar Córdoba and the Pensión Antonio to R on **Calle Olivo**. Continue diagonally ahead and reach the road marked to Bujalantes.

Turn R. Pass Guardia Civil barracks, turn R behind petrol station and then turn R up gravel road marked '**Cordel de Córdoba a Granada (Camino de Córdoba)**'. KSO up track, straight uphill, leading out into open country. KSO. Pass **Cortijo Viahornillo** and descend. *After a while the village of Espejo is visible to the L, perched on a mountain top between two hills on the horizon.*

KSO for some 4km (from the Guardia Civil barracks) and then turn R on second track to L, leading to a road 100m away (by a 'bend' sign). *Cereal fields to either side – the olive groves stop here.* Turn R along the road (A309), shortly before KM39. 600m later turn L onto CP183 (signposted 'Córdoba'). KSO. After 2km pass sign to R 'Camino de Garcicalvo.' KSO on road.

4km (from main road) pass modern *cortijo* (on L) with old-style electricity tower. 300m later cross broad bridge over river (probably dry), and on the other side turn L onto gravel track leading through fields (ruined house to R). 500m later reach a junction with an electric pylon and a steep hill ahead (with a farm on top of it); turn L here. At junction turn R uphill then KSO(L) at fork. *River below (with water in it) is the Guadajoz.*

KSO uphill at next crossing to plantation of olive trees at top *(river below you to the L here has an island in it)*. Continue ahead on this not always very clear track up and downhill then, before you get to a line of electric cables, turn L fairly suddenly to follow a line of fence posts to the RH side of a plantation then follow a much clearer track to R. Pass a concrete structure to R.

2.5km (approx.) from bridge reach gravel road crossing at right angles in front of the **Cortijo Castelejo** *(a farm)*. KSO on other side and go downhill. 500m later reach a crossing with wide gravel road and a signpost telling you that it is a 3 hours' walk (back) to Castro del Río, and 5 hours and 30 minutes' (forwards) to Córdoba and, if you turn L here, 1 hour 15 minutes' (5km) to **Santa Cruz**.

If you want to break this very long stage of 37km into two parts you can sleep in Santa Cruz (2 hostales: La Galga and La Bartola, one on either side of the main road).

The following day you do not need to retrace your steps completely but can pick up the route again (after 7km road walking) a bit further along.

Otherwise: *KSO downhill, cross river via the single arch* puente romano *and continue uphill again on the other side and cross small gravel road at top and KSO on other side. KSO, ignoring turns all the time.*

4km after signpost reach tarmac road. Cross over and KSO ahead uphill on track. 4km (after road) reach the **Cortijo Torre de Juan Gil Alto** *(a farm). This is a sort of mini-oasis in an otherwise bleak landscape, with solar panels, trees and a generally very green landscape. Here there is another signpost indicating the distance that you have already come from Castro del Río (5 hours 10mins) and that which remains to Córdoba (3 hours 20mins).*

From here onwards the track follows the CP272 (a road) and you KSO, literally, for 11km, up and downhill between cereal/cornfields, passing the entrance to an occasional *cortijo* and then a small flying club. The last 400m are tarmac, after which you reach a T-junction with a slightly bigger tarmac road. Turn L here, veering R 1km later to cross the road bridge over the motorway on the outskirts of Córdoba. KSO ahead on the other side on a very long street (**Calle Acero del Río**), after which the yellow arrows stop.

Continue at the end along the **Avenida de la Diputación** (waymarked as the 'Ruta del Califato'). This leads you to the **Plaza de la Iglesia** and straight into the **Plaza Santa Teresa** *(bars etc.).* Cross over onto the RH pavement (**Acera del Arrecife**) and continue past small(ish) brick church on R to the **Torre de la Calahorra** *(daily visits) – sitting area on R.* Continue to cross **Río Guadalquivir** by the **Puente Romano** in

---

37km Córdoba 124m, pop. 314,034 (162/241)

Large town with all facilities. Plenty of accommodation in all price brackets, especially in the area surrounding the Mezquita-Catedral (tourist office has list of pensiones). Youth hostel. RENFE, direct buses to Madrid, Granada, Seville, Barcelona and many other parts of Spain. Three tourist offices: Plaza de Tendillas, Campo Santos Mártires (opposite cathedral) and one in the railway station.

Apart from the *Mezquita* (mosque) here are many places of interest worth visiting, whether of Roman, Jewish, Arabic or Christian origin and it is worth spending two days here. Iglesia de Santiago (Calle Agustín Moreno) has a tile Matamoros figure in the porch and a painting of Santiago Peregrino above the altar. Office hours seem to be 20–20.30 hours (for sello).

The route through Córdoba (as is the case with urban areas from here onwards) is not waymarked. It is therefore suggested that you obtain a good street plan to help you find your way out of the town, as well as for visiting its sights.

Cathedral/Mezquita and Puente Romano over Río Guadalquivir, Córdoba

Puerta del Palacio, southeast portal of west façade, Cathedral/Mezquita, Córdoba

The following instructions are given as a fairly direct way of crossing the town but as long as you head for the **Avenida Blas Infante** (where the arrows start again) you can adapt the route as you think best.

You can also decide whether to walk as far as Cerro Muriano (18km but where there is no accommodation apart from R&F) and then return by bus to sleep in Córdoba. The city bus (green) service 'N' leaves (and returns) to the RENFE station every one and a half hours in the week: journey time 45 minutes (but although it is nearly 20km by road it is classified as an 'urban' journey and so only costs the same as a ride in the city!). In Cerro Muriano it leaves from the Bar Cinema on the main road. This is also a very strenuous stage ('cerro' = hill) as, apart from the last kilometre which is downhill, most of the other 17km are all uphill (easier without a heavy rucksack!).

The Asociación de Amigos del Camino de Santiago en Córdoba has information sessions every Wednesday and Thursday evenings (apart from the first fortnight in August when the Casa de Galicia is closed) from 20.00 to 21.30. These are held in the Casa de Galicia, Plaza San Pedro 1 (by the church of that name, in the old part of town).

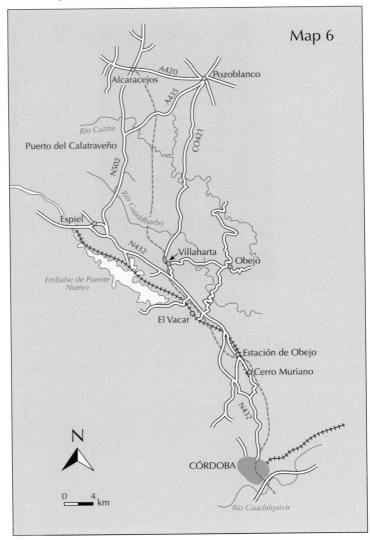

After entering Córdoba and crossing the **Puente Romano**, go to the **Plaza del Triunfo** on the other side of the river and then turn R into **Calle Luis de Cerna**, along the side of the Mezquita-Catedral. Continue on **Cardenal González**, cross Calle San Fernando and continue along **Calle Lucano**. Turn L up **Calle Carlos Rubio** (but to visit the *Iglesia de Santiago* KSO ahead here along *Calle Don Rodrigo and Calle Agustín Moreno*, then retrace your steps).

Continue to **Plaza de la Almagra** and then along **Calle Gutierrez de los Ríos** (a very long street) and turn R at the end into **Calle** and then (small) **Plaza Realejo**. Continue ahead on **Calle Santa María de Gracia** to the church and **Plaza San Lorenzo**. Pass to RH side of church on **Calle María Auxiliadora** to the **Plaza Corazón de María** with large church on L *(Convento de los Trinitarios)*. Turn L here along the **Ronda del Marrubial** *(remains of town walls to L)* and then turn 1st R up the **Calle de Sagunto** and fork 6th L opposite the Cruz Roja (ambulance) HQ up the **Avenida Cinco Caballeros**. Cross the **Avenida Carlos** III (outer ring road) at end and KSO ahead (staggered) up the **Avenida de Blas Infante** and at the first junction (with **Calle Guaraní**) you will find the first yellow arrow on lamp post on LH side. KSO (central reservation is tree-lined), passing the prison (on your R).

Go downhill at the end of the road and turn L under the railway line. Pass the end of the reconstructed Roman bridge over the **Arroyo Pedroche** (on your R) and continue ahead up bank and turn R at top in front of a large bus depot. Turn L at end to traffic lights (petrol station to L). Cross to the other side of main road and then turn hard R onto the old main road. Cross (old) bridge over **Arroyo Pedroche** then KSO on other side, veering L to cross canal and then go uphill ahead into open country. *The next section is well waymarked but is very fiddly and there are not many distinguishing features.* Veer R and then KSO(R) at fork by pylon. This leads you downhill to go under the N432. *Note a sign on bridge surround which says 'Aviso Paso de Ganada. No tocar ni saltar el alambre' – 'Cattle crossing; do not touch or climb over the barbed wire.'*

Turn L on other side, // to road at first, uphill, and then a much better track starts *(watch out for large-scale quarrying operations which may still be in progress)*, // to road over to L all the time. At the top of the hill turn L and then KSO(L) on gravel road to a red and white barrier. Fork R immediately on other side (under cables) onto earth track, leading to a gravel lane. KSO(R) along it and KSO ahead, passing eucalyptus woods (on your R). Cross similar track shortly afterwards and then turn R along a (proper) asphalt road: this is the CP319.

Immediately after RH junction *(road is La Colina)* fork R up earth track uphill (a short-cut) then return to road for 100m then fork of it to R on FP *(whole area to L of road looks set to be developed with a housing estate in near future)*. Continue on path for a short while then cross road and continue on other side, gradually > a wider track. *You are playing hide-and-seek with the road a lot in this area.*

Cross asphalt road and KSO on other side (area is 'El Guido' – *a lot of dogs, both loose and tied up, live here*). KSO(L) at fork 100m after last house then L at next and then turn L along track coming from R and that leads to road at a bend. Cross a gravel track and KSO, descending to meet road again at a bend. Turn R onto it to cross bridge then turn L immediately *(unsuitable for bikes after this)* on wide, clear track earth track alongside river/stream.

500m later note Roman bridge to L by gates to private property. Fork L here to pass by end of it then continue on FP closer to river and with fence to L. Fork R away from it by telephone cables, veering R to continue on rocky path high up and // to clear earth road to R to begin with but then veering L slightly uphill. *This part of the camino coincides with the* Cañada Real Soriana *again and also with long-distance and local waymarked walks as well.*

KSO, fairly high up, in a straight line all the time *(in sort of old slate-mine area). If you look back behind you at top of hill you can still see Córdoba below.* KSO. KSO(L) at fork when the track starts to level out. *The N432 is now on the same level as you but on the other side of the valley, 1km away.* At the top of the next hill a huge quarry is fenced off to the R. Another track joins from back L – KSO ahead here. Pass second set of quarry entrance gates and KSO ahead on wide gravel road, still uphill all the time.

1km later reach main road at a bend. Turn R along it (uphill) for 100m then fork R up a disused railway line and KSO(L) along it for 50m before crossing over to other side. Continue on FP between rocks and pass plaque to L *in memory of the late Don Vincente Benavente de Mora, former president of the Córdoba 'Amigos ' and who really set the waymarking of this part of the route under way.*

Return to road when it does a sharp LH bend and then at next bend (to R) KSO ahead up clear track uphill. Reach a small yellow building at the top (a *chiringuito* – refreshment stall) and see Cerro Muriano below you ahead. Continue ahead, downhill, on FP. Wide track joins from back R. KSO downhill and KSO(R) at fork, reaching main road by roundabout *(with bar/rte)* and fork R (on the **N432A**) into

---

18km Cerro Muriano (180/223)
'Pueblo calle' with everything – bars, shops, rte – concentrated on the main road. Green buses (service 'N') to Córdoba and back, every 1½ hours, from Bar Cinema. Bar 'H' has a sello. [R&F: Local Parroquial, párroco.]

KSO on main road through village, passing (modern) **church of Santa Barbara** (on L) and KSO to end. Fork R opposite the **Guardia Civil barracks** down street over old railway line. KSO here, on long street being laid out with new housing estate. Cross railway line again at end, KSO and join road coming from back L. KSO along it and also when another joins from back L as well (N432A). Pass military base and KSO until you reach

3.5km Estación de Obejo (183.5/219.5)
Former railway station. Small Embalse de Guadanuño is visible to L.

Fork L (to RH side of former bar), veering R to continue to LH side of road. KSO (*the Cañada Real Soriana again*). *Landscape begins to change, with* encinas *(holm – i.e. evergreen – oak) and* jara *(cistus – the bush that smells like church incense).*

KSO (road to R but often hidden), undulating, for 3km until the main N432 gets nearer in front of you on your L and the N432A crosses a railway line. Go downhill and KSO ahead on wide earth road coming from back R. Go under railway line *(the earth road leads to a big* cortijo *called Dehesa de Campo Alto)* and KSO(R) ahead on same sort of track as before, // to railway line. Cross railway line nearly 1km later and continue on track on its RH side. KSO, with railway line to L and main road to R.

KSO for 6km (from going under the railway bridge) until you reach the village of

8.5km El Vacar (192/211)
Castillo on hilltop. Bar/shop on L on road at entrance to village and several other bars. No accommodation. [R&F: former railway station, keys Casa Laura.]

KSO on track to LH side of N432 *(this still coincides with the GR40, the Cañada Real de Soria), sparsely waymarked with red and white flashes).* After 1.5km (road km 240) cross over to its RH side but then cross back again 500m later, by petrol station *(cafetería and small shop, mesón opposite)* and continue on its LH side again. After that veer L down to valley and up again, to emerge on local road (A433) 150m before a 'stop' sign. Turn R along it then turn L to continue // to N432 again (on track on LH side) then 1km later return to road at junction – turning area and beginning of section of old main road.

KSO along it, up and down, // to new road, until you reach the top of the hill, the

4.5km Cuesta de la Matanza (196.5/206.5)
When you get here **BE CAREFUL**.

Between here and Monterrubio de la Serena the route has been changed because of problems with motorway construction and difficulties in finding suitable alternatives to the road in the area near the Embalse de Puente Nuevo. Instead of continuing west to Espiel and Peñarroyo Pueblonuevo before turning north to Monterrubio de la Serena (i.e. going L along the bottom of a 'square' and then going up its LH side), the route now turn north here and then turns L along the top side of the 'square'). From where you are standing it goes directly north to Villaharta (the village in front of you to the L on the other side of the main road) and from there northwest to Alcaracejos, Hinajoso del Duque and Monterrubio. The route is waymarked, but not consistently.

Look out for a RH turn just beyond the brow of the hill, by a road sign marked 'con hielo,' fork R down a gravel track, *ignoring yellow arrow on the road sign inviting you to continue on the old main road*. Continue downhill (the new main road and its fencing is to your R) and as you go you will see the village of Villaharta ahead, nestling in the hills on the other side of the main road. KSO(R) slightly uphill at fork *(yellow arrow shortly afterwards)* and continue on clear *camino de tierra* with road and fence above you to R.

Ignore 3 tunnels under the main road to R and 1.5km from the **Cuesta de la Matanza** reach a junction where you turn R under the new road. Turn R on other side, veering L to pass below line of old workers' cottages *(main road and cement works are now to your L)*.

Reach junction with road coming from **Pedrique** *(village with* casa-museo *of the sculptor Aurelio Teno)* and turn L, cross bridge and continue on gravel road, passing stone wayside cross (on L). 500m later reach the **CO420**, the local road leading from the N432 to Pozoblanco, at the beginning of the village of

4.5km Villaharta 600 (201/202)
Shop(?), bars. hostal/Rte El Cruce, 400m to your L at the road junction, has rooms but ring first to reserve (957.36.70.75). [R&F: Casa Parroquial, Párroco Nuestra Señora de Piedad.]

   Tip: if the hostal is full you can go to Espiel (13km further along the N432) instead and stay either in the (curiously-named) Hostal Descanso del Volante (957.36.30.98, inexpensve) or the Hostal Juan Carlos Primero (957.36.33.36) but phone ahead in both cases. There are buses in both directions approximately every hour, all day long (journey time 15mins) as this junction is on the route of several bus services from Córdoba (to Peñarroyo, Don Benito, Badajoz, etc.)

Note: there is no way of splitting the 38km stage from Villaharta to Alcaracejos into shorter sections – you have no choice but to do it all in one go – so make sure you have enough food and water with you as there are no facilities at all en route.

Cross the CO420 and continue (forking R) on track on other side. (If you slept in the Hostal Cruce turn R up the CO420 for 400m to the junction with the road to Pedrique on your R.) *For the next 25km (from here to the granite wayside cross 1.5km after crossing the Río Cuzna) the route continues to coincide with the GR40 (that goes to Pozoblanco).* Rejoin road very shortly afterwards, then 300m later, at LH bend (opposite sign for *Vía Pecuario*) turn L uphill on FP to join clear *camino de tierra* (the Cañada Soriana) which continues below the road towards the village itself. Just before you reach it, veer R uphill by low stone wall to public garden and then turn L up slope to road. KSO(L) along it, fork R (marked 'Pozoblanco 34') by building with clock on it and continue ahead out of the village on the **Carretera de Pozoblanco**.

When you reach the top of the hill *(1km later, by a notice board about the Valle del Guadiato)* fork (not turn) R onto FP which descends to cross the Arroyo de las Seranas and then returns you to the road at bend you can see ahead – a shortcut of only some 200m. 500m after returning to road, opposite junction with a *camino de tierra* on R, fork L off road, uphill, passing behind a farm (the **Cortijo de la Capilla**, now on your R) onto a grassy *camino* (marked with the GR40 signposts to 'Pozoblanco 10H'). Join a bigger track at end of farm and KSO, up and then (mainly) downhill. KSO, ignoring turns to L and R, with splendid views all round on a clear day.

After passing **Las Narváez** (a small farm), cross stream 300m later and then turn R at T-junction uphill 150m after that. Go through gate and 700m later reach the

7km Río Guardalbarbo (208/195)
Nice place for a (short) rest. You can normally cross the river (shallow) without any problem, via stepping stones, but if it is too deep go 200m (L) upstream where you should find a FB.

Continue on similar track on other side, passing through gate, uphill. Pass breeze-block barn (L) and some farm workers' cottages (R) and KSO, gently uphill all the time. At the top (1km from river) go through some gates and track levels out a bit. 1km after that (i.e. 2km from river) reach a T-junction with a much wider track/*camino de tierra* and turn L along it. KSO for 4.5km until you reach a small road bridge with concrete bollards.

7km Bridge over the Arroyo Lorito (215/188)

KSO for 250m more then, at bend, turn R onto a narrower *camino de tierra*, passing between olive groves, climbing gently all the time and with the stream to your R. 1km later reach a fork where the LH option *(leading to the* Puerto del Calatraveño *on the N502)* has gates: take the RH fork but then at the next fork shortly afterwards KSO(L) ahead on a rocky track that may not be clearly waymarked. KSO ahead uphill all the time. Another track joins from back L, after which the surface improves and another track joins from back L as you pass under the telephone wires. 500m after that (and 1.5km from the fork by the gate) pass site of former mine workings with houses and – beware! – the **Ventorro del Cachorro** (kennels?), where several very large dogs live. Track levels out here for a while.

KSO, track > a gravel road, climbing all the time, until its levels out and 1km after the mine workings reach a wide, flat area with a junction of paths where the road you are on bends L: here you are level, at 750m, with the pass on the main road away to the L, the

4km Junction near the Puerto del Calatraveño (219/184)

The track you were on bends L here and leads to the N502. KSO ahead, instead, on a *camino de tierra*, level at first then gradually losing height. *The landscape begins to open out a little, as you descend and > slightly more inhabited. The plains of the Valle de los Pedroches are now visible ahead. Track marked with green 'V.P.' (Vía Pecuaria) posts from time to time.*

The section from here to Alcaracejos is not well waymarked at present though it is easy enough to follow.

2.5km (from the junction at the top) reach a junction with a wide unsurfaced road and turn R along it. 250m later, when the fencing on your LH side stops, turn L onto a *camino de tierra* again (still the Cañada Soriana). 800m after that, in valley, cross stream by stepping stones and KSO ahead on other side, uphill again, with a perimeter fence on your R. Cross the entrance lane to the **Cortijo Corromenos del Valle** and KSO ahead again on other side.

800m after that, at the top of a hill, go through a *cledo* (waymark on gatepost) and then go down towards the large house ahead of you (this is the **Cortijo de la Hoyarza**), veering L to reach T-junction by wall. Turn R here then KSO(R) ahead at fork, veering L to go uphill and through gates in the *cortijo's* perimeter fence. Turn R immediately on other side. KSO, descending rapidly most of the time, and 1km later reach the

6km Río Cuzna (225/178)
This is a shallow (though fairly wide) river which can normally be crossed via stepping stones to R.

Continue uphill on other side alongside fence and KSO for 1.5km until you come to a junction with a granite wayside cross known as *La Quemá. This is the point where the Camino de Santiago and the GR40 part company (the latter turns R here to Pozoblanco).* Turn left here along a *cañada* between fencing, on the **Camino de Alcaracejos**. KSO, undulating gently, and 2km later reach a local road, the

4km A435 (229/174)
This leads (L) to the N502 and (R) to Pozoblanco.

Cross over and continue on similar track until you reach the

5km Ermita/Merendero (234/169)
Small chapel to L of road and picnic area opposite, the site of local *romerías.* Covered seating area on R useful for rest in hot or bad weather.

At 4 large pillars 100m later turn L onto wide unsurfaced road and KSO for 4km, until you reach the fourteenth-century **Ermita de San Sebastián**, on the LH side of the road, overlooking Alcaracejos below you. Continue downhill, KSO(L) at fork on road that > the **Calle San Sebastián**. Turn L at end to reach the main road in

5km Alcaracejos 1400 (239/165)
Very small town with shops, bars, banks, rtes. Hostal/Rte Fonda Nueva (957.15.64.11) and Hostal Las Tres Jotas (957.15.61.21) have rooms, both at junction of N502 and A420 in centre. [R&F: Parroquia de San Andrés.]
From here onwards the landscape opens out, is much flatter and the Camino Mozárabe becomes much less strenuous.

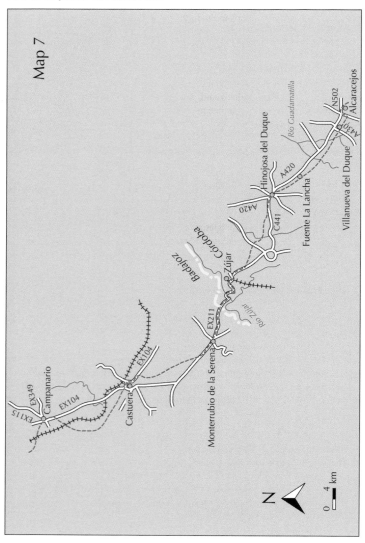

Map 7

From the main crossroads in the town (N502 and A420) go along main road in the direction of Córdoba and then turn R between **Talleres Galán** (a garage) and house no. 20 down a lane, passing granite wayside cross 200m later. 300m after that KSO at crossing with old-style electricity transformer. KSO ahead on walled lane between fields, // to the A420 over to your R.

KSO ahead, ignoring turns until you reach the entrance to the village, continuing along the **Calle Reyes Católicos** and passing the **Cruz de la Fuente Vieja**, an iron wayside cross mounted on a granite pedestal, in

3.5km Villanueva del Duque (242.5/160.5)
Shops, bar (at end of village), banks (CD inside?). Note the solid double front doors in the old-style houses in the villages, with a cupboard-door type of judas-window in the RH door. Church of San Mateo.

Continue to the **Plaza de la Iglesia** and the church, veering L to the *ayuntamiento*, then pass to the side of it down the **Calle Mora Figueroa**, a long street, not named at start. Cross a road and continue ahead on other side on the RH of two forks, between a metal cross *(on L, similar to the one at the entrance to the village)* and the Bar Rancho Grande (on R). Then cross the main road to Peñarroyo and continue on other side down a gravel lane.

Continue ahead, ignoring turnings. Pass farm buildings and then go through slightly rockier landscape. *Occasional trees offer shade for a rest.* 1.5km later pass large cattle farm (on R) and continue ahead, with stream to your L, and then pass to RH side of stone smallholding. KSO between fencing.

1km later, by junction of electric pylons/cables, 200m from road over to your R and by a small field with a group of trees in it and granite posts round its edge, turn LEFT 50m afterwards to ford the **Arroyo del Lanchar** and continue on a *camino de tierra* on other side. KSO on this for 3km until you reach

6.5km Fuente La Lancha (249/154)
One of the smallest villages in the province of Córdoba. Bank, unmarked shop (near church), café/bar on road at end of village.

The track you are on is joined by another coming from back R. KSO, passing a sitting area and track that runs into the **Calle del Calvario**. Continue along it, turn R at the end into the **Calle María Auxiliadora**, which then > the **Calle Virgen de Guía** and reach the **Plaza de la Iglesia** with the **church of Santa Catalina** and the *ayuntamiento*. Continue ahead down the **Calle Nueva** and KSO to end of village at junction with a granite wayside cross and a lane coming from back R. *(Turn hard R to road here if you want to visit the café/bar and then retrace your steps.)*

500m later reach the main road, turn L along it for 200m to a deserted house then cross over and fork L down a *camino de tierra* with wall to LH side. 300–400m after that KSO(L) at fork (RH option leads to a farm) and continue between fields, // to the road over to your L. 1km later reach the

3km Río Guadamatilla (252/151)

Cross to other side (go up to road bridge if necessary) and KSO ahead on similar track. KSO for 6.5km, ignoring turns and going through the occasional *cledo*, until you return to the road by the

6.5km Ermita de la Virgen de Guía (258.5/144.5)
Small chapel/shrine with picnic site. Covered sitting area useful for rest in very hot/bad weather.

Turn R along road for 500m then fork L off it by road KM121 onto track that passes behind the *naves* (i.e. hangars) on a small industrial estate *(the last building is a mesón – i.e. bar/rte)*. KSO for 2km more, entering Hinojosa via a street lined with factories. Reach a junction with the remains of the fountain of the **Pilar de los Llanos**, dating from 1570.

If you want to sleep in the Hostal El Cazador turn hard R here then R again when you reach the main road.

Continue ahead down street to LH side of park (or go through it), turn R at end then first L down **Avenida Corredora**, a very long street leading to the **Plaza del Catedral** and the **church of San Juan Bautista** in the centre of

3.5km Hinojosa del Duque 7000 (262/141)
Small town with shops, bars, rtes, banks etc, with a lot of factories specialising in the production of ham and *embutidos* (cooked sausage). Tourist office (Plaza San Juan), hostal/Rte El Cazador (on main road) has rooms (Avda Marqués de Santillana 112, 957.14.04.43 & 637.57.39.34). [R&F: Parroquia de San Juan.]

> Church of San Juan Bautista (also referred to as the 'Catedral de la Sierra'), convent church of the Purísima Concepción, Ermita de San Sebastián, Ermita de San Isidro.

Pass to RH side of church (**San Juan Bautista**) into the **Plaza de San Juan** behind it, pass to RH side of tourist office down the **Calle Jesús** and reach the **Plaza del Duque de Béjar** with the **Convento de la Concepción** on your L. Continue ahead into the **Calle Monjas** but then fork L immediately into the **Calle Isabel la Católica** (not named at start). Turn second R into **Calle Ramon y Cajal** then turn L at end into **Calle Juan XXIII** and continue onto **Calle Pius XII**, passing the *matadero municipal* (slaughterhouse, on your R).

KSO at end onto road into open country *(yellow arrows start again here)* and KSO ahead at bend along lane following line of electricity pylons. 500m later minor road joins from back R by cement works: KSO ahead along it and 1km later, at road KM2, turn R onto wide track, veering L (industrial building now to your L). *Landscape is more or less flat, pasture land.* KSO, ignoring turns, for 2km more, then ford the

4km Arroyo de la Dehesa (266/137)
The stream, like many others, is visible ahead due to the bushes/small trees that line its banks.

KSO ahead on other side and continue for 3.5km, passing *encina* groves (on L), until you reach a cattle farm *(El Coto Chico)* – dogs! 300–400m after the first building, after a small stone house and before a white concrete one, turn L down small stony track under telegraph wires and along line of electricity pylons and 200m later reach the

4km Arroyo del Cohete (270/133)

Ford this *(if the water is too deep at the crossing place try going R downstream where there are some rocks)* and KSO ahead on other side. Reach a minor road 2km later *(if you look R here you will see the keep in the castle complex in Belalcázar de la Serena)*. KSO for 5km *(after 3km you can see Monterrubio ahead on a clear day)*. *This is a very nice quiet section in good weather, very slightly uphill all the time, with* encina *groves to either side.*

When you (eventually) reach a farm KSO(L) at crossing and 500m after that reach another minor road. Turn R along it for 3.5km *(hardly any traffic at all)* until you reach a T-junction with a

10.5km Local road (280.5/122.5)

Turn L, veering R and then L downhill and then up to cross the railway line 1km later *(former Zújar station below to R)*. KSO for 3km more until you reach the bridge over the

4.5km Río Zújar (285/118)

The river forms the boundaries of the autonomous regions of Andalucía and Extremadura and the provinces of Córdoba and Badajoz though on the *camino* you continue for 2km more until you actually cross from one to the next. Ermita de Nuestra Señora de Gracia de las Alcantarillas (patron saint of Belalcázar) on hill above bridge, built in the thirteenth century on the site of a Roman fort and an earlier Iberian settlement, enlarged (with Gothic-style apse) in the sixteenth century. Splendid views all round on a clear day and a good place for a rest.

Immediately after crossing bridge fork L up hill on track to visit *Ermita* then continue ahead on track leading back down to the road again. KSO along it for 8km. *An easy walk to Monterrubio, with nice views in good weather, though it is all gradually uphill and the wind is often in your face.*

8km Monterrubio de la Serena 878m, pop. 3220 (293/110)

A very long thin small town with shops, banks, rtes etc., whose main industry is the production of olive oil. Pensión Balsera, Calle Constitución 47 (924.61.00.04), Hostal Vatican, Plaza de España 15 (924.61.06.33) plus Hotel Coto de la Serena*** (in former Casa del Cordón near church, 924.63.51.69). [R&F: Parroquia.]

Sixteenth-century church of Nuestra Señora de la Concepción, Ermita de San Isidro (modern), eighteenth-century Ermita de los Cuarenta Martires de Levante (the town's patron saints).

On entering the town KSO ahead, passing to R of petrol station and continue for 700–800m to a crossing (the road you are on is marked here as **Calle Cruces**). Turn L to church and centre of town, KSO ahead to continue.

Pass **Bar El Paso** (on R) and KSO on main road for 700–800m, pass junction with traffic lights then, just before the town exit boards, fork R down a minor road (a former *camino de tierra* that has been tarmacked), passing to RH side of **Disco Oli-Bar**. KSO, ignoring turnings *(very little traffic)* for 15km, passing through the **Reserva de los Berciales** *(nature reserve). There are with olive groves to either side then, later,* encinas. *The village of Benquerencia de la Serena is visible in the hills ahead.*

After 10–11km reach a minor road (marked 'Pista Benquerencia–Puerto Hurraco 12km'). Cross over and KSO ahead on other side. After this you have a plunging view of the landscape ahead and can see the beginning of Castuera on the 'bump' on the horizon, with houses on it. From here you see more *encinas* and the landscape becomes rockier, but with more houses dotted about in it.

After 15km (i.e. 4.5km later) the tarmac stops at a junction of houses. KSO here, road > a *camino de tierra*. 700m later cross a stream and veer R to continue. Reach the road 1km later on the outskirts of Castuera *(note large cactus 'hedges' over to your R)* and turn R along it to the town.

18km Castuera (311/92)
Small town with shops, banks, rtes etc. Hotel Paraíso, Calle Santa Ana 15 (924.76.014.50 is in centre of town, Hostal Los Naranjos (924.76.10.54) and Hotel Barón del Pozo (924.76.10.48) are both on the Carretera Villanueva–Andujar on outskirts. [R&F: *ayuntamiento/polideportivo* (sports hall).]

Eighteenth-century Iglesia de Santa María Magadalena, Palacio Condes Casa Ayala, Plaza de San Juan, Ermita de San Juan, tourist office.

Note: if you are thinking of taking a bus from Campanario to Don Benito check timetables in bus station here in Castuera.

Turn R at road junction at start of town *(Guardia Civil post on R)* and then fork L down **Calle Huertos**. Continue ahead at end into the **Plaza de España** with church, *ayuntamiento*, post office and tourist office, and then continue on other side along the **Calle de la Constitución**, **Calle Marties** *(passing small church of Nuestra Señora del Buensuceso on R)* and **Calle Ana**. When you get to the end turn L behind a small *ermita* down the **Paseo de Santa Ana**, along the RH side of a public garden, and at the end KSO ahead down **Calle Zurburán**, past petrol pumps (on your R). Reach a roundabout *(with a real aeroplane on a stand in the middle of it)* and the Cruz Roja (Red Cross) post to your L.

113

Continue ahead on main road to Campanario then 200m later turn L down tarmac lane marked 'Centro de desinfección de véhculos', passing behind the **Salon Ovino** *(a big building used for agricultural fairs)*, veering R into the open countryside. *This path, as far as the former railway station at Quintana de la Serena, is known as the 'Senda del Rey.'*

Fork R *(no arrows at start)* by house called 'Huerta del Prado' uphill along a *camino de tierra*, past electricity transformer. KSO, on ridge, ignoring turns, with open vistas to all sides.

4.5km from Castuera reach the metal railway bridge (on your R) over the **Río Guadalefra**. Ford the river and KSO on other side, keeping railway line on your R. (If you DO need to cross the river via the railway bridge do so extremely carefully, especially if, like the author of this guide, you do not have a good head for heights.) 1km later reach the

---

6km Former railway station at Quintana de la Serena (317/86)
Station buildings now used as an *albergue*.

Pass to L of *albergue*, cross minor road coming from village of Quintana de la Serena over to your L and KSO ahead on track to LH side of railway track. 2.5km later pass a level-crossing sign (just after railway marker 365/4 with a 'stop' sign: a track turns R here but yellow arrows invite you to continue ahead.

KSO on track that moves away from the railway line but which, 3km before Campanario, it eventually crosses. KSO uphill on the other side *(more houses and other buildings dotted about here, large granite quarry to R)* and shortly before you each the main road *(you can see Magacela from here, the pointed hill on the horizon ahead)* turn R onto a *camino de tierra* which leads you to it, at first running // to it on a *cañada*-style path then later continuing on the road itself. After passing a *vertadero* (municipal tip, on R) continue to a junction marked (to R) 'centro urbano,' after the town's place name boards, at the entrance to

---

14km Campanario (331/72)
Small town with shops, bars, banks etc., but no official accommodation as such. Lady at house no. 55 opposite the Guardia Civil may have rooms or you may be able to sleep in the *polideportivo* – ask in *ayuntamiento*. Casa del Diablo.

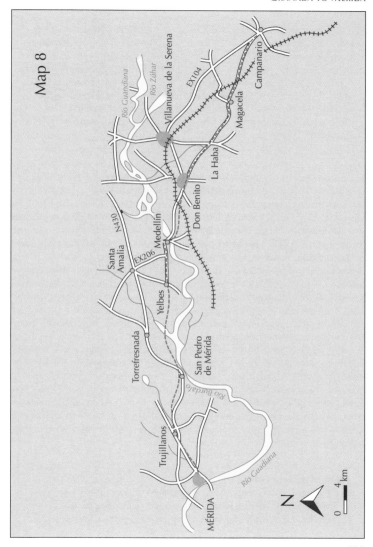

Map 8

Río Guadiana

Río Zújar

Villanueva de la Serena

EX104

Campanario

Magacela

La Haba

Don Benito

N430

Santa Amalia

EX206

Medellín

Yelbes

Torrefresnada

San Pedro de Mérida

Río Burdalo

Trujillanos

Río Guadiana

MÉRIDA

N

0   4 km

If you don't feel like continuing for another 23km to Don Benito (the next place with anywhere to sleep) you could consider taking the bus to Don Benito, sleep there and return to Campanario the following morning to walk back to Don Benito. Be careful, however, if you decide to take this option, that a) you avoid Sundays (when there are far fewer buses) and b) you arrive in Campanario by about 13.30, in time to find the bus stop and catch what may be the last bus of the day (around 14.00 – you can check this out in the bus station in Castuera). The bus stop in Campanario is at the end of a public park, almost opposite the *Casa de la Cultura*).

At the entrance to Campanario turn R (marked 'Centro urbano'), turn first L and then second R down **Calle Espronceda**, passing to LH side of a public park. Turn R past bus stop *(waiting room is dug out underneath park)* and then, if you want to visit the town, KSO(R) ahead on **Calle Los Benites** and **Calle Plazuela** to the **Plaza del Carmen** with two churches and the **Plaza de Espana** and the *ayuntamiento*. Retrace your steps (to the start of the **Calle Los Benites**) and turn R. Take the LH of two streets, the **Paseo de Extremadura**, downhill, and turn L opposite **Muebles Soria** (a furniture factory) down a *camino de tierra* leading to the main road. Turn R and then immediately L beside a tile and paving stone factory down a minor road through fields. *You are now on the* **Colada del Camino de Zalamea***, formerly a wide earth track but now tarmacked. It is marked as 'Ruta 9, Campanario–Don Benito,' with a noticeboard at the start. (The whole section from here to Don Benito is now, unfortunately, on tarmac, though this part has hardly any traffic at all.)*

KSO for 7km then cross the railway line and KSO ahead again on the other side. When you reach the first houses in the lower part of the village (this is the Barrio del Berrocal) KSO(R) ahead at fork. Follow road round through village then turn L by house no. 12 to fountain and lavadero *in the middle of the street. Veer L uphill here (Calle Arroyo de la Fuente), cross a road (shop on R) and go up* **Calle Alfarerías** *on other side. Turn R on local road (BA084). 200m later fork L up towards what looks like a factory or a grain silo from a distance but which is, in fact, a (modern) church, at the beginning of*

10km Magacela (341/62)
Bar(?), shop, bank (+CD) but no accommodation.
    Small village perched on hilltop with a *castillo* dominating the entire region, built on site of prehistoric settlement. Ermita de los Remedios, Iglesia Santa Ana

(built on site of former mosque) of former Convento Prioral, fifteenth-century Ermita de San Antonio, sixteenth-century Cárcel vieja, Casa del Intendente (Casa-Palacio) of Intendente of Orden de Alcántara, sixteenth-century castillo, dolmen with megalithic burial ground.

Continue steeply uphill ahead on **Calle Pedro de Valvivia**, passing Guardia Civil barracks (on R), veering L near top into small square. To visit the Castillo and take a walking tour of the historic part of the village, turn second L here (up **Calle Don Enrique Ramirez**) and then retrace your steps afterwards.

To continue: turn R and then reach large open esplanade *(seats)* with splendid views over the whole area. KSO ahead and continue out of village on road ahead, downhill, passing public garden on your L. This is the BA084, a local road without too much traffic. *(There is, in fact, a* camino *over to your L which will take you to La Haba but is it frequently waterlogged.)* KSO for 6km, until you reach the junction with the EX346 in

8km La Haba (349/54)
Settlement founded in the sixteenth century, belonging to the Orden de Alcántara. 3 bars on road (one to L, 2 to R).

Turn R onto EX346, marked 'Don Benito 7' and then KSO(L) at junction (RH option is for Villanueva de la Serena), passing petrol station (on L) and crossing the Arroyo del Campo. KSO on road (you can walk on tractor tracks on L for part of the way) and continue until you reach the entrance to **Don Benito**, at a roundabout by an electricity substation.

Continue for 300m more to a second roundabout *(with a metal statue of the Virgin Mary in the middle)* and turn R down **Calle Cruces** to visit the town. However, if you do not want to do so, continue ahead on main road (**Avenida Canosas** and then **Avenida Eduardo Dato**) until you come to a roundabout (the **Plaza de Hispanidad**, *bar to L)* at the beginning of the **Avenida de Badajoz, where the yellow arrows start again.**

6km Don Benito, pop. 30,000 (355/48)
Medium-sized town with all facilities. 5 hotels, 1 hostal and 1 pensíon but only the Hotel Miriam 1* (Calle Donosco Cortes 1, 924.81.15.39), the Hotel Miriam

2** (Calle Donosco Cortes 2), the Hotel Ortiz* (Calle Fernan Pérez, 28, 924.81.04.45) and the Hostal Galicia (Plaza Sánchez Cortes s/n, 924.80.35.28) are in the centre of town, near the Plaza de España; the others are all on the outskirts, on the main road to Villanueva (Hotel Veracruz, 924.80.13.62) and Pensión Olivo, 924.80.00.06), both at KM 101, and on the Avenida de Badajoz (Hotel Vegas Altas***, 925.81.00.05 – you pass this leaving the town). [R&F: Parroquia.]

The town takes its name from its founder and benefactor, Don Benito. There is a thirteenth-century Iglesia de Santiago Apóstol, with painting of Santiago Matamoros in the middle panel of lower of two rows of paintings in reredos and an almost life-size statue of Santiago Peregrino on RH side altar, with halo as well as hat (and scallop shell), stick, calebase and scallops on his cape. Mass daily at 10.00 and 20.00. Barrio de San Sebastián. Don Benito also has an interesting Museo Etnográfico, located in the Casa del Conde.

Read the section from Medellín to San Pedro de Mérida before you walk any further.

To continue into the town: from **Calle Cruces** *KSO(L) at fork into* **Calle Virgen** *(turn L here then R then L to visit San Sebastián, the oldest church in Don Benito, then retrace your steps). Continue ahead, passing the* **Capilla de la Virgen de Guadalupe** *(on R) and reach the* **Plaza de España** *with the ayuntamiento, Iglesia de Santiago and (modern) Casa de la Cultura (note storks' nests on roof).*

To leave: go back down the **Calle Virgen***, turn R into* **Calle Bustos***, continue along* **Calle Arrabal** *and at roundabout KSO(R) along* **Calle Luna***. KSO(R) at fork along* **Calle Argentina** *and reach the* **Plaza de Hispanidad** *and the junction at the start of the* **Avenida de Badajoz** *(and the start of the yellow arrows).*

Cyclists take the EX105 to Mengabil and Guareña (27km) from here and then the EX307 via Valverde de Mérida direct to Mérida (22km).

Continue along the **Avenida de Badajoz**, passing the *feria* (agricultural fair) site and KSO(L) at junction with roundabout in direction of Medellín. Pass petrol station (on L) and 500m later cross railway line. *(Fortress in Medellín now visible on top of LH of three hills on skyline ahead.)* Fork L at bottom of slope into service road until it stops some 400–500m later. KSO on LH side of road for 500m more then turn L and immediately R onto a *camino de tierra* at small junction on L with 'stop' sign. KSO, // to road but not next to it, until you reach a T-junction 700m before you reach the entrance to **Medellín** *(petrol station over to your R on road)*. Turn R and each entrance to town by junction with statue of Quintus Cecilio, the town's Roman founder.

8km Medellín 251m, pop. 2347 (363/40)
Small town with shops, bars, rtes, banks (+CD). Hostal/Rte Río (924.82.26.70) at end of town has rooms.

 Castillo of Arabic origin, well preserved and dominating the area all around. The town was founded in 70 BC by consul Quintus Caecius Metellus Pius, and named Metellinum after him. Birthplace of Hernan Cortés (founder of the Mexican city of Veracruz). Thirteenth-century Iglesia de San Martín, built on the site of a temple dedicated to the Roman god Pluto. Thirteenth-century Iglesia de Santiago, now closed for services but used as a visitors' centre for the Parque Arqueológico, and the parish church of Santa Cecilia (sixteenth century, built in part with recycled stone from Roman theatre). Seventeenth-century Puente de los Austrias, 400m long with 20 arches, built beside the remains of the original Roman bridge over the Río Guadiana. Tourist office (open evenings only) [R&F: Parroquia de Santa Cecilia.]

Read the description of the route from here to Mérida before you proceed any further.

 Continue ahead up **Calle San Francisco** then turn R opposite a bank by traffic lights, to square with the **Torre del Reloj** and the *ayuntamiento*. Turn L after first part of paved area to visit *church of Santa Cecilia (note storks' nests on its roof – penthouse-style as the church tower is much lower than its roof)* and then retrace your steps. Go up cobbled path in top RH corner of square to T-junction, then turn R to visit *Iglesia de Santiago* and remains of first-century-BC Roman theatre *(church was built on theatre's 'stage' area)*. Continue up paved path to visit the Castillo.

 To visit the inside of the towers and the inner courtyards you need an entrance ticket when the Castillo is open (evenings only?), but at other times you can walk round most of the outside; it is worth the climb for the 360-degree views, during which you can see clearly where you have come from and where you are going next.

 Retrace your steps to the T-junction between the two churches and turn R to visit the twelfth-century *Iglesia de San Martín (it was restored in the fourteenth century and its side chapel added in the eighteenth century; Hernan Cortés was baptised here (font still exists) in 1485).*

Turn R at bottom of paved track past the ruins of the **Porta Coeli** *(a former Roman gateway demolished in the nineteenth century, and the obligatory gate to leave the town and cross the Puente de las Austrias over the river – i.e. on the* calzada Córdoba–Mérida). Site of former Ermita de San Pablo.

Go downhill, veering L at bottom and then turn R to cross the bridge over the Río Guadiana. *Swimming area to L. Arrows start again here.* 200m before you reach the end of the bridge fork L onto a stony track that veers L and then continues // on the EX206, which is now over to your R. 800m later you will reach a T-junction with a tarmac road.

*Here (walkers only) you have two options open to you, according to weather and season, one of which involves fording the Rio Bordalo. (****Cyclists*** *should take the second option, via Santa Amalia.)*

Option A
In July and August the water is low enough to enable you to ford the river – a shorter, quieter option than the 7km longer alternative via Santa Amalia. When you reach the T-junction turn L (despite obliterated arrows) along the minor road marked 'Yelbes 4'. KSO ahead, cross **Arroyo Caganchez** and after 2km, on a clear day, you can see the medieval bridge over the Río Montanchez over to R in the distance. Continue ahead on the road to

> **5km Yelbes**
> Small village with 3 bars, shop.

KSO to end of village to T-junction of tarmac road and sign saying 'Canal Secundario No. 4'. Cross over and KSO on *camino de tierra* ahead, veering L. KSO for 1.5–2km and then turn L at T-junction of similar tracks. *Flat all round, swampy fields to both sides.* KSO. At another T-junction 500m later *(farm with two plastic green-houses over to your L)* turn R then, after crossing an irrigation canal, turn L at next T-junction 20m later. At fork shortly afterwards (by another bridge), KSO(R) ahead, then KSO ahead at crossing 300m after that. *The line of trees you can see ahead of you is the Río Bordalo.*

1km later reach a road (5.5km from Yelbes). Turn L and 500m later, at crossing *(with another road back to Yelbes)*, turn R towards the line of trees ahead. Turn L 1km later at junction of similar tracks. KSO for 1km then, 150m before a farm, fork R down grassy track through fields, towards the line of trees by the river, then KSO(L) alongside them until you reach the river. KSO(L) alongside them until you reach the fording place at the

9km Río Bordalo (377/19)

Cross the river, choosing carefully where you 'land' once you are on the other side, as parts of the opposite bank are at present very overgrown. Pick up a not very clear track leading L to start with, but which > fairly quickly more distinct and which, after a crossing 300m later, > a very clear *camino de tierra*. KSO ahead on this, west all the time, with the motorway away to your R, the river wending its way along over to the L. *Waymarking only very sparse but the route is not hard to follow.*

Continue ahead, ignoring turns, for 3.5km until you reach a T-junction with the motorway, which is now immediately ahead of you. Turn L here and 500m later reach another junction. Turn R on gravel road leading under the motorway, veering L uphill on other side.*** KSO(R) at fork *(handy seat under tree to L)*. Continue uphill, passing cemetery, and enter village of **San Pedro de Mérida** (5km).

Option B

In months other than July and August, turn R at the T-junction and then L to continue along the hard shoulder of the EX206. Cross the **Arroyo La Galapaguera** and KSO for 4km.

Due to the many irrigation channels in this area there are unfortunately no suitable alternatives to long stretches of tarmac. However, if you decide you would prefer to take a bus to Mérida bus station you can do so from Medellín, Santa Amalia or Torresfresnada, but note that the last bus leaves in the middle of the afternoon (Villanueva de la Serena–Don-Benito–Mérida service) and check times carefully beforehand, especially for Sundays and holidays.

When you reach road KM82, opposite the white gates of a *finca* with no name on it, turn L onto a farm track, passing an old-style electricity transformer. Cross a bridge over a stream/canal and turn R at junction on other side. Return to the **EX206** by a bridge 300m before its junction with the N430, but then KSO(L) at a bend on a section of the old road leading towards a petrol station *(bar/rte)* on the outskirts of

8km Santa Amalia (371/32)
Small town with shops, bars, rtes, banks (+CD) etc. Hostal Trebole in town centre, Hostal Caribe on outskirts (near petrol station).

To visit the town: *cross the N430 (very carefully) and KSO ahead up road to RH side of petrol station. Retrace your steps afterwards to continue.*

121

To continue without visiting the town: veer L when you each the **N430** and continue along its hard shoulder. When you see the fork marked 'Torrefresnada' KSO(L) along it into the village.

9km Torrefresnada (380/230)
Bar.

KSO ahead on road out of village and then on the *vía de servicio (an earth track // to the motorway and used for droving animals)*. Continue on it until you reach the outskirts of **San Pedro de Mérida**. Continue on track to RH side of motorway and KSO(R) at fork *(handy seat under tree to L)*. Continue uphill, passing cemetery, and enter village of

9km San Pedro de Mérida (389/14)
Hostal Juan Porro has rooms (924.325.010/198), 2 bar/rtes, all by petrol station on main road. [R&F: Albergue municipal, contact Guardia Civil.]

Continue ahead along the **Calle Mayor**, then fork L uphill by small garden. *Turn L here up Calle Iglesia (not marked at start) to visit church then retrace your steps.* Veer R to the *Plaza España* and *ayuntamiento (public WC)*. *(Turn L here along the Avenida Virgen de la Albuera if you want to go to the hostal or one of the bar/rtes then retrace your steps to continue.)* KSO ahead up **Avenida de Mérida**, passing the Guardia Civil barracks on R and continue uphill *(passing more handy seats on R!)* to the top, 1km from village, with junction by bridge over the motorway. KSO ahead here on its service road to RH side, pass another bridge (on your L) and then another at the entrance to

6km Trujillanos (395/8)
Hostal Rte Asador de Tomás on main road has rooms (924.32.70.05). Bar Centro in village itself reported to be very pilgrim-friendly.

KSO ahead on service road all the time, passing hostal and bus stop and reach junction with bridge over the motorway. The arrows then lead you ahead on the service road again, until you come to the **Arroyo Téjar** 2km later, where you go under the motorway, picking up a road on the other side which you turn R along it into Mérida.

Roman theatre, Mérida

However, you may find it just as easy, though not quite as quiet to start with, if you cross the motorway via the bridge at the end of Trujillanos and then turn R onto the old main road (NV). KSO, pass Camping Mérida *(open all year)* on L after 4–5km and enter the town, just past a very large hotel on the L, on the **Avenida María Auxiliadora**. KSO ahead at a large roundabout with fountains playing, past the **Ermita de Nuestra Señora de la Antigua** (on your R), on the **Avenida Juan Carlos I** (marked 'Centro urbano').

Continue ahead, passing the **Circo Máximo (Hipodromo)** on L and the **Acueducto de San Lázaro** on R. Veer R to continue on **Avenida de Extremadura** (stay on LH side of road), continue on raised walkway, go through pedestrian tunnel under a road and 400m later reach a public garden on your L (**Parque de Lopez Ayala**). Fork (not turn) L to cross it diagonally then continue through a second garden, uphill to the **Plaza Puetra de la Villa**, a six-point junction at the top.

KSO ahead down **Calle Santa Eulalia**, passing to R of tourist office *(building with a clock on it)* and continue down to the **Plaza de España** with the cathedral and *ayuntamiento* in the centre of **Mérida**.

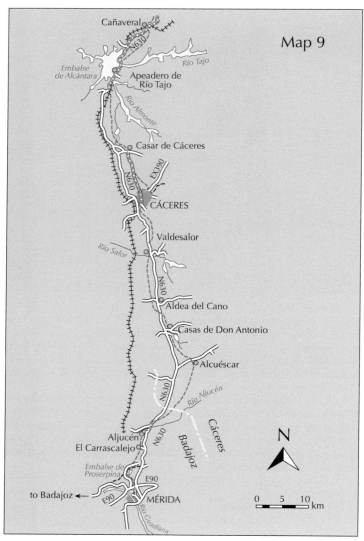

Map 9

8km Mérida 218m, pop. 51,600 (220.5/779.5)

All facilities, RENFE, buses to Madrid, Seville, Cáceres, Salamanca. Capital of the autonomous region of Extremadura. No pilgrim-only accommodation but several hotels and hostales, including Hostales Senero (Calle Holguín 12, tel: 924.31.72.07), Nueva España (Avenida de Extremadura 6, 924.31.33.56), El Alfarero (Calle Sagasta 40, 924.30.31.830, El Torero (Avenida de Alange 1, 924.37.17.89), Anas (Avenida Reina Sofía 9, 924.31.11.13) and Pensión Alameda (Calle Magadalena 1, 924.30.04.74). Hostal Los Pinos, Avenida Vía de la Plata s/n (924.31.15.50) on way out of town, reported to have one room as pilgrim dormitory). Tourist offices: one in Calle Saenz de Burnaga s/n (near Roman theatre), another at the top of Calle Santa Elena (off the Plaza de España, i.e. the main square).

Mérida was founded in 23 BC as a settlement for veterans of the Iberian wars (hence its name: Augusta Emerita). It contains more important remains of Roman antiquity than any other town in Spain and it is worth spending a whole day here. Roman amphitheatre, theatre (still used), bridge over the River Guadiana (one of the longest of its kind), National Museum of Roman Art (free at certain times), Visigothic Museum (free), Trajan's Arch, Alcazaba, church of Santa Eulalia (the city's patron), church of Santa María. Note, however, that to visit the major Roman and Christian monuments you have to buy a combined ticket for all of them; individual tickets are not available. (Ask for reduced rate if you are over 60.) A good place for a rest day before continuing on the main Vía de la Plata.

At the time the present edition of this guide was prepared the route through Mérida, formerly waymarked, no longer had any yellow arrows visible. The original route is described here, however, with the names of all the relevant streets, and is easy to follow.

After crossing a Roman bridge over the **Río Guadiana** continue ahead past Puerta del Puente and a small public garden (R) and then fork L up **Calle del Puente** to **Plaza de España** *(Cathedral of Santa María to L,* ayuntamiento *opposite)*. Then (with your back to the cathedral) leave by the top LH corner along **Calle Santa Julia**, veering R and then turn L into **Calle Trajana**, passing under **Trajan's Arch (Arco de Trajano)**. Turn R and then immediately L into **Plaza de la Constitución**, in front of the post office, and continue ahead into **Travesia de Almendralejo**. Turn L into **Calle Almendralejo** in front

Stage and scenery, Roman theatre, Mérida

of the police station and then turn R into **Calle Calvario**. Continue to very end *(bar on L opens early)*, turn R and go under the railway line via an underpass. Turn L and immediately R to cross the **Río Albarregas** via Mérida's other bridge of Roman origin. The **Acueducto de los Milagros** is now on your R. *It was built by the Romans to bring water into the city via an underground channel coming from the reservoir (Proserpina) 5km away. The aqueduct was originally 838m long and 25m tall at its highest point. The area around it has now been landscaped as a public park.*

Continue on **Avenida Vía de la Plata** for 100m on the other side then fork (not turn) L, leading to a roundabout. KSO ahead there up **Âvenida del Lago** past the Pan Emerita bread factory.

The waymarking here has 'EP' – Embalse de Proserpina – in yellow, one of the two reservoirs of Roman origin (the other, Cornado, is to the northeast of the town) as there are, in fact, two pilgrim routes out of Mérida. The one described here is the EP route; the other, marked 'CR' and following a section of the calzada romana, has to return to the N630 a lot of the time, due to new road construction, including coming back to El Carrascelejo via the road. The route via the Embalse de Proserpina is much quieter and, after the reservoir itself, goes through beautiful countryside with *encina* and cork plantations. Here, as earlier on, you will find the black, brown and grey *cerdos ibéricos* grazing on the fallen acorns below.

KSO at the roundabout (the Mérida–Badajoz road crosses R to L). KSO. Cross the motorway and continue ahead on a minor road leading downhill, marked 'Embalse de Proserpine'. After 1km pass a metal wayside cross on top of a stone *rollo* at top of hill. KSO, KSO at a small roundabout, passing campsite on L. KSO at a small roundabout (RH turn leads to an *urbanización*) and continue by the side of the Roman embankment of the

7km Embalse de Proserpina (227.5/772.5)

Now a tourist attraction with water sports, several cafés, *chiringuitos* (open-air snack bars), rte and campsite (open April 1st to September 15th). The reservoir supplied Mérida with drinking and other water in Roman times.

At the end of the wall leave the road and continue along the shore *(N.B: bars not open early)* and then return to the road to cross the bridge. Pass a Red Cross post (R) and KSO on the road (very quiet, very little traffic), undulating between fields with *encinas*, becoming increasingly rocky. 4km after the reservoir and 300m after an isolated white house on L, turn L off the road onto a *camino de tierra*, undulating through trees.

KSO(R) at the first fork, KSO(L) at the second and then continue between fences. 1km later cross a cattle grid and KSO alongside the wall, then cross another one 2.5km later and KSO. Go through a gate and veer R up into the village. Turn R along the main street to the church in

Roman Acueducto de los Milagros in evening light, Mérida

Roman dam, Embalse de Prosperpina

7.5km El Carrascalejo 308m (235/765)

Fountain, church of Nuestra Señora de la Consolación but no other facilities.

Turn L downhill after the church, veering L behind it down to cross a bridge over a small river. Pass wayside cross (L) with red cross on top, cross another track at right angles and KSO(R) ahead on the other side, through undulating vines. When you go down into a dip and meet a new road coming from R cross over (staggered) and KSO uphill, passing wayside cross, then go down into

2.5km Aljucén 270m (237.5/762.5)

Two bars, shop, farmácia, fountain, Casa Rural 'La Boveda' (Avenida de Extremadura 25, 924.31.28.23) on LH side of main street (ask there for key to the municipal *refugio*, the Albergue Analena, in Calle Andres 23).

Church of San Andrés has Santiago crosses on all its pedestals (inside the building).

Make sure you have enough water before you leave Aljucén.

Continue down the main village street *(Avenida de Extremadura)* and follow the road round to R at the end, leading to the N630. Cross a bridge over **Río Aljucén** and just before the petrol station, 2.5km from Aljucén *(café, but not always open)*, and opposite a turning to 'Las Navas de Santiago, 17' turn R onto a path leading through trees, following to L of the fence.

Between here and Alcuéscar you leave the province of Badajoz and enter Cáceres. For the next 15km you will not pass a single building and are unlikely to meet anyone at all. This section is well-enough waymarked but watch out carefully for the yellow arrows as the route is not always as straightforward as you might expect. Like many other areas of the Vía de la Plata this one is a paradise of wild flowers in the springtime.

After 1.5km KSO(L) ahead at a fork with another tall metal wayside cross, still following the line of fence to L. 300m later go through a wide gate (or cattle grid to L of it) and continue ahead on a track with fencing posts to RH side at first, then veering L, and KSO(R) ahead at a fork. 500m later the path continues alongside a drystone wall and 500m after that you reach another wide gate. Fork L on other side, slightly uphill, and continue ahead at the top, on the level.

500m later (after a gate) reach a crossing and KSO ahead, descending, with fence to your R. 200m later fork L and 200m after that fork R. 100m later turn L and then R, veering R to turn L at a fork with a track you are now on *(there are a lot of cistus bushes in this section)*. 500m later go through a *cledo* and KSO. 1km later KSO(R) ahead at a fork and 300m later go through a gate. At next junction KSO(R) again at a fork. Continue uphill.

KSO for 3km, with a fence over to your L all the time, and reach a fence with a large, wide and open level space behind. Go through it on a track. 2km later (at end) fork R through a gate and KSO. 2km after that reach the

15.5km Cruz de San Juan/Cruz del Niño Muerto (253/747)
Stone wayside cross, so named because on one such feast day (June 24th, Midsummer's Day, celebrating the anniversary of St John the Baptist) a young shepherd boy coming to the fiesta from the Valle de la Zarza was eaten by a wolf.

KSO for 3km, ignoring turns, then, when you are nearly at the top of the hill, before a group of white buildings on R, fork R downhill down gravel lane beside a fence on your L. At the bottom, 1.5km later **you can either**:

a) turn R along walled lane past white electricity 'sentry box.' This option leads you to the centre of Alcuéscar, 1km higher up, **or**

b) if you intend to sleep in the Residencia, turn left here (also waymarked but not very clearly). When you reach the road turn R along it to the junction and you will see the Residencia on the L.

6km Alcuéscar 489m (259/741)

Shops, bars. Casa Alejandro in upper part of village and Bar Cuesta lower down both do meals. Accommodation (for pilgrims with *credencial* only) at the Residencia for handicapped men, run by the Hermanos Esclavos de María y de los Pobres at the bottom of the village on the way out. (Note, however, that they do not charge but you should leave a donation.) Hostal Canuto, Hostal Olivo and Hostal de la Herrerías are located at KM249 on the N630 at the junction with the local road to Alcuéscar, 3km to west.

If you would like to visit the isolated Visigothic church of Santa Lucía de Trampal you can do so by following the well-signed track, out of the Plaza de España in Alcuéscar, 2.5km each way.

Leave by turning R in front of the Residencia if you have come from the top of the village (or L if you have slept there). 500m later fork R then at the next fork KSO(L) ahead and at the next KSO(R) along a walled lane between fields.

After 1.5km pass between two sets of gates and KSO. KSO(R) at the next two forks and KSO(L) at the next one after that. 800m later reach a crossing and KSO ahead. 500m later KSO(R) at a crossing and KSO(R) at the next.

Approximately 1km before the village (visible ahead) the track becomes asphalted. 200m later turn R onto a *camino de tierra* leading to the village, crossing a Roman bridge over the **Río Ayuela** *(three central arches and five square ones. Note two defunct telegraph poles nearby, with stork's nests on top).*

10km Casas de Don Antonio 413m (269/731)

Bar in village and another (not always open) on N630 at exit. No accommodation. Ermita de la Virgen del Pilar (with statue of Santiago Matamoros) at exit.

To visit the village: *cross the local road and go uphill, veering L (bar in centre). Follow the main street down to a second church to rejoin the local road.*

To continue without visiting the village: turn L on the local road and continue to the N630 *(bar opposite)* and turn R on a track on its RH side, // to it. KSO for 2km. *300m after road KM580 (castle behind road is the Castillo Arquijuelas de Arriba) there is a Roman* miliario, *still standing and in good condition except that its inscription is now very faint.* 800m later veer slightly R to cross a small Roman bridge over the **Arroyo de la Zafrilla** *(one curved central arch and one square one to either side of it, three in all).* 200m later the track returns to the road; cross over and continue on a similar track on LH side.

300m later, near a field of large trees (and when you can see Aldea del Cano) the *camino* veers L away from the road. Pass another *miliario* just after crossing a dried-up river bed and 150m before a group of six eucalyptus trees.

If you want to go into Aldea del Cano – for example to eat – you can make your way to the N630 from here along the LH edge of a field opposite or otherwise go 200m further and turn R down an unpaved road opposite a large barn, 300m in each direction, emerging on the road between cemetery and Centro Cultural. To return to the camino, *though, you can fork R partway up this road on your way back and turn R beyond the barn.*

7km Aldea del Cano 396m (276/724)
Fountain, shops, bars in centre of village on other side of road. Bar/rte 'Las Vegas' on N630 has key for basic R&F in school nearby. Casa Rural. Church of San Martín.

KSO, cross a minor road and KSO towards *encina* plantations *(not much shade to walk in though plenty to sit in).* KSO(R) at a fork and then again at a second fork and KSO ahead. Fork L at a junction *(view of another castle ahead over to R, the Castillo de Arquijuelas de Abajo)* and continue uphill. At the top, when it levels out, KSO(R) at a fork and continue ahead in the direction of a tall red and white pole on the horizon.

Reach **Cáceres flying club** then continue to climb gently for 1km more, keeping straight on ahead. Cross a track at a crossing and begin to descend. KSO at a crossing *(Castillo de Mayoralgo visible over to R)* and continue ahead. When you get near the village veer R to cross a Roman bridge over the **Río Salor** *(14 arches though not all are visible)* and turn R to the main road in

11km Valdesalor 380m (287/713)
Shop, bars, bar/rte by petrol station. R&F in ayuntamiento; ask in Hogar del Pensionista. Church of San Pedro.

Cross the N630 and continue on a track // to it. KSO for 3km until you reach a minor tarred road coming from R. Turn L along it to the N630 just before the road KM562. Cross over and continue on a FP on the other side, below the road, widening out to a track after a while.

Continue up to the top of the hill, passing a wooded area on the L and crossing the entrance road to a property on your L and then continue // to the main road when it bends L. Just after road KM560 (2km from the bottom of the hill) the track veers R to the main road.

Cross over and KSO diagonally on the other side, down the track alongside a wire fence on LH side, marked 'Zona militar, no pasar'. KSO, keeping // to the fence on your RIGHT. 700m later, near some farm buildings over to your L, the track divides. KSO(R) ahead on a smaller track between fields. Pass the *finca* San Antonio and 300m later, at a fork, KSO(R) ahead alongside fencing on RH side. 200m later cross a track coming from R and fork R down **Calle Océano Atlántico** at the start of an industrial area *(where all the streets are named after seas)*.

KSO until you reach some traffic lights after the local road (C520, Carretera de Don Benito) joins from the back R by a petrol station *(bar/rte on L)*. Cross over to RH side and fork R down the **Ronda San Francisco**, a very long road, passing a large hospital (on L) before you reach, abruptly, the foot of the old part of the town in front of you.

12km Cáceres 464m, pop. 69,193 (299/701)

All facilities, RENFE, buses to Madrid and places on the Gijón–Seville service. Accommodation in all price brackets, including Albergue Turístico (Calle Margallo 36, 630.50.41.95), Hostal Almonte (Calle Gil Cordero 6, 927.24.09.25), Hostal La Rosa (Calle Sanguno Michel 8, 927.22.17.50), Hostal Al-Qazeres (Calle Camino Llano 34, 927.22.70.00), Hostal Plaza de Italia (Calle Constancia 12, 927.62.72.94), Pensión Carretero (Plaza Mayor 22, 927.24.74.82), Pensión Márquez (Calle Gabriel y Galan 2, 927. 24.49.60), Pensión Virgen de Fátima, Avenida Virgen de la Montaña 17, 2 piso, 927. 21.18.44), Pensión Castilla (Calle Rios Verdes 3, 927.24.44.04) and Pensión Cuesta de Aldana (Calle Parras 31, 927.21.44.35) but no pilgrim-only facilities. Tourist office: Plaza Mayor 33. Bike repairs: Bicicletas Cáceres, Calle de Badajoz 10. *Sello*: church of Santiago or ayuntamiento (entrance at rear).

City founded in Roman times with the old town (the whole of which is classi-fied as a *monumento histórico*) dating from the thirteenth century onwards, completely self-contained within the modern one. Surrounded by its walls with gates and towers, it has many monuments worth visiting, whether churches, palaces or other imposing houses (two-hour guided walking tour of the historic quarter available from tourist office in the mornings). Church of Santiago (just outside the old city centre, like those in Salamanca and Zamora and as was often customary for pilgrim churches) has a bas-relief of a pilgrim with staff, scrip, hat and shell, and a Santiago Matamoros in the main altarpiece (see Appendix B for other Santiago references in Cáceres). Another place worth spending a whole day.

When you get to the very end of the **Ronda San Francisco**, arrows point you to pass to RH side of a bridge and then KSO ahead, up the **Calle San Ildefonso**, veering L up to the **Plaza Las Candelas** and then veering L again up **Calle de la Consolación** (not marked at start) to the **Plaza de Santa Clara** *(with stone crucifix in centre)*.

Leave by the top RH corner, turn L into **Calle Puerta de Mérida** and continue along the **Calle Adarve del Padre Rosalio**. Turn L at end under the THIRD archway, down a short flight of steps, into the **Plaza Mayor** *(tourist office,* ayuntamiento).

From the **Plaza Mayor** (with your back to the tourist office and the old town) turn R (opposite the *ayuntamiento*) into **Calle Gabriel y Galán**, with the **Plaza Duque** at the end, then L into **Calle Sancti Espiritu**, continuing on **Calle Margallo** to the **Plaza Argel** and the **Plaza de Toros** (bullring). Cross over and continue down LH side of the bullring on the road signposted 'Casar de Cáceres', veering L to the **Calle Carretera de Casar** (not marked at start) and then R down the central reservation *(seats)* of **Calle Brunete**. When the buildings end KSO on the road. NO SHADE AT ALL in this section, either to walk or sit in.

Pilgrim bas-relief above north portal, church of Santiago, Cáceres

Some 6–7km after Cáceres yellow arrows lead you off the road to the L, // to it but at a distance. KSO ahead until you reach a new road bridge in front of you. Veer R and then turn L underneath it and turn R on other side (service road). 100m before the road to Casar de Cáceres turn L along another *camino de tierra*, // to though not beside the road.

Pass a petrol station *(useful for cold water in hot weather)* 500m before entrance to village and veer R at end to junction at entry to

> ### 11km Casar de Cáceres 369m (310/690)
> Shops, bars, bank, post office. New *refugio* in square opposite the ayuntamiento (20 beds, showers, kitchen: contact Bar/Rte Majuca opposite for key). Hostal Las Encinas 3km away on N630, near KM542 (927.29.02.01); if you stay here you will have to return to the village to continue on the Camino, picking up arrows again near the Ermita de Santiago (on the northern outskirts of the village).
> Iglesia de la Asunción (parish church, in centre of village) has a Baroque wood painted Santiago on LH side of main altarpiece with fine Santiago Peregrino complete with staff, gourd, hat and scallop and modern but inverted black scallop in grille of SW chapel. The town also has four *ermitas*, one each to its north, south, east and west; Santiago, to the north, has modern Santiago Matamoros with a giant sword above the altar while those to the south, east and west are dedicated, respectively, to San Bartolomé, Los Mártires and La Soledad.

At the entrance to Casar de Cáceres continue down the walkways of the public garden *(Paseo de Extremadura – well kept, various sorts of trees)*. At the very end cross the road and KSO ahead down **Calle Larga Alta** to the **Plaza de España** and *ayuntamiento*.

Turn L into **Avenida Constitución** and then R into **Calle Santiago** to the end. Turn R then L to the **Ermita de Santiago**. Pass to its LH side and KSO on an untarred road out into open country. KSO(R) when you reach the round hut that is the *Centro de Información Pecuaria*. KSO for 2–3km then KSO(R) at a fork by a farm. *NO SHADE AT ALL but a very nice walk in the early morning if you like being 'on the roof of the world' in wide open spaces. More* miliarios *in this area.* KSO for several kilometres. Cañaveral *visible ahead on mountainside in distance and if you look back you can see Cáceres too, on a clear day.*

50m after the entrance to the **Finca La Higuera** (9km from Casar de Cáceres) reach a fork, both options with gates. Go through LH set of gates and then KSO(R) ahead on the other side, veering L uphill. 500m later go through more gates and KSO ahead alongside a fence. *Landscape becomes increasingly rockier, some very large, with*

Ermita de Santiago, Casar de Cáceres

unusual formations. 700m later, near a farm on R, go through more gates and KSO straight ahead on the other side in a straight line. DO NOT go through the gates on L but continue ahead on the track and 500m later go through more gates. KSO, go through some more gates and continue on a walled lane, then continue between gate posts out into open heathland, passing in front of an isolated house on L.

Shortly afterwards (5km from the Finca La Higuera) you reach a single concrete gate with TWO sets of waymarks. Here you can either continue ahead, joining the road and continuing on a FP to its RH side until the bridge over the *Río Almonte* or turn R and use a section of the *calzada romana* whose course has been passing to the R of the track you have been on until now but is overgrown and impassable up to here. This option is waymarked, though not all that well; it is NOT suitable for bikes and is not described here. Both options meet up before the road bridge (the only means of crossing the two rivers). *View of the Embalse de Alcántara ahead from here.*

KSO ahead, veering L and cross a cattle grid. ***Cyclists:*** KSO here and continue north on the N630 (turn R onto it) until the former *Hostal Miraltajo*. **Walkers:** immediately after crossing the cattle grid turn hard R towards the N630 (at road KM527) and continue on a FP, clear, that goes // to the road below to your L, up and down, undulating, clearly marked *(good views)*.

Rejoin the **N630** just before road KM525 (2km later). Cross over to LH side (VERY carefully – there is a huge amount of very heavy traffic) and cross a road (and rail) bridge (nearly 1km long) over the **Río Almonte**. *Over to your L you can see the Torreón de Floripes, the only remains of the village of Alconeter which was flooded to make the reservoir.*

Unfortunately the only way to cross the two rivers *(until some enterprising person sets up a pilgrim ferry service, at least...)* is via the N630 and the road/rail bridges – a total of 5km. After crossing the **Río Almonte** KSO for 3km, passing the **Apeadero del Río Tajo** *(a railway halt). There is one train a day (7 days a week) from here to Cañaveral (on the Madrid–Badajoz line); it leaves Cáceres at 14.30, passes the halt at 14.50 and arrives in Cañaveral at 15.07.* Cross the ***Río Tajo*** then KSO on the other side for 1.5km to the (now closed)

> **20km Hostal Miraltajo 250m (330/670)**
> Pilgrims interested in Roman bridges may like to make a 4km detour from here to the huge, imposing Puente Mantible/Puente Alconétar which was re-sited in a valley beside the N630 when the reservoir flooded its original position. Take the gravel path to the north end of the hostal terrace and follow it down to the banks of the reservoir and then nearly all the way to the bridge: you may need to scramble up to the N630 for a short distance to avoid cliffs.
>
> Albergue (turistico) de Alconetar, near reservoir and not far from the hostal: ask in Cáceres Tourist Office for details.

Turn R off the road opposite the hostal onto a *camino de tierra*, climbing gradually all the time *(good views as you go)*. Cross a cattle grid and KSO on a level track, isolated and high up. About 2km before you get level with Cañaveral KSO(L) at a fork and then KSO(R) at the next. KSO. *Loose cattle may be on the route.*

When you come level with Cañaveral in an open area there are two sets of waymarks:
 a) **to go into the town itself** turn L steeply downhill on a rocky path (marked 'Caña'). At bottom turn L onto track and go through a gate, continue on a *camino de tierra* and go over the restored fourteenth-century **Puente de San Benito**. KSO uphill on other side, up walled lane, to main road (N630) at entrance to Cañaveral. Turn R onto the pavement.
 b) **otherwise**, if you do not want to go into Cañaveral (i.e. to eat or sleep) continue straight ahead here (marked 'CR'), passing Cañaveral railway station *(bar)* and the industrial estate, veering L to join the N630 2km beyond the town near the Ermita San Cristóbal.

> **14km Cañaveral 362m, pop. 2100 (344/656)**
> Bars, shops, bank (+CD), post office, Hostal/Rte Málaga (927.30.00.67) on main road towards end of town. Small *refugio* in old building in centre of town (ask in

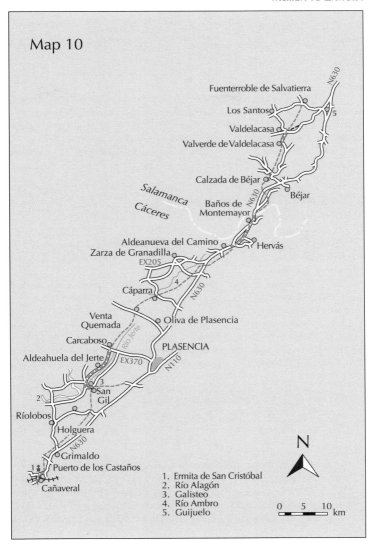

Map 10

Fuenterroble de Salvatierra

Los Santos

Valdelacasa

Valverde de Valdelacasa

Calzada de Béjar

Béjar

Baños de Montemayor

Salamanca

Cáceres

Aldeanueva del Camino

Zarza de Granadilla

Hervás

EX205

Cáparra

Venta Quemada

Oliva de Plasencia

Carcaboso

PLASENCIA

Aldeahuela del Jerte

Río Jerte

EX370

San Gil

N110

Ríolobos

Holguera

N630

Grimaldo

Puerto de los Castaños

Cañaveral

1. Ermita de San Cristóbal
2. Río Alagón
3. Galisteo
4. Río Ambro
5. Guijuelo

N

0   5   10 km

137

WAY OF ST JAMES: VIA DE LA PLATA

ayuntamiento) with new, larger one planned in another location.

Fourteenth–sixteenth-century Iglesia de Santa María, sixteenth-century Ermita de San Roque.

After turning R onto the pavement you can either KSO on the N630 (**Calle San Benito**) or, quieter, fork L on the other side up **Calle de Monrobel** *(fountain on L)*. KSO to the square in front of the church and then turn R, passing to RH side of the *ayuntamiento* up **Calle de Centro**. Turn L and then R into a long unmarked street leading to the N630. Turn L.

Continue on the N630 out of town for 1.5km (road KM508), pass a turning (on R) to Cañaveral railway station *(bar)* and 500m later reach the

2km Ermita de San Cristóbal (346/654)

Cyclists may prefer to continue on the road here, although there is no hard shoulder until you reach the pass, as the path, short-cutting many of the bends, is very steep and will be bumpy.

Turn L off the road and then turn R in front of the chapel and L uphill alongside a wall over to your R, picking up a clear track coming from L and go under some electricity cables uphill.

Follow a wide, clear track uphill, veering R and then L past a new *depósito de agua* (water tank), which then veers R, climbing very steeply at first. KSO along it when it levels out and reach a minor road coming from the transmitter on top of the hill over to your L. Turn R along it and then R along a bigger minor road coming from your L, and reach the

4km Puerto de los Castaños 500m (350/650)
No facilities at all at present.

The next section (as far as Galisteo) is NOT suitable for cyclists, even on mountain bikes. Cyclists should continue on the main road for 3km more, until just after Grimaldo *(bar)* and then turn L on a minor road to Holguero. KSO at a crossroads with the Torrejoncillo–Riolobos road and then turn R at the next cross-roads along another minor road more or less following the Río Alagón to Galisteo.

The *camino* leaves through the woods on the north side of the former hotel, through a gate to the LH side of the N630. Watch waymarks carefully and follow the line of either the barbed wire or the walls, in more or less a straight line, on a fairly clear track to start with. KSO, sticking as closely as you can to the fence on your L, though you will have to veer R from time to time to cross ditches/streams. After 2–3km the fence begins to veer R and path goes downhill and you can see (briefly) the village of Grimaldo over to your R on the main road above.

100m after going under electric cables reach a gate in a corner. Go through it, veering R down to stream by several big trees *(nice shady place for a rest)*. Cross it via stepping stones and then KSO ahead alongside wall to R *(road bridge visible to R above you)*. **To go to Grimaldo** *(castillo, small refugio – 927.30.06.05 – ask in bar)* turn R through the second gate after the stream.

Otherwise, continue alongside fence to start with, then veering away from it (to L). *Crash barriers of new road visible above you to R by now.* KSO ahead all the time *(not many arrows in this section but a lot of plastic tape markers – watch out carefully for them)* and 700–800m from stream, reach what was formerly a minor road but which looks as though it is being converted into either a slip road for the motorway or an upgraded local road *(extensive roadworks were in progress at the time this edition was being prepared)*. Cross over and go through a gate on other side, to RH side of fence to start with but then cross over to its LH side as soon as possible and continue on that side (or you won't be able to get out at the end).

500m later cross a ditch and then go through a gateway in the fence. 200m after that go through a gate onto the entrance road to a 'finca particular,' a large private property on L with big metal tanks on the horizon and white pillars on either side of its gateway (on your L). Cross the entrance road and continue straight ahead immediately on other side through a *cledo*.

KSO ahead here on grassy track close to the fence on your L. 1.5km later go through another *cledo* and 100m after that pass to the RH side of a gate with white posts (do NOT go through it) and continue ahead on a slightly raised track between fields (is this the course of a *calzada romana*?). 700–800m later go through (or over) another *cledo* and continue ahead on path closer to the fence on your R all the time. 1km later go through/over another *cledo* and continue ahead, still staying close to the fence all the time.

After this **be particularly attentive**, especially after the path begins to go downhill. Some 1km after that last *cledo* and before you reach the valley bottom watch out for another one by an open area to your L known as the 'cuatro terminos' (though there is nothing as such to indicate it). Here waymarks indicate a RH turn through a *cledo* in the fencing. Go through it and then continue on FP to RH side of fence, undulating, and 300–400m later go through a gate. Continue ahead on other side beside the fence (on your L). Some 800–900m later go through a *second* gate and KSO on other side, still with fence (and now a wall) on your L, undulating all the time.

139

800m later reach TWO gates, side by side. Go through the bigger, RH one, and continue on other side on clearer track that has now joined you from back R, still with a fence to your L. 500–600m after that reach a fourth gate in front of you (i.e. some 3km after turning R through the *cledo* at the 'cuatro terminos'). DO NOT go through it but go through the one on its LH side instead. *View of the walled town of Galisteo, still some three hours' walk away.* Turn R to continue alongside wall (now on your R), though there is no clear track, through rocky field with *encina* trees. Continue for 600–700m then go through another gate on RH side and continue after that on its RH side (i.e. with the wall now to your L).

KSO. After nearly 1km (having kept as close to the wall as was practical) reach a large *cledo* (very close to the wall) and go through it, slightly downhill all the time. 1km later, when you see a small reservoir below to R, arrows indicate that you should stick close to the wall but you can in fact (and less complicated) continue on the track you were already on as they meet up anyway 50m later and keep veering L, sticking close to the wall/fence all the time. When the fence bends L, turn L alongside it and follow close to it all the time. Shortly before you reach the valley bottom (about 1km from where you were above the reservoir) you go under some electric cables and then be careful. Part of the path by the fence has subsided into the trough/pit in front of you so veer R down to the dip and then make your way back up to the fence again as soon as is practicable. Reach a gate, go through it, turn L onto a *camino de tierra*, cross a small river (stepping stones if needed), turn L again and then go up a bank (by a large drain) onto the local (tarred) road ahead. (**Cyclists** should KSO here then turn hard R later onto the road.)

Turn R along it for 700–800m then turn L up a track to a white gateway and cattle grid, set well back from road, to the **finca Valparaíso** and continue uphill. At a junction at the top KSO ahead, veering L alongside a fence downhill. *Here the landscape changes abruptly, becoming much greener and giving way to fields full of tobacco, beetroot, sunflowers, and irrigated by a system of canals.* Fork R at a junction at the bottom and continue uphill.

Cross a canal via a bridge and then turn R along its LH bank for 1km, passing a ruined house. Just before a bridge turn L, through some gates, pass to RIGHT-HAND SIDE of barn (despite arrow to L), pass to LH side of row of deserted farm workers' cottages and then pick up a track with an irrigation channel to its LH side. Go through three sets of gates, pass to the LH side of a pond, after which the track becomes an unsurfaced (non-tarred) road and on L, at a bend, there are some willow trees and a seat *(nice place for a rest)*.

Go downhill past a barn, cross a bridge (800–900m after leaving canal) and after passing a large barn on R and going between irrigation channels on both sides of the road, turn L. (**Cyclists** seeking a flatter option should KSO here then turn L in *San Gil* to continue along the road to Galisteo.) Turn R 100m later, uphill between fields on an unsurfaced road. KSO at a crossing. (Camino then > a *camino de tierra*).

Walled town of Galisteo

1km later (after turning L through irrigation channels) reach a road. Cross over, continue ahead and cross another road, turning L in front of *Bar/Rte Los Emigrantes* and then turn R under an archway (the **Puerta del Rey**) into the walled town of

22km Galisteo 308m (372/628)

Small town with shops, bars, bank, Hogar del Pensionista (in main square, does simple food). Bar/Rte 'Los Emigrantes' at entrance does meals and has rooms. Two *refugios*: a) municipal, next to campsite but ask at Plaza de España 5 for key; b) Refugio El Trillo (private); ask in Mesón Rusticiana (outside town walls) for key. Camping Merendero by old bridge leaving town (also serves food when open).

The town has a complete set of walls, with a *paseo* both along the top and round the outside, an alcázar and church of Santa María with Mudéjar apse and scallops in groups of five in decorative ironwork in north portal. Take a walk round the ramparts (several access points) to get a good view of the town and its surrounding area. Most of the town is inside its walls. Its three *puertas* are still intact: Puerta del Rey, Puerta de Santa María and Puerta de la Villa.

Turn L (after going through an archway) and then R into **Travesia del Rey**, leading to the square with the *ayuntamiento*, and then turn L into **Calle Gabriel y Galán** and leave the town by the **Puerta de la Villa**. Fork R into **Calle Huerto de los Olivos**. Go downhill to the bottom, turn R onto a local road, pass **Camping Merendero** (on R) and cross a bridge over **Río Jerte** *(note stork's nest on memorial in middle of bridge)*. 200m later turn R onto a slightly bigger local road. KSO(R) at a junction and KSO for another 5km. *Style of farm buildings begins to change, with a lot of brick barns (often decorative).*

6km Aldeahuela del Jerte (378/622)
Bar, shop, *farmacia*.

Continue ahead through the village on road and KSO to

5km Carcaboso 271m (383/617)
Bars, shops, bank (no CD), Rte Los Golondrinas. Bar Ruta de la Plata (on main road) has inexpensive rooms. Modern church of Santiago Apóstol with glass roundel of Santiago Matamoros above west door.

Note: if you do not want to walk the 38km to Aldanueva in one day (there is nowhere at all to sleep en route), the Hostal Asturias (on the N630 near the junction to Jarilla, some 6–7km away from Cáparra but only 2km from the route the following morning) will collect you from the arch (at Cáparra) between 16.30 and 17.00 if you telephone the evening before (927.47.70.57) – or the owner of the Bar Ruta de la Plata in Carcaboso will telephone for you if you stay there the night before. You can then walk the 2km back to pick up the *camino* again the next day.

Make sure you have enough food and water before you leave here.

Plasencia (11km to the east, all facilities) is not on the route of the Roman Vía de la Plata, as explained in the Introduction, but is well worth a visit. (Note, however, that the only buses there from Carcaboso leave early in the morning.) Hotel Rincón Extremadura, Bar Micasa, Pensión Blanco and Hostal Muralla all have rooms. Its *casco* antiguo contains the old and new cathedrals, several churches and historic houses and the town had seven pilgrim hospitals in medieval times.

Cyclists should continue on the local road to Valdeobispo and then turn R onto another one leading to the Venta Quemada (marked *** below). *Please note that the walkers' route is NOT suitable for bikes of any sort.*

Walkers cross the **Carretera de Plasencia** and fork R up **Calle de la Iglesia**, passing the (modern) **church of Santiago Apóstol** (on R). Turn L at the end into **Calle Real** and then R into **Calle Pozo** then KSO(R) at a fork out of the village. KSO(R) at a fork by three modern concrete wayside crosses (on L), cross a river and follow a lane as it veers L, alongside stepped sections of an irrigation canal on R.

At a junction (marked 'Bombay') and opposite a small *finca* on your L there is now only one waymarked route and which is much more straightforward than the former RH option. KSO ahead with the irrigation channel on your R and continue for 1.5km. Pass empty house on L, cross channel and KSO with it on your L. *This section was badly waymarked at the time the present edition was being prepared but it is easy enough to follow.* 500m later channel crosses under track and returns to RH side. KSO.

3km after Bombay reach a minor road *(small house hidden under trees to L)*. Turn L along it for 200m then turn R over irrigation channel and go through gates. Veer L uphill on clear wide track inside the *finca*, veering R uphill, with stone wall to your R all the time, through rocky *encina* woods. Continue uphill and after it levels out go through some metal gates. 300m after that, when track bends L, fork R under trees and continue alongside wall to your R.

1km later, at end of field (wall in front) reach a gate in the corner. Turn R through it then L and continue with wall on your LH side. After 3km go through/over a makeshift gate in wall ahead (at end of field) and 500m after that pass to the R in front of a cattlepen made of orange breeze blocks. Then turn L behind it in order to be able to continue ahead to the RH side of the wall as before. At end of field go through another makeshift gate, go through a gap in the wall at the end of the next field and 200m after the orange breezeblock enclosure, just before a road (you will have to climb over/through the makeshift gateway in the top LH corner of the field) reach the

---

13km Venta Quemada (396/604)
Isolated house at side of road. No facilities of any kind. The next stretch of the *camino* is very beautiful, quiet and peaceful, along a very wide walled lane, with a fair amount of shade and good views into the distance (the Embalse de Gabriel y Galán and a national park are over to the west).

Cross the road and KSO ahead down a very wide walled lane for 6km. Pass houses on R and the lane becomes narrower, reaching the **Roman arch** at

Triumphal Arch, Cáparra, in evening light (photo: author)

6.5km Cáparra 400m (402.5/597.5)

Remains of ancient Roman city with four-square triumphal arch; this is no mere museum piece, though, and the *camino* actually passes underneath it, surrounded by fields. It has now become more 'touristy', but you can now get into the increasingly extensive ruins of the adjacent town and it also has a visitors centre.

KSO down the road ahead and 350m later fork R down a walled lane. KSO for 2km (gate halfway down) and at the end go through a gate into open rocky countryside with *encinas*. KSO ahead.

1.5km later reach more gates. 200m later cross the end of a gravel road and KSO alongside the wall on R. 700m later cross a river (some stepping stones). Pass the end of another gravel road and KSO. Cross a river (bed may be dry) and then go through a *cledo*. 500m later go through another one and turn L onto a minor road. KSO (literally) for 5km on a path on its RH side. *Note all the storks' nests on each electricity pylon in the very long line of them to the RH side of the road.*

Turn R onto a local road coming from back L and 800m later KSO(L) at a fork ('no entry' sign – 'excepto servidumbres'). 1.5km later the tarmac ends and the N630 is above you, 20m ahead. Veer to L then cross river (via stepping stones if needed) and then arrows direct you under a road bridge under the N630 on RH side of river/stream. *The mountains of the Sierra de Gredos are over to the R in the distance.*

144

a) **Walkers**: on the other side, on your L, is a set of gates (may be locked). Climb over/go through them and head for first electric pylon in field on other side. From there go through gate in the wall in front (at right angles to N630) and turn R alongside wall. In corner go through gateway and turn L, continuing diagonally R, veering L in front of a ruined building (on your R) then reach a wall by a gateway (on its other side). Climb over wall and turn L – you are now on the *calzada romana,* a wide walled lane, undulating. *This a very nice quiet section with quite a lot of shade – to rest in at least – and which will take you all the way to the outskirts of Aldeanueva del Camino.*

KSO for 4km then go up a cobbled slope, veering L. Pass farm and KSO. 500m reach the motorway and continue beside it for 300m until you reach a road bridge across it. Turn R and then L to cross the motorway via this road, veering L at end. Turn R 150m before you reach the N630 onto a long street (unnamed at start) with an old-style electricity tower on the corner and a ceramic map (of the route). Continue until you reach a square (**Plaza de España**) in the centre of **Aldeanueva del Camino**.

b) **Cyclists** *(but not those on touring bikes, who should continue on the road to Aldeavueva)*: do not go under the bridge but continue ahead on a *camino de tierra* and then turn R onto a local road leading to the N630. 1km later, at the side of bar/rte *Casa Basilio*, go up the *camino de tierra* to pick up the *calzada romana* 1km later and turn L along it.

18.5km Aldeanueva del Camino 529m (421/579)

Shops, bars. Hostal/Rte Montesol at end of village (open all year) has inexpensive rooms (927.48.43.35) and is the only place in the village that does meals. New *refugio* (ask in ayuntamiento, Bar de la Union or in the *churrería* in the Plaza España for key, no charge but donations). Fountain with good (chlorine-free) drinking water (hard L on entry).

San Servando, one of the town's two parish churches, has modern tiled Santiago panel above high altar.

Continue straight ahead, over a bridge *(dried-up river, second ceramic map to R)* and continue ahead past the *ayuntamiento* on **Calle de Severiano Masids**. KSO(L) ahead down a long street with first floor balconies, passing church (on L), to the very end, where you join the N630 at road KM438. Pass **Hostal Montesol** and 300–400m later reach roundabout. Take second RH turn and cross bridge over motorway. On the other side go quarter of the way round the roundabout (to the L) and then turn L down a gravel track that runs // to E205, marked 'Hervas 5' (on its RH side, separated by a *wire fence). The section from here to Baños de Montemayor is basically on the road, though you can walk on the verge on its RH side for some of the time.*

After 4.5km you pass the first turning (bar opposite) to **Hervás** (pop. 3500, accommodation available, including *albergue turístico* Vía de la Plata, Paseo de la Estación s/n, 927.47.34.70) which is worth a detour (total 8km). Apart from the Palacio de los Dávilas, the Convento Trinitario and the church of Santa María, it contains the best-preserved *judería* (Jewish quarter) in Spain. To return to the Vía de la Plata do not retrace your steps to the N630 the way you came but rejoin it further to the north by taking the SECOND turning back to the N630.

After the second turning to Hervás *(bar/rte opposite) walkers* can use a small FP on RH side of the road (**cyclists** stick to road), joining a wider lane for a while before returning you to the road. Cross over and continue on LH side for 350m then, shortly before road KM430, fork L down a lane // to the road. This returns you to the road 800m later. Cross over to RH side, go back a few steps to cross a ditch and then turn L to pass BEHIND the **Ermita Santísimo Cristo de la Miisericordia** *(so as not to walk on road at dangerous bend). Seats, wayside cross. In use but kept locked: you can see inside through the windows. (The dip in the skyline ahead is the Puerto de Béjar, where you will be going after leaving Baños.)*

> ### 10km Baños de Montemayor 708m (431/569)
> Small spa town with shops, bars, banks, and plenty of accommodation for its size (one hotel, five hostales, four fondas) and an *albergue turístico* (Calle Castañar 40, 679.22.82.08, 10 Euros). Campsite 'Las Cañadas' (Cat.1) at KM432 on N630. Tourist office in the ayuntamiento.
> A rather touristy place with old-style Hotel Balneario and where people still go to 'take the waters' and a lot of basketwork *(cestería)* is on sale. Thermal baths of Roman origin (with small museum), famous for the cure of respiratory and muscular complaints. Church of Santa María.

Continue on the pavement then fork R off the N630 *(fountain on R)* near the former **church of Santa Catalina** *(now a municipal auditorium). However, if you are feeling hungry note that all the bars with food are on or near the main road so you will have to deviate from the* camino *as waymarked through Baños if you want to eat.* Pass to LH side of church (this is the **Calle Mayor**: another fountain partway up on R). Continue to the top then fork L to a square with the *ayuntamiento* (and tourist office inside).

Pass in front of the *ayuntamiento* (it is on your R), turn L into **Calle Castillejos** and then turn first R, veering L steeply uphill (this is still Calle Castillejos), joining the **Carretera de la Estación** (coming from back R). 100m later, at a 'hairpin' in the N630, fork R ahead up a restored section of the *calzada romana*, which short-cuts many of the zigzags in the N630 that you can see over to your L. (**Cyclists** it is worth pushing up this section.)

The *calzada* stops after 1.5km, reaching the N630 100m before the border between the autonomous regions of Extremadura and Castille-León and the provinces of Cáceres and Salamanca. Cross over and continue on road up to the

3.5km Puerto de Béjar 870m (434.5/565.5)
Refugio in preparation in old school. Casa rural?

300m past the petrol station *(with café)* fork L down a lane, cross local road *(sign for sello and meals in Casa Adriano on L)*. KSO on other side and go under motorway. KSO ahead on other side on walled lane, cross a local road *(motorway now to your R)* by junction with pillar inscribed with 'CXXXLL.' KSO on walled lane downhill, passing fountain on R and ignoring turnings, down to cross the **Río Cuerpo de Hombre** by the

4km Puente de la Magdalena (Malena) 650m (438.5/561.5)
Many *miliarios* nearby in this section.

Turn R on the other side along a sandy lane (the *calzada romana*) that continues // to a small tarmac road on its L for some 3km, climbing gently all the time. Join the road shortly after the **Colonia San Francisco** (a former farm) and continue along it for 250m to a sharp RH bend by some houses. KSO ahead here up a stony lane (GR100 continues here, GR10 turns R on road) that zigzags its way fairly steeply uphill at the start and then more gently. Pass a cemetery and chapel *(sign says 'Humilladero', indicating a devotional place, normally marked by either a cross or some other type of image)* and enter the village of

5.5km Calzada de Béjar 796m (444/556)
Bar, fountain, shop?, casa rural, new private *refugio* at entrance to village. Church of Nuestra Señora de la Asunción.

Enter the village by **Calle Baños** and KSO along the main street and then along **Calle Salas Pombo** to the end of the village *(fountain and* lavadero *on R)*. KSO ahead on a minor road then 500m later, at RH bend, KSO ahead down a grassy walled lane, straight as a die. 1km later cross a minor road and KSO ahead.

Grass gives way to sandy/stony lane, in a wide plateau with walled cornfields to either side and mountains in the distance. Gradually the landscape becomes more rocky. (The steel-grey cows you see in this area are not a cross between black and white ones but a breed of their own.)

Cross a dried-up riverbed and shortly afterwards reach a minor tarred road. Turn R along it for 150m then turn L up a sandy track. KSO for 2km, KSO at a crossing over a (dry) riverbed, pass a wayside cross (R), take RH option at a fork and enter

9km Valverde de Valdelacasa (453/547)

Fountain, bar at end of village in Hogar del Pensionista (unmarked, in former school). Church of Santiago. Former pilgrim hospital in house with '1704' over the door and Santiago sword in coat of arms.

Enter the village via **Calle Salas Pombo** (RH fork after wayside cross), pass another wayside cross (R) and the **church of Apóstol Santiago** (R) and KSO ahead to L of the church (**Calle Iglesia**). Turn R at end *(Calle Altozano)* and then immediately L (unnamed street) and L again at the end. Turn SECOND R behind an old school into **Calle Las Eras** onto road and turn R along it. Stay on the road to

3.5km Valdelacasa 964m (456.5/543.5)

Two bars, shop behind church, meals in Centro del Día on road at end of village. Originally there was only one house here – hence the village's name.

Cyclists may wish to make a 10km detour here to Guijelo for accommodation (shops, banks, Hotel Torres 923.58.14.51, Pensión Comercio 923.58.00.37). If so, you can return to the camino the following day by taking the minor road to Fuenterroble de Salvatierra: from the N630 cross the railway line, turn R and follow its windings for 6km to Fuenterroble.

Turn L at an entry on the road marked '10 Guijelo' and then immediately R into the **Calle Camino Real de la Plata** out of the village. Continue on the road for some 2km and then, at a junction with two *caminos de tierra* to L, turn (not fork) L onto a sandy track, veering R. *Large information board about the Vía de la Plata here and very* *large boulders on RH side of road; this is the* termino *(boundary) of Fuenterroble de Salvatierra –* milias *(Roman miles) 147–151, measured from Mérida.*

KSO, ignoring turns and climbing gradually all the time. *Look out for more miliarios in his area.* When the track levels out KSO at a crossing (with gates to either side of the track). KSO, climbing gradually again, and when you level out reach a crossing of similar tracks. Turn R and then L onto a minor road *(Fuenterroble is now visible 1km ahead, over to R).* Continue downhill and enter the village via the **Calle Larga**.

7.5km Fuenterroble de Salvatierra 955m (464/536)

Two bars, one with shop, the other does meals. *Refugio* in Casa Parroquial, run by Don Blas, the very helpful parish priest; part of the ashes of the late José Luis Salvador Salvador, former president of the Seville 'Amigos', are buried in the front wall of the building.

Fortress church of Santa María la Blanca has been impressively restored and is now in use again as the parish church after being closed for decades, and is worth a visit. Inside there is an enormous modern statue (in wood) of Christ risen from the dead which was taken on a pilgrimage around nearby villages before being placed in situ and others of the Apostles of the Resurrection. (Useful information board near church and parque *temático* showing the construction of Roman roads and explaining Roman burial customs, miliarios and the Vía de la Plata.) Ermita del Santo Cristo.

Pass the *ermita* (on L) and continue to a junction with Casa Parroquial on the opposite RH corner *(very large freestanding wooden cross outside)* and turn L (signposted 'Liñares'), L, R and L again. KSO for 1.5km *(this is the road to Casafranca)* then turn R onto a *camino de tierra* at a crossing with another one on LH side of the road. KSO along a wide walled lane, ignoring turnings, for 5–6km.

Reach an area with scrubby trees and then a track crossing diagonally. Go through a gate, fork L and 100m later turn R alongside a fence then turn L 20m later alongside a fence on L. 1km later, at a break in the fencing when a wide track joins from back L, KSO and 100m later go through a gate and KSO ahead (track turns L here but do not take this).

There are a lot of roaming cattle in this area *(ganadero suelto)*. You will also notice, if you have not already, that the route appears to be waymarked (in white) in reverse in this area and elsewhere; as explained in the Introduction, this is not, in fact, done for pilgrims' return journeys (though cyclists in particular make use

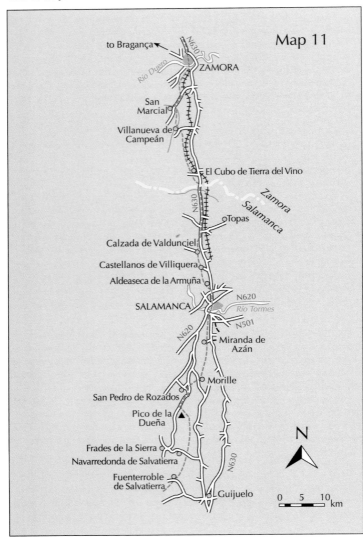

Map 11

to Bragança
N630
Río Duero
ZAMORA
San Marcial
Villanueva de Campeán
El Cubo de Tierra del Vino
Zamora
Salamanca
N630
Topas
Calzada de Valdunciel
Castellanos de Villiquera
Aldeaseca de la Armuña
SALAMANCA
N620
Río Tormes
N620
N501
Miranda de Azán
Morille
San Pedro de Rozados
Pico de la Dueña
Frades de la Sierra
Navarredonda de Salvatierra
Fuenterroble de Salvatierra
N630
Guijuelo

N

0   5   10 km

of them) but was prepared in the mid-1990s when the old drovers' route from Asturias to Cáceres was reopened (and used) for the transfer of large numbers of animals from one area to another in search of new pasture land.

After 1km you join a gravelled track and then cross a minor gravelled road leading (L) to *Navarredonda de Salvatierra*.

Cyclists: turn L here, continue to *Frades de la Sierra* and then turn R onto another minor road which will take you all the way to a turn-off 2km before *San Pedro de Rozados*. Alternatively, you can continue to the cattle grid* and deviate from the walker's route from there.

Walkers: KSO ahead then 300m later fork L and KSO until you reach a gateway and a cattle grid.* Turn L here uphill alongside a wall. Keep as close to it as is practicable and then continue below the wall (RT) and the fence (on L). *There are (at present) four very large wayside crosses en route, the beginning of a Vía Crucis (Stations of the Cross). A new one is added each year on Good Friday until the series is complete. The existing cross atop the Pico de la Dueña will become no. 14 (the final one).* Continue uphill for 3km until you reach the

15.5km Pico de la Dueña 1140m (479.5/520.5)
Highest point on the route between Seville and Astorga, with spectacular views on a clear day. The 'pico' itself is now surmounted by a modern cross of the Order of Santiago and forms a sort of 'Cruz de Ferro' for the Vía de la Plata.

Continue ahead, gradually downhill, keeping the wall to your R, passing a large wooden wayside cross (some 3m high). Reach a local road 700m later and turn R along it *(very little traffic and a lot of the time you can walk on its very wide verges)*. KSO on the road for 5km to

5.5km Calzadilla de Mendigos 950m (485/515)
A large pig farm on the road (it has its name on it)

Continue on the road for 6km to a junction. If you want to go into **San Pedro de Rozados** (2km, to eat or sleep) turn L here. Otherwise, KSO on the road and take the next turning on R (opposite non-tarred road on L) to Morille.

Sword of Santiago on Pico de la Dueña (photo: author)

8km San Pedro de Rozados 980m (493/507)

Two bars, panadería, shop but no fountain. Basic *refugio* in former schoolroom – ask in Bar Morena (in Calle Oriente, which also does hot meals on request and has a pilgrim stamp and book) and also about the new Casa Rural.

Enter the village via **Calle Eras Viejas** then turn third R (**Calle Oriente**). Turn R at the end (or turn L to visit the church) and KSO, the street becoming a sandy *camino de tierra*. Cross the road to Salamanca and KSO ahead down another sandy *camino de tierra* then turn L 150m later on a similar track, // to the road.

KSO for nearly 3km and just before the entrance to Morille fork R along lane and KSO. Cross a tarmac road and KSO ahead all the time, continuing down **Calle Salas Pombos**. Cross a stream and reach square with *ayuntamiento (the building with a clock)* and *Consultorio Médico* in

4.5km Morille (497.55/502.5)

Fountain, bar (opens late). For pilgrims going all the way to Santiago from Seville this is roughly the halfway point on their journey. Small *refugio*.

Continue up the street to LH side of the *ayuntamiento* (**Calle Mayor**) and KSO into open countryside, passing a cemetery and a large pond (on R). KSO. 3-4 km later go through a *cledo*, and then through a gate and go downhill through *encina* woods. KSO, gently downhill all the time, and 1km later go through gate and 500m after that reach a farm by a road. Go through gates, cross road and go through more gates on the other side. Go downhill in narrow field with walls to either side and continue on stony track to LH side of wall.

Go through another *cledo* and turn L on other side then veer R to continue // to fence on R. When this bends R KSO ahead and pick up track coming from L that continues to RH side of wall, gradually uphill all the time. Continue ahead when wall stops and go through another *cledo* into lane between fences, still gently uphill all the time. At the top a track joins from R; veer L here to farm.

Go downhill on earth road on other side and 3km later pass a RH turning to

10.5km Miranda de Azán (508/492)

Two bars (simple food available), shop

To go into the village (300m each way) turn R here and then retrace your steps to continue. **Otherwise** KSO.

At a crossing after turning to *Miranda de Azán*, KSO ahead over a bridge and continue for 3km towards the cliffs of the **Alto de Zuerguén** *(good views of Salamanca in the distance)*. Go uphill to rocks *(cyclists dismount briefly. Nice place for a rest if not too hot)* and continue ahead towards cathedral towers in front of you.

When you reach a T-junction by a ruined building (2km later) turn R then L onto a track coming from R and KSO, passing isolated tree. *(The N630 is getting closer all the time, over to your R.)* When you reach a new road near the top of the hill *(hotel and N630 over to your R)*, climb up onto it and continue ahead, under electricity cables and head towards blocks of flats. Cross the **Avenida Virgen del Cueto** and continue ahead down **Calle Villar del Profeta** *(pedestrianised)* // to the N630, to the end. Fork R over a railway line and KSO on **Calle Camino de Miranda**. At the end turn R and then L (in front of the *parador*) to a roundabout with a fountain at the bottom of the hill. Veer L here alongside **Río Tormes** and cross it by the Roman bridge. Turn R on the other side, past the church of Santiago, and then L, up **Calle Tentenecio** to the cathedral. Continue along the **Rúa Maior** *(sic)* to the **Plaza Mayor** in

Salamanca Cathedral reflected in the Río Tormes

154

10km Salamanca 808m, pop. 167,000 (518/492)

All facilities, RENFE, buses to Madrid, Zamora, León and other parts of Spain. Accommodation in all price brackets (but always very difficult at weekends), including Hostal Peña de Francia (Calle de San Pablo 96, 923.21.66.87), Fonda Barez (Calle Melendez) and Pensión Estefania (Calle, Jesús 3–5). Albergue Juvenil (youth hostel) on outskirts of town to west (Calle Escoto 13-15, 923.26.91.41). Campsite 2.5km out of town towards Zamora (turn L at roundabout after football stadium). New pilgrim-only *refugio* in the Huerto Calisto y Melibea, between the cathedral and the river: turn R after crossing the Puente Romano. Bike repairs: Bicicletas Palacios, Avenida de los Reyes de España 6, Bicicletas Gilfer, Calle Bólivar 43 and La Cadena, Calle Vitigudin 17. Stamp for pilgrim passport: the cathedral sello is available from the ticket kiosk inside or, alternatively, a *sello* can be obtained from the office of the church of San Marcos (on the way out of town), 12.30 to 13.30, Calle San Marcos (small street at back of church).

Another place to spend a whole day. Tourist office in Plaza Mayor (ask for leaflet with walking tour of city). Two cathedrals (Old and New), university (founded by Alfonso IX in 1218), Plaza Mayor, Patio de las Escuelas, Casa de las Conchas, and many churches and convents, including church of San Tomás de Canterbury, Capilla de Santiago (twelfth-century Romanesque–Mudéjar style) outside historic quarter, by river. Museum in Old Cathedral (fee) has statue of St James.

To leave Salamanca: *from the Plaza Mayor leave by the big arch and go up the* **Calle Zamora**. *Pass the* **Iglesia San Marcos** *(L) and KSO. When you see the* **Plaza de Toros** *ahead of you veer L onto the main road (N630) to Zamora. The arrows start again on the R, just before the city boundary. KSO and pass the* **El Helmántico football stadium** *on the R (*bar/rte on opposite side of road has rooms*). At the roundabout just after the stadium* (campsite 800m to L), *cross carefully, watching out for arrows, KSO on the N630 and go under road bridge. KSO.*

Note: *in the section between Salamanca and Zamora there is VERY LITTLE SHADE at all.*

Just before road KM335 fork L onto a *camino de tierra* // to the road and KSO into the village of

6.5km Aldeaseca de la Armuña 820m (524.5/475.5)

Bars, shop, rte behind petrol station, *farmacia*, bank (+CD), fountain in public garden.

Enter the village via **Calzada de Zamora** and **Camino de la Plata**, continue to **Plaza Mayor**, continue ahead and then turn SECOND L *(Calle Iglesia)* to the church, passing behind it. KSO and take the SECOND *camino de tierra* on R, the **Camino Mozodiel**. 1km later, at a junction of similar tracks, turn R, passing a large walled enclosure and KSO. 1km later reach crossroads of similar *caminos de tierra*, KSO but then 200m later R (i.e. third R after walled enclosure) veering L *(trees over to R)* and KSO to

---

5km Castellanos de Villiquera 830m (529.51/470.5)
Two bars, shop, *farmácia*.

Enter past the cemetery along **Calle de los Santos** *(small wayside cross at start)*. Turn R at the end by water tower and then L to the church, pass in front of its entrance and then turn R down **Calle Calzada** between the *Casa Consistorial (bar in street behind it)* and the church. Continue right to the end, cross a minor road and continue ahead (slightly staggered) on a *camino de tierra* into open countryside. KSO for 3km, cross a local road and enter

---

4.5km Calzada de Valdunciel 807m (534/466)
Bar, shop, bank, fountain in square. New *refugio* (eight beds, key from house behind Casa Consitorial). Hostal/Rte El Pozo has rooms (923.31.00.16), as does the Hostal/Rte La Ruta, both 500m to east on N630.
   Church of Santa Elena contains altar to Santiago Peregrino.

From here **cyclists** will find it easier to turn R to the N630 and continue on it until *El Cubo de Tierra del Vino*.

KSO to a square with a *frontón (turn R here for church, bars, shops)*, pass in front of **Casa Consistorial** *(sello)* and KSO ahead, over the river and out into open countryside again. KSO. 800m later fork R at a junction (badly signed) and KSO, getting closer to the N630 over to your R. When a track comes to an end in a field turn R alongside a fence to the road (N630) at KM323. Turn L along a rough track, first below and then above the road, for 2km, returning to the N630 at a turning to *Topas (big grain silo over to R)*.

Continue ahead on the road (though it is possible to continue below it, to L, or on the embankment above it, but it is a bad FP), cross **Río Ribera de Cadoña** *(probably dry)*. Continue on the road to KM318 *(bascula pública – public weighbridge)* and then cross over to RH side to walk on a track alongside a railway line on your R.

KSO for 3km then watch out for yellow arrows on the other side of the road. 500m before you reach the beginning of the *Topas centro penitenciario* (high-security prison) complex *(its observation tower is visible well ahead)* go down to the road (i.e. before the track you are on finishes), at the end of a section with a crash barrier and cross the N630 (very carefully). Turn L on other side up farm track // to road but inside a field, veering L, and then turn R up track between fields. KSO towards some houses (nearly 1km away).

Pass to LH side of houses, KSO ahead and go through the gates into some woods (not well waymarked at the time this edition was being prepared). Go through a second and then a third set of gates and KSO. Go through a *cledo*, cross a lane leading to the N630 (to your R) then a second one and continue on the lane between fencing. Cross an area of open ground and at the end, at a T-junction, turn R to return (over a cattle grid) to the **N630**, just past road KM311.

Turn L and KSO for 3km. Turn L at road KM308 for 1km into

20km El Cubo de la Tierra del Vino 846m (554/466)

Three bars, shop, *farmacia*. Rooms available in Bar Santo Domingo (does food). Small *refugio* in church (ask priest). The village takes its name from the fact that this area, south of the Río Duero, is rich in vines, whereas the region to its north, the Tierra del Pan, is mainly cornfields. You are now in the province of Zamora.

Note: first of a series of decorative terracotta plaques in the village, indicating its position on the Vía de la Plata. As explained previously, these have been placed in the prominent places of any size along the route in the province of Zamora by the Fundación Ramos de Castro. They are all in the same general style but each one provides information and references specific to the situation and local history of the place in question.

Enter the village via **Calle Mayor** to a square with the *ayuntamiento*. Continue L ahead, passing a church *(on L, picnic area on R)*, cross a bridge and turn L onto a wide *camino de tierra* that continues // to the railway line. When the railway line bends sharp L KSO on a sandy *camino de tierra* // to the railway all the time. KSO for 5km until you reach a T-junction with a bigger *camino de tierra* and where the railway bends sharp R. Turn L and then 100m later turn R. KSO for 3km to a T-junction on a ridge, with woods to L and R in front ahead and KSO(R). *Good plunging views of plain ahead on a clear day.*

Continue on the ridge, passing a fenced-in enclosure on L, ignore LH turn and KSO ahead, veering L downhill. KSO, ignoring turns. *Note three Vía de Plata stone pillars at intervals along the way (there are two more on leaving Villanueva).* At a fork

157

WAY OF ST JAMES: VIA DE LA PLATA

by a line of trees KSO(R) and then KSO(L) at the next and continue between fields, ignoring turns to L and R, undulating then descending. 6km after the T-junction on the ridge reach the small village of

---

13km Villanueva de Campeán 765m (567/433)

Fountain in main square, shop. The very pilgrim-friendly Bar Jambarina is now closed due to the owner's ill-health but a new bar has now opened in the village, which also does food. Very small *refugio* with bunks and hot shower. Another of the series of decorative terracotta plaques in main street

---

Enter the village by the cemetery (R). *(Ruined building over to R is the former Monasterio de Nuestra Señora del Soto.)* Continue along **Calle Calzada** (for church turn second R into *Calle El Señor*). Continue along it to the end of the village, cross a minor road and continue out into open countryside, straight ahead on a *camino de tierra. Flat everywhere around, on all sides.* Shortly afterwards fork R and KSO.

There are **two waymarked routes** after Villanueva: one that by-passes the village of San Marcial, the other (**cyclists** will find this easier) that leads directly to it.

a) Go over several crossings and KSO all the time, reaching the village of **San Marcial** *(5km, bar at entry, on road, does simple food)*. Turn R onto the road (**ZA313**, *Carretera de Ledesma*) and KSO for 2.5km. *Zamora visible ahead at top of hill.* At a bend after KM7 (and just before the turn-off to *Tardobispo*) KSO(L) ahead on a *camino de tierra* towards Zamora ahead *(group of trees to L).*

b) Watch out for a waymark indicating a RH turn at one of the above crossings, leading you to a small river and bringing you up to the top of a hill with a view of Zamora ahead. Turn L here and 20m later when you reach the **ZA313** proceed as above (1km to a bend from here).

KSO for 2.5km, ignoring turnings and crossings and passing farm buildings (on L). 300m after this turn L onto a minor untarred road. 300m later, at a crossing after a water pump and stone drinking troughs (on L: ignore old arrows pointing R before the pump house), turn R along another *camino de tierra*. At the next crossing, 600m later (fenced-in enclosure ahead) turn R, veering L and then R towards (gradually) the railway line coming from R. (When you get close to it, it veers off to R under road bridge.) KSO, veering L towards industrial estate (over to L).

Cross a road (leading to the industrial complex to L) and at a turning circle continue ahead on a track leading towards a line of tall trees ahead on R. Pass to L of them and continue between farm buildings uphill. Turn R at another T-junction and KSO until you reach the **C527** (a by-pass).

Cross over, KSO ahead and enter the former pilgrim district of **San Frontis** *(shop, church of San Frontis)*. Turn R along the **Río Duero** *(bar to L in park by river)* to cross it by the **Puente de Piedra**. Turn R into the **Calle del Puente** and then into the **Plaza Santa Lucía**, turn R behind the church (a few steps) and then second L into **Calle Herreros**, which will lead you up to the **Plaza Mayor** and the *ayuntamiento*.

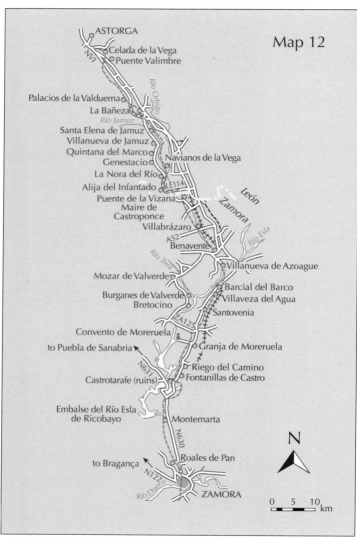

Map 12

ASTORGA
Celada de la Vega
Puente Valimbre
Río Órbigo
Palacios de la Valduerna
La Bañeza
Río Jamuz
Santa Elena de Jamuz
Villanueva de Jamuz
Quintana del Marco
Genestacio
Navianos de la Vega
La Nora del Río
Alija del Infantado
LE114
León
Puente de la Vizana
Zamora
Maire de
Castroponce
Villabrázaro
A52
Benavente
Río Esla
Villanueva de Azoague
Mozar de Valverde
Río Tera
Barcial del Barco
Burganes de Valverde
Villaveza del Agua
Bretocino
Santovenia
A125
Convento de Moreruela
to Puebla de Sanabria
Granja de Moreruela
N631
Riego del Camino
Castrotarafe (ruins)
Fontanillas de Castro
Embalse del Río Esla
de Ricobayo
Montemarta
N630
N
to Bragança
Roales de Pan
N122
Río Duero
ZAMORA

0   5   10
km

19.5km Zamora 658m, 64,421 (586/414)

All facilities, RENFE, buses to León, Ourense, Madrid and other parts of Spain. Plenty of accommodation: 8 hotels, 10 *hostales* and 12 *pensiones*, including Bar El Jardín (near church of San Torcuato, 980.53.18.27), Fonda Padornelo (980.53.20.64) and Hostal la Reina (Plaza Mayor, 980.53.39.39) but no pilgrim-only accommodation. *Sello*: Cathedral, Policía Local (in Plaza Mayor) or parish churches (such as San Ildefonso). Bike repairs: La Madrileña, Calle San Andrés 19.

Note: There are NO CASH DISPENSERS before Benavente if you are going to Santiago via Astorga.

Town situated on north bank of Río Duero, developed and expanded by the Romans on the site of an existing centre of population. Cathedral and 19 Romanesque churches: Santiago del Burgo (Santiagos Matamoros and Peregrino on main altar reredos), San Juan de Puerta Nueva, Santa María la Nueva, San Cipriano, San Ildefonso, La Magdalena, Santa María de la Horta and Santo Tomé,

Head of Santiago Peregrino, predella of the altarpiece of San Ildefonso, Cathedral museum, Zamora

as well as the cathedral, are all open to the public daily except Mondays, from 10.00 to 13.00 and 17.00 to 20.00 (slightly earlier in winter); San Claudio de Olivares (contains statue of San Roque as a pilgrim) and Santiago de los Caballeros, both on the western outskirts, are open the same hours but July–September only. San Esteban is now the Museo Baltasar Lobo, exhibiting the sculptures and drawings of the internationally renowned Zamoran artist who died in 1993. The other churches (with the exception of San Leonardo, which is privately owned) are open at mass times.

Zamora is also well known for its week-long Semana Santa (Holy Week) processions (accommodation very difficult during this period) and many of the floats used, both modern and historic, are in the Museo de la Semana Santa (others are located in different churches). Castillo, ramparts, Palacio Episcopal, Palacio del los Momos, Parador de Turismo in former palace of Dukes of Conde and Allots, Hospital de la Incarnation (now headquarters of regional government). Museo Etnográfico de Castilla y León, Museo Catedratico, Museo Provincial. Tourist offices: next to Cathedral and also at Calle de Santa Clara 20 (980.52.69.53); organises guided walking tours of the town – in Spanish – every morning in summer except Mondays). Worth spending a whole day here.

Cyclists can use the walker's route from here as far as Tábara (on the route via Ourense) or Barcial del Braco if going via Benavente.

*Leaving Zamora: from **Plaza Mayor** go down **Calle Costanilla** (to R of the ayuntamiento), continue, veering L, into **Calle Feria** and cross **Ronda de Feria**. Continue up **Cuesta de la Morana** (church of San Lázaro on R; first yellow arrow after this). KSO(R) at a fork up **Avenida de Galicia** (N122), leading to a roundabout and the N630 at KM275 (bar in hostal/rte by petrol station is open 24 hours). KSO along the N630 (but watch out carefully for any new waymarks as there were major roadworks here at the time the present edition of this guide was being prepared): the Vía de la Plata coincides with it for 5km more, as far as*

6.5km Roales de Pan 700m (592.5.5/407.5)
Farmacia, bar, rte on N630.

Fork L onto a minor road // to the N630 by a factory just before entry to the village, opposite a road sign (pointing R) to 'Valcabado'. KSO (**Calle General Franco**) to the *ayuntamiento* and church (*seats, another decorative plaque*).

DO NOT turn L here but KSO ahead on the main street to the end of the village. Then KSO ahead along a *camino de tierra*, with a main road over to R but at a distance. Turn R at the next junction and 200m later turn L // to the road again. KSO, through undulating cornfields (and occasional sunflowers) stretching to infinity. *No shade at all (this area is the Tierra del Pan).*

Note: as there is often nowhere else to paint arrows, watch out for them on the concrete slabs that end the drain pipes of the irrigation system at junctions *of caminos.*

KSO for 3km, in a straight line all the time. Then KSO ahead, very slightly L, at a prominent junction. KSO for 4km. When Montemarta comes in sight in the distance *(buildings, groups of isolated trees)* the *camino* begins to veer L (west), away from the road. At the next junction after this turn R and KSO. 1.5km later *(with road and petrol station over to R)* KSO ahead at a junction. *(However, to eat or sleep in bar/rte Hostal El Asturiano at road KM289 on main road – see below – turn RIGHT here.)* Otherwise, KSO.

Turn SECOND R after a farm (on your R) and then veer L at a fork towards a *depósito de aqua* (water tower, this one on legs). Continue along the street (**Calle Adrial**). *At a junction with a grassed area you will see another of the plaques put up by the Fundación Ramos de Castro explaining the history of the Vía de la Plata and its associations with the place in question.*

KSO then turn second R down **Calle de Reblo** *(passing shop, R)* to a junction with a church in

---

12.5km Montemarta 690m (605/395)
Bar, shop and *farmacia* in village, near church, and others bar/rtes on main road. Bar/Rte El Asturiano (980.55.01.82) at KM289 on main road has rooms (this is the one you passed earlier, near the petrol station).

Turn L here down **Calle Ermita** past the *farmacia* and then R along the side of the *frontón (pelota court)* and then L behind it. Cross a reservoir via a causeway (if it is dry) and go up a FP to **Ermita de la Virgen del Castillo**, on the hill ahead of you. (**Cyclists** dismount or continue to road and back-track.) However, if the reservoir is flooded you will have to go round to the church via the road bridge opposite and then fork L uphill. *The ermita is a good place for a shady rest (outside the entrance door) with good views and stone seating.*

Continue past the cemetery (on L) and then turn L uphill on the middle of three tracks, joining the RH one at the top of the hill and passing concrete building on L surrounded by barbed wire (marked 'Exco. Ayuntamiento 25.4.1994'). KSO ahead.

KSO for 3.5km, ignoring turns. Two TV masts (*repetidores*) can be seen over to L on the skyline. The path then begins to go uphill into an area of scrubby trees and cistus bushes. When it starts to veer sharply to L, just before a line of telegraph wires at right angles to you, turn R onto another track (// to wires now), leading gently downhill to a road by a noticeboard explaining the division of the main road into the N630 and N631.

Cross over, go down a local road ahead, veering L and when it veers hard R KSO ahead along a *camino de tierra*, // to the main road and alongside more cables. 700m later return to the **N630**, cross it (carefully) and continue ahead on a similar track. (**Cyclists**, however, may find it easier to continue on the road from here to Fontanillos de Castro.) KSO at a crossing and fork R past a small concrete hut, slightly uphill. When you get to the top you will see the Embalse de Ricobayo ahead of you below, with bright blue water if full, and on a hill at the end of it the ruins of Castrotarafe.

The arrows, in fact, lead you into the water (if there is any), in order to take you (on the other side) to the ruins of *Castrotarafe*, but unless the water is low enough to walk/wade across you will have to take the upper of two tracks which leads you past some houses and then to the main road, where you can cross the dam by the bridge. *(The remnant of a building sticking up by water's edge was an old mill.)*

Continue for 100m on the other side of the bridge and then, just after road KM253, turn L down a track, passing to R of two buildings. This takes you round the side of the *embalse* (reservoir), // to it but slightly above, and leads you, round a small hill, to the ruins of Castrotarafe. *The route is well-enough waymarked but the paths are not always very distinct and cyclists will find it easier to continue on the road for 1.3km more and then turn L down a wide track, signposted in purple (as for historic monuments) to 'Castrotarafe.' Ruins are not very far (200–300m) from there and are clearly visible.*

10km Castrotarafe (615/385)
Remains of a town, possibly dating from Roman times, and inhabited until the eighteenth century, controlling the traffic crossing the Esla. Its *castillo* was the seat of the Knights of the Order of Santiago.

From the ruins (with them on your L) you can either continue by path to the village of Fontanillos de Castro or (if you are hungry, for example) go back to the road and turn L (there is a *bar/rte* on L, *next to a petrol station*), 700m before the entrance to

---

2km Fontanillas de Castro 725m (617/383)
Bar/rte by petrol station, fountain.

Ruins of the castle of the Knights of Santiago, Castrotarafe

Turn L into village if coming from road (first street on L is **Travesia del Cemeterio**) then R at the water tower (or straight on if coming directly from Castrotarafe) down **Calle Cementario** past the church (*with another decorative plaque, explaining local history and the historical importance of the castro*). Turn L (staggered) downhill and L at the bottom opposite house no. 12 *(fountain opposite no. 14)*. KSO to the end of the village (this is **Calle la Barca**) and then turn R down a *camino de tierra* at a junction. *Riego del Camino is visible ahead.*

KSO, KSO at the next junction (1km later) and fork R after a large group of trees. Fork R again at a large isolated tree and by the first building cross a *camino de tierra* coming from R diagonally. Continue ahead on a small but clear FP between fields, alongside the wall of a building along **Calle Ferrabal** to the main road in

4km Riego del Camino 705m (621/379)
Bar on main road (with simple food), basic *refugio*.

Turn L and then fork second R between buildings and KSO on a *camino de tierra* again. Turn R up the *camino de tierra* after the last house towards a white silo and KSO(L) at a fork, // to the road (**N630**) over to your R.

KSO (quite literally) for 6km. At the end turn R at a T-junction to the village. Veer L over a bridge and turn R on a concrete lane leading to a main road. Turn L and continue to the church in

165

6.5km Granja de Moreruela 708m (627/373)

Three bars, two on main road. Bar El Peregrino, which does meals and has pilgrim book and *sello* and has the key the Casa de la Cultura (basic accommodation), is uphill (ring bell if closed), on the way out of the village on the Astorga option. Shop.

> This is where the two *caminos* divide, one continuing ahead (north) to Astorga, the other turning left (west) to go directly to Santiago via Puebla de Sanabria and Ourense. For the second option see 'Route via Puebla de Sanabria and Ourense', page 181. To continue via Benavente and La Bañeza to Astorga proceed as described here.

From here a detour to the west to visit the ruins of the Convento de Moreruela is suggested. This was the first Cistercian convent in Spain, founded in 1158, with a pilgrim hospital added in the sixteenth century. To do so, turn L off N630 (signposted) just before entry to village, which takes you directly there, 3.7km each way. The convent is on private land but it is accessible and worth the detour.

Cyclists: to avoid the fairly long section on the N630, you can follow the walker's route for the next 2.5km as far as the ZA123 (to Tábara), turn L along it and then, shortly after crossing the bridge over the Esla, turn R along a local road through Bretocino, Olmillos de Valverde, Burganes de Valverde, cross the Río Tera in Mozar de Valverde and turn R to Santa Cristina de Polvorosa and enter Benavente from the west. This route is slightly longer but very much quieter that the N630.

Turn L by the church (*decorative plaque explains the separation of ways*) into **Calle Dr González Galindo** and then first R up **Calle San Juan** *(waymarked 'Astorga')*. Fork second L uphill to the village square and make for the prominent grain tower and TV mast, where you take a *camino de tierra* // to the main road. KSO on this, ignoring turns, for 2.5km, until you reach a local road, the ZA123 to Tábara. Turn R and then just before the road junction with the N630 turn L onto a *camino de tierra* which veers round to R, // to the road.

4km Junction with the road to Tábara (ZA123) (631)

Bar/Rte Hostal Oviedo (980.58.60.80, meals and rooms), on R just after junction at road KM237/238.

Convento de
Moreruela

KSO. From the junction you can stay on a clear track a short distance from the N630, except possibly near KM236 (where it may be boggy) all the way to Santovenia.

2km before the village you get your first view of Benavente over in the distance to the northwest. You will continue to see it away to your left until you reach it, though you often appear to be going east, away from it: this is because there is no road bridge over the Río Esla until you reach the outskirts of the town itself.

4.5km Santovenia 715m (635.5)
Bar/Rte Esla (980.64.70.14) has rooms, another bar, two shops. Fountain at end of village on R.

The 'Santovenia' of the village's name refers to Santa Eugenia la Mozárabe (see plaque on church).

Continue on the main road past the church (*seats – nice place for a rest*). Stay on the road for 1km to a cemetery at the top of the hill then continue on a *cañada* to RH side of the **N630**. This section is not very interesting as you walk between the irrigation channel and the road as far as

6km Villaveza del Agua 700m (641.5)
Bar at end of village (on road).

Continue through the village on the road, fork L just before **Bar La Huerta** and pass behind it. KSO ahead (staggered) at a junction towards **Barcial del Barco** (*church with its octagonal tower visible on hill ahead*). When you reach the road again at a crash barrier at the bottom of the hill KSO(L) ahead underneath the church, turning R uphill just after you have passed it. Veer R and at the top turn L along the main road into

> **2.5km Barcial del Barco 717m (644)**
> Three bars. Village takes its name from the ferry service that used to operate to connect the two banks of the river Esla.

Continue to the end of the village and when you are on the level of a large grain silo fork R (**Calle Toro**) in front of a café-bar and continue to a level crossing.

Cyclists: continue ahead on the old road via *Castropepe* to cross the bridge over the *Río Esla* at the entrance to *Benavente* (12km).

Walkers: fork L here, along the disused Zamora–Astorga railway line (*tracks still there so you can walk on the sleepers; it is 8km to Benavente from here by this route*). KSO along the railway track and after 1km cross a metal bridge over a tributary (probably dry) of the **Río Esla**. Here you can either KSO on the railway line (*very tedious, especially if your stride and the spacing of the sleepers do not coincide, and it also gets increasingly overgrown as you proceed*) or go down an embankment on LH side immediately after crossing a bridge and take the *camino de tierra* that follows the railway line to its L all the time. 2km later you will see a black water tower to RH side of the railway line (on its level) and a dilapidated white building on LH side on field level: go up a bank to a metal 'box' bridge and use it to cross the **Río Esla**.

Immediately after crossing the bridge, turn R down a FP and KSO(R) along a track through a poplar plantation and on a shady path beside the river. Take the second R turn along a *camino de tierra* with concrete irrigation channel alongside it and then turn L 500m later, cross a road and enter the village of

> **6km Villanueva del Azoague (650)**
> Bar in Plaza Mayor.

KSO, following the street (**Calle Huerta**) as it veers L, turn R into **Calle Mayor** which becomes **Calle de Benavente** – a very long street with a large *azucarería* (sugar factory) on the LH side (*the Museo del Azúcar is located inside*). At the end (2km), cross the main road (N525) – carefully – and KSO ahead on the other side past a large bathroom fittings showroom (L) to another junction (with the *Vía del Canal*) and then to a third (not waymarked at the start) with the **Avenida General Primo de Rivera**. Turn R along it into

3km Benavente 747m, pop. 12,500 (653)

All facilities. Accommodation in all price brackets (three hotels, eight hostales, five pensiones), including Fonda California (Primo de Rivera 32, 980.63.38.34), Hostal Ría de Vigo (Primo de Rivera 27, 980.63.17.79), Hotel Bristol (General Mola 16, 980.63.16.93) and Hostal Paraíso (Calle Obispo Regueras 64, 980.63.33.81). *Refugio* in former RENFE (i.e. railway) station. *Sello:* ayuntamiento, between 08.00 and 15.00. Tourist office in Calle Fortaleza 17.

Note: Many of the street names in Benavente have recently been officially changed to avoid those which had associations with the former Franco regime. As a result it may be difficult to use a street plan for the time being.

Old town has churches of Santa María del Azoque and San Juan del Mercado (both open for visits 10.00 to 13.00 and 17.00 to 20.00), Hospital de la Piedad (former pilgrim hospice with cloister and pilgrim door knocker in early sixteenth-century entrance) and Ermita de la Soledad. Castillo de la Mora (only tower remains of original building) is now the parador. Modern octagonal church of Santiago in northern suburbs.

Turn L (off Avenida Primo de Rivera) up **Calle Agucero** (middle of three streets) at a prominent junction. Turn R up **Calle Ancha**, passing (R) the church of **Nuestra Señora del Carmen**.

Then, **walkers**: fork L up **Calle Zamora**, veer L and then R to **Plaza Nuñez Granes** and ahead along **Calle Conde Patilla** to the **Plaza de España** and the *ayuntamiento.*

Cyclists: fork R into **Calle Cervantes** to the end, turn L up **Calle General Mole** and immediately R (**Calle General Aranda**) to **Plaza de España**.

From there (**Plaza de España**) go back through **Calle Conde Patilla**, turn R into **Calle José Antonio** to the **Iglesia de Santa María**. From the **Plaza de Onesimo Redondo** (on its northwest side) go down **Calle Aguadores**.

Walkers: *this is the old (formerly well-waymarked) route and is very quiet, fairly shady (in the mornings) and is easy to follow.* Continue (not well-waymarked) and then turn fourth R down some steps into. Turn R at the bottom towards an old railway station *(marshalling yard behind has been made into a park, with seats)* and continue past it *(it is now a* refugio*).* When the tarmac road bends R KSO ahead on a *camino de tierra*, with remains of railway line to your L at first and then to R. 1km after the station KSO ahead at a junction by a farm and 1km later, when the *camino*

169

Pilgrim knocker on
hospital door,
Benavente

de tierra bends L 200m after a small house), go up to railway line on R and continue on a small but clear and obviously well-used FP. This does a detour away from the track from time to time but then returns. *River below to L is the Órbigo.* KSO for 1.5km.

Just after the railway marker 289/6 the FP widens out and goes downhill towards the road which comes from under the railway line (from the R). Continue on a *camino de tierra* coming from your L from a bridge over the *Río Órbigo* and continue on it to LH side of the road for 500m. When it comes to an end (first yellow arrow here, where a line of telegraph poles crosses the road) cross over and continue on the *camino de tierra* on RH side.

Cyclists: *the walker's route described above is NOT suitable for bikes (of any sort).* So, turn first R out of the **Calle Aguadores** into **Calle Sancti Spiritu** which becomes the **Calle del Perú** and then runs into the **Carretera de Acubilla**. KSO along it and you will go under the railway bridge referred to in a) above, veering R.

Both cyclists and walkers: when this road begins to veer L (1km from the railway bridge) by a lay-by, fork R uphill, veering L to a level crossing sign, and then R uphill to cross the railway line. *This is the Teso del Peñón, the area where, it is thought (and based on evidence from aerial photographs), the Roman mansio Brigeco was located.* Fork L uphill on the other side and KSO(L) ahead when another track joins from your R. KSO at a junction, go over another level crossing, go under the motorway, KSO ahead and then turn R opposite the cemetery into

8.5km Villabrázaro 710m (661.5)
Large bar at entrance to village (has pilgrim book and does simple food), unmarked shop in main street (RH side), fountain in centre of village. Simple *refugio* for those with pilgrim credencial. *Sello* in the ayuntamiento. Plaque informs you that the village was a *mansio* on the Vía de la Plata in Roman times.

Go through the village on the main street and out again on the other side on a very minor tarred road. KSO for 4.5km. At a junction KSO ahead, ignoring turns, to

8.5km Maire de Castroponce 748m (670)
Bar in Casa Consistorial (on LH side of road)

KSO through the village and KSO at the end on a minor road ahead, leading to a bridge over the **Río Órbigo**.

3km Puente de la Vizana (673)

Original bridge of Roman origin but with later additions and alterations. Boundary of provinces of Zamora and León. Picnic area with trees, campsite. Hostal Puente La Vizana has rooms and bar/rte (987.69.20.63, closed after 16.00 Mondays Oct-May). From here to La Bañeza the landscape becomes much greener, though there is not necessarily more shade to walk in.

The path from here formerly took you through the fields but it is nearly always waterlogged so now you KSO on the road until you reach

3km Alija del Infantado 740m (676)

Bars, shop, farmácia, bank (+CD), small simple *refugio* above Hogar del Pensionista – ask in tourist office (which also has *sello*). Rte (expensive) at entrance to town.

Iglesia San Estéban (thirteenth–fourteenth centuries), Iglesia de San Verísimo (twelfth–sixteenth centuries), Castillo-Palacio (first–sixth centuries), Fuente de Mendaña. Fuente de San Ignacio of Roman origin, with water with medicinal properties (digestion, obesity, kidney problems), Rincón de la Judería (former Jewish quarter) with a lot of restored *bodegas* (on top of hill near fountain). Small *ermita* on LH side of road at entrance to village by children's playground was formerly in private hands but is now owned by an organisation that is constructing leisure and sports facilities there for the village. Ermita del Cristo at end of village on R and on hill at end, above it, Cruz de Peregrino (with Santiago sword).

KSO to the end of the village (*worth climbing up, L, to Fuente de San Ignacio to drink cool water, fill bottle and have a good view*). When the road veers R, the old waymarking takes you straight ahead on a track to LH side of the road, roughly // to it and rather overgrown. You will find it easier, however, to continue on the road for 2km (not much traffic) to the turn-off, to the L, to

3.5km La Nora del Río (679.5)

Small village wedged in between the rivers Jamuz and Órbigo. Unmarked bar in centre.

Here you have a choice of THREE routes, whether you are on foot or on a mountain bike (**cyclists** should take the road option). Options A and B enter La Bañeza from the south, C from slightly further east.

A. Road option KSO ahead on road and stay on it, passing through the villages of **Genestacio** *(4km, bar)*, **Quintana del Marco** (2km), **Villanueva de Jamuz** *(3km, bar in Hogar del Pensionista)*, and **Santa Elena de Jamuz** *(4km)*, from where you continue as described on page 174 below. *This route is sparsely waymarked, but is very easy to follow and there is not a lot of traffic.*

B. Riverbank option *This option follows the Río Jamuz until 5km before La Bañeza and has been waymarked recently. It is quiet, shady in places and is extemely straightforward and easy to follow.*

Turn R over bridge towards *La Nora del Río* but then turn L immediately on other side onto a *camino de tierra* along the RH bank of the **Río Jamuz**. KSO, quite literally, ignoring turnings *(track is tree-lined all the way on the LH side)*. Pass vehicle bridge (on L) after 2.5km and KSO. Pass a second bridge 1.5km later (the *camino de tierra* to L leads to the village of *Genestacio (bar)*). KSO ahead all the time. 2km later continue on concrete lane (leading to third bridge) in

6km Quintana del Marco
Two churches. Bar opposite church on other side of bridge.

Continue ahead on RH side of river and 2km later pass a fourth bridge. KSO ahead and reach a 5th bridge on outskirts of

3km Villanueva de Jamuz
Bar in Casa Consitorial (on road). Village over to your R is San Juan de Torres.

KSO. Pass sixth bridge 2km later. Then, **cyclists** *can turn L here, turn R along LH bank and then, when this track bends L, continue to road if they want.* **Walkers** *can turn R here, turn next L, turn R 'por el monte' and then go over the motorway into La Bañeza (i.e. connecting up with option C).*

Otherwise: KSO ahead here and 1km later, at poplar plantation, turn R and then L to pass to back of it, // to river, on grassy track. Pass several such plantations. The track has a kink in it by a water pump (after which it > partly gravelled) but otherwise KSO ahead all the time.

700–800m from first poplar trees track joins from back R. KSO and reach FB (on L) on outskirts of **Santa Elena de Jamuz**. Turn R up clear track here and 200m later turn L along hillside and crossing of similar tracks. Continue ahead and emerge at road just past bridge over the **Río Jamuz** at the end of the village of

4.5km Santa Elena de Jamuz

After turning R KSO on the road, climbing up after leaving Santa Elena. When you reach a large grain silo (now a scrap yard) on your L, turn R over a railway bridge, veering L, and continue down **Calle Santa Elena** (not marked at the start), a long street. At a junction turn L (opposite house no. 35) and then turn R immediately into **Calle San Julián**. (Turn second R off here into **Calle San Roque** for the *refugio*, on the corner with **Calle Bello Horizonte**.)

Turn first L from **Calle San Julián** into **Calle San Blas** and immediately R into **Calle Santa Lucía**, veering L downhill. KSO at a junction along **Calle Lope de Vega** to a junction with **Calle Ramón y Cajal** in **La Bañeza (4km)**.

C. Motorway tunnel option. Turn R over a bridge, follow the road round, veering L, skirting but not entering La Nora del Río. *This is the route that follows the course of the original calzada romana. It was waymarked in the early 1990s but due to the reorganisation of land boundaries most of them have now disappeared. It is not hard to follow if you are attentive to the instructions given below and is an easy ride for mountain bikes.*

After crossing a bridge veer L and then turn L after RH bend, up the *camino de tierra* that follows the LH bank of the **Río Órbigo** to start with. KSO(L) at RH fork (leading into woods) and KSO, ignoring turns, into

3.5km Navianos de la Vega (683)
Two bars (not open early).

Continue on the road you entered on and KSO through the village, passing a public garden (L) and continue along **Calle de Arriba**. Fork R at the end and continue on a *camino de tierra* out into open countryside between fields.

KSO(R) at the first fork (600m) and 400m later, by a group of trees (small brick hut over to L) where the track joins from back L, pass a turning to R. Continue ahead. *(Village over to L in distance is Genestacio, with water tower and fort.)* 200m later KSO(L) at a fork.

At a T-junction by a much larger group of trees and concrete irrigation tanks turn L, and then turn R 100m later onto a long, straight track between fields. KSO (literally). After 500m pass the first crossroad *(village to L is Quintana del Marco)* and the second one 800m later. 750m after that turn L at another T-junction, between concrete irrigation channels, and then R alongside another one. KSO *(you can see houses in San Juan de Torres ahead here)*. Pass a large group of trees 100m away to R.

KSO and 1.4km later KSO at another crossroads. KSO ahead (irrigation channel still on L). *Village over to L is Villanueva de Jamuz.* 750m later cross a crossroads and KSO and then 700m afterwards reach a T-junction at a road linking *San Juan de Torres* and *Villanueva de Jamuz* (6.5km from Navianos).

Turn L towards a white building *(electricity transformer)* and 200m later turn R to cross a bridge over an irrigation channel. Turn L and then turn R after the white building and 300m later turn L. 200m later turn R, passing large metal barn on R, to circumnavigate a hilly area on R.

At a junction with a *camino de tierra* coming from L, veer R and 300m later KSO(L). 1.5km later cross a road leading (to L) to *Santa Elena de Jamuz*. KSO and 1.5km after that cross a disused railway line and 500m later go through a tunnel under a motorway. Continue straight ahead all the time and 1.3km later you will reach the **N630**. Turn L along it for 150m then fork L down **Calle Libertadores** (a long street). Cross the **Plaza de los Reyes Católicos**, continue (R) ahead down **Calle Juan de Mansilla** to the **Plaza Mayor** in

---

15km La Bañeza 777m, pop. 8501 (697)

All facilities. Buses to Madrid, Santiago, León, Seville and other parts of Spain. Hostal/Rte Astur (Calle Astorga 9, 987.64.04.15), Hostal Madrid (Calle Angel Riesco 3, 987.64.00.21), Hostal Roma (Calle Astorga 56, 987.64.05.89), Pensión Astelena (Calle Lepanto 4, 987.64.11.13), Fonda Industrial (Calle Ramón y Cajal 12, 987.64.10.42), Fonda El Nistal (Calle El Salvador 15, 987.64.00.69), Pensión Bar Johnny (Calle la Fuente 18, 987.64.07.26); otherwise accommodation is on the outskirts of the town on the NVI. Large *refugio* in converted school (corner of Calles San Roque and Bello Horizonte). Tourist office: Calle Padre Miguelez s/n. Bike repairs: Gonzalez de la Torre, Calle Antonio Bordas 16.

Iglesia de Santa María, Iglesia de San Salvador (both are parish churches), Capilla de Jesús Nazareno, Capilla de las Angustias. The church of El Salvador, of Romanesque origin, is on the site of one of the earliest pilgrim hospitals, founded in AD 932 (barely 100 years after the discovery of the tomb of St James in the location that was to become Santiago de Compostela).

To go into the town centre and the Plaza Mayor: turn R down **Calle Ramón y Cajal** (and then retrace your steps to continue).

Otherwise: cross **Calle Ramón y Cajal** and continue along **Calle El Salvador** past church. Continue to the end of the street *(public garden opposite)* then turn R (**Calle Primo de Rivera**) and then immediately L into **Calle José Marcos de Segovia**. KSO, veering L over a level crossing, and continue ahead on **Carretera Villalis**.

At a small junction by the town exit boards (and entrance signs for Santiago de la Valduerna some 20m later), fork R onto **Calle la Mesta**. KSO at crossing on *camino de tierra* and take second L (do NOT cross railway line) and then fork R up FP to cross the **Río Duerna** by a metal 'box' bridge. KSO on FP on LH side of railway track and when a *camino de tierra* starts, coming from L, turn L here, past a barn. KSO(R) at fork 150m later and head towards the motorway.

Turn L at a T-junction at end and then R to go under motorway, veering R and then L on other side. KSO(R) ahead at junction (motorway is now over to your R). Continue ahead, turn fourth L (just before the track you are on veers R) and then turn next R.

Continue ahead through fields *(Montes de León begin to be visible in the distance)* for 1km to

6km Palacios de la Valduerna (703)

Bar (unmarked) on main street on L near public garden, shop, farmacia. Tower over to L is remains of fourteenth-century fortress.

Turn R after crossing the canal, L up a lane, L again then R and R again towards the church. Turn hard L *(Calle Santa María)* to the *ayuntamiento* then KSO(L) along the main street (**Calle Carretera Tabuyo**). The *ermita* is on LH side towards the end. At a fork with a sitting area and fountain turn R down a more minor road (**Calle Camino del Monte**). Fork R in front of the cemetery and KSO on a *camino de tierra* across open heathland with occasional plantations of vines.

The mountains are very clear now in the middle distance, the road away over to R all the time. The Santuario de Nuestra Señora de Castrotierra is over to L on a hilltop, the focus of an annual local pilgrimage on March 25th and, every seven years, the start of a journey on foot to Astorga, with the Virgin carried in procession on the shoulders of the participants.

KSO(L) at the first crossing. KSO ahead at the next. Cistus trees begin.

When you get to a 'stop' sign with a tarred road crossing diagonally (7km from Palacios de la Valduerna), turn R along it *(do NOT continue on the clear track ahead or you will need a 6–7km detour to get back on course again)*. At the next junction (600m later) KSO straight ahead on a *camino de tierra*. KSO, gradually getting nearer to and then alongside the motorway. Turn R underneath it (via a tunnel), go towards the next tunnel but then turn L along a track (in the direction of the big white Norgasa factory ahead) leading to a motorway slip-road.

Cross it, continue to RH side of the slip-road signed 'La Coruña' then turn R to an old road. Cross it and walk along it for 20m then turn R down a minor road marked 'Estación de Valderrey 0.7'. Turn L along a lane by an old-style electricity transformer tower and KSO. Approximately 1km later, after passing between two lines of poplars, you will come to the

12km Puente Valimbre (715)
Four-arch bridge of Roman origin over Río Turienzo. Restored on several occasions, most recently in 1998. **Cyclists** stay on N630 from here to Astorga.

Cross the bridge and veer L uphill to the road. Cross over and continue ahead on the track that goes alongside it, not always very near. Just before the top of the hill (large modern house, isolated, in front) return to the road at a 'stop' sign.

First view of Astorga cathedral from here. After this, because of new motorway construction, you have to continue on the **N630** for the last 5km to Astorga.

3km Celada de la Vega (718)
Bar/mesón at junction, Hostal/Rte La Paz (987.61.52.77, rooms) on same side further on.

Bishop's Palace, Astorga

Continue on the road until you reach the edge of Astorga. Fork R into the **Plaza San Roque** and then go up the staircase into the **Calle del Angel** which then > the **Calle La Bañeza**. (*Cyclists* wait to turn R up the *Bajada del Postigo*). KSO up the **Calle La Bañeza** to the **Plaza de España**. Continue ahead via Calle Pio Guillón, Calle Postas and Calle Santiago, pass in front of the **Palacio de Gaudí** and reach the cathedral in

3km Astorga 899m, pop. 14,000 (722)
All facilities, RENFE, buses to Madrid, Santiago, Seville, León, Ponferrada, Villafranca del Bierzo and other parts of Spain. Tourist office near cathedral. Two *refugios* in centre of town (both large), a municipal one near the town walls and the private San Xavier near the cathedral. Plenty of other accommodation.

A town dating from Roman times, with extensive remains of its original walls. Astorga was (and still is) the junction of two pilgrim routes, the Camino Francés and the Camino Mozárabe or Vía de la Plata. This explains the unusually large number of pilgrim hospitals formerly in existence (there were 22 in the Middle Ages), the last of which, the Hospital de las Cinco Llagas (the Five Wounds), burned down early in the twentieth century. Gothic cathedral with interesting choir stalls and museum, Bishop's Palace built by the Catalan architect Antonio Gaudí, with pilgrim museum on ground floor and chapel upstairs. Several other interesting churches, Baroque town hall, Museo del Chocolate (Astorga was once the chocolate capital of Spain). It is worth spending half a day here.

From Astorga those who wish to continue to Santiago now 'turn left' along the Camino Francés for another 250km and in many ways this part will seem much easier. There is an extensive network of refuges, getting your pilgrim passport stamped is much simpler and you will also meet a lot of other pilgrims, though many people experience something of a shock when they leave the relative solitude of the Vía de la Plata to be plunged into the busy hustle and bustle of this much more frequented route. There are also a lot more fountains and bars on the Camino Francés, and once you enter Galicia the weather is usually considerably cooler as well.

The continuation from Astorga to Santiago is described in, *inter alia*, the present author's *The Way of St James: Pyrenees–Santiago–Finisterre* or, for cyclists, John Higginson's companion volume *The Way of Saint James: A cyclists guide*, both published by Cicerone Press.

Pilgrim street sign, Astorga (photo: author)

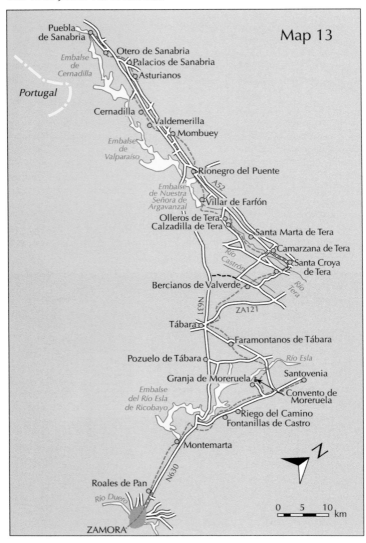

ROUTE VIA PUEBLA DE SANABRIA AND OURENSE (CAMINO SANABRÉS)

6km Granja de Moreruela 708m (627/373)
From here you have two options to reach Puente Quintos: the waymarked route or a more direct alternative that is not yet waymarked but which is 2km shorter and very easy to follow.

a) **Waymarked route:** turn L by the church (**Calle Dr González Galindo**) and KSO ahead. KSO(R) at a fork and continue for 1.4km in open countryside. Take the SECOND RH turn uphill. KSO for 3km (having passed two LH turns) and then when you do not expect it, turn R. 1km later turn L at a T-junction (you can see the ZA123 ahead of you here) and continue along it, veering R downhill to a road. Turn L along it and continue to cross the bridge over the **Río Esla**.

b) **Shorter route:** turn L by the church but then turn R uphill on the route marked 'Astorga' to the *Bar El Peregrino*. Continue to the top of the hill by the telephone pylon, where pilgrims taking the Astorga route turn R. Turn LEFT here instead (on track that comes up from the village to your R) and then KSO ahead, quite literally, ignoring all turnings. After a while the track veers L a little and you will see the ZA123 (the road linking the N630 with Tábara) over to your R.

1km before you reach the bridge over the *Río Esla*, the waymarked route joins from the L. Continue steeply downhill, veering R to road and continue on it to the

7km Puente Quintos (643/366)
The original route crossed the Río Esla some 500m downstream, as you can see from the remains of the old bridge positioned where you will turn away from the river after your detour to cross the present bridge.

a) **Cyclists:** this section is NOT suitable, even for mountain bikes, and you should continue along the road here until Faramontanos de Tábara.

b) **Walkers**: on other side turn L behind the crash barrier and continue on a small
   FP through rocks, leading down to the shore. Walk alongside the river until
   you are level with the remains of the old bridge and then fork R steeply uphill
   by large cliff-like rocks next to the river. *Be very careful if the weather is misty.*

Go uphill (small FP, well waymarked) // to the river to start with then veering R up
to the top of the cliff ahead of you (*good view of old bridge if you look back as you
climb*). At the top turn R through trees by a ruined house, after which a proper track
starts. KSO along it.

1km later turn L at a T-junction and continue through heathland, ploughed up in
part, with a lot of encina trees (and therefore quite a lot of shade). KSO, ignoring turns,
for 1.5km then KSO(L) uphill on a track joining from your R. KSO, ignoring turns, until
you reach a junction by the large white gate posts at the entrance to the

5.5km Finca Val de la Rosa (639.5/360.5)

Turn R here. 1km later cross tarmac road and KSO. 800m later turn L, turn R at T-
junction shortly afterwards and KSO, gently downhill all the time. KSO at first crossing
and 1km late, at second crossing, turn R. KSO (quite literally) into

8km Faramontanos de Tábara (647.5/352.5)
Two bars (one with shop), another shop, *panadería* but no accommodation.
Church porch good place for a rest.

Enter the village on **Calle Prolongación Benavente** and then head on to **Calle
Benavente**, KSO along it, following it round to L, KSO(R) at a fork and then turn R into
Calle Pozo, passing a church (R) and continue on it towards small modern *ermita*. The
yellow arrows keep you on this road, then indicate that you turn L over the bridge and
then turn R to cross the ZA123, thus going round two sides of a triangle; **instead** you
can pass to the R of the *ermita* down a lane, cross the ZA123 and continue ahead down
a *camino de tierra*.

KSO for 3km then turn L at third crossing. 700m later turn R on wide *camino de
tierra*. KSO for 2km and at end, when track bends L,***KSO ahead under electricity
cables and continue on grassy track with walled field to L. When this comes to an end,
turn L for a few metres then R, to pick up track that goes over a concrete bridge. Follow
this as it passes a poplar plantation (on R) and then veers R to a T-junction. Turn L here
and 50m later reach another. Turn here if you want to continue. Otherwise, turn L to

church and main road in Tábara (cross over to enter centre of town, shops).

***If you want to sleep in the Hostal Galicia in Tábara you can go there directly by turning LEFT here (instead of straight on). 500m later turn R at T-junction and reach main road just before petrol station.

7.5km Tábara (655/345)

Bars, shops, bank (+ CD). New *refugio* (ask in *ayuntamiento*). Hostal Galicia (600m out of town by petrol station on road to Zamora, 980.59.01.36) has rooms and rte. Buy food here for next day.

Site of a famous monastery in Visigothic and Mozárabic periods though only a few remains and the tower are left. Two churches: eleventh-century Romanesque Iglesia de la Asunción (no longer used for services) and parish church.

To leave: *retrace your steps past the church to the T-junction where you turned L to enter the town and KSO out into open countryside on a wide camino de tierra. KSO for 1.5km in direction of windmills on the skyline. Turn L at a crossing and KSO to road. Cross over, continue on similar camino de tierra on other side then turn R at first crossing. KSO, ignoring first two crossings, to top of hill.*

Here you can **either** turn R to road then fork L down *camino de tierra* **or** KSO for another 200m to junction where the (marked) *camino* from the road joins from back R and the track you are on veers L. KSO ahead here, downhill.

700–800m later grassy track joins from back L: KSO ahead on it, through wide valley. KSO. Track > a *calzada* and then a *camino de tierra*, undulating. Ignore two LH turns, one crossing and one RH turn then turn R when you reach a crossing of similar track. Turn L at junction 600m later and 400m after that, at a small white house, turn R. 700m later, at a crossing of similar tracks, turn L. KSO to the road (1km). Cross it and then turn R to the village, passing a church. KSO(R) along **Calle Mayor** into the centre of

14km Bercianos de Valverde (669/331)

Unmarked bar (no food).

Turn L in the square (with *ayuntamiento*) and continue along a lane with trees to one side. Cross a bridge over the **Río Castrón** and turn L in front of the last group of poplar plantations. *(Good place to rest before going uphill, where there is little shade.)* Turn R 250m later then L and then R again uphill past *bodegas*.

At the top a track veers R above old quarry workings. KSO(L) at a fork. KSO, ignoring all turnings, KSO(R) at a fork and continue for 2km, until you cross the canal and reach the road leading into *Santa Croya*. KSO(R) along it and follow the road into the centre of the village and the *ayuntamiento*.

7km Santa Croya de Tera (676/324)
Bar, two shops, bank, farmacia, fountain. Nice green and shady public garden is also a good place for a rest. Private refuge (Casa Anita), Calle Santa Marta 30, just before bridge over the Tera at end of village.

KSO on the very long main street through the village to the end. Cross the bridge over the **Río Tera** *(swimming area on R)* and enter

2km Santa Marta de Tera (678/322)
Two bars (neither does food), shop. No *refugio* as such but large clean room with mattresses and hot showers in municipal building near church. *Sello* from priest, who lives in modern house by church. No other accommodation but in Camarzana de Tera, 5km further on (on main road but you can access it from the camino) there is the Hostal Juan Manuel (980.64.94.46, open 24/24) and the Pensión Amanacer (980.64.93.16).

Twelfth-century Romanesque church with famous eleventh-century Santiago statue in south portal (the one reproduced opposite and on the cover of this book). Church open for visits daily in summer, Fridays, Saturdays and Sundays only in winter, 10.00 to 13.00, 17.00 to 20.00 or at mass times (20.00, for example); building next to church is former summer palace of Bishops of Astorga.

From the church turn L along a terrace-like road with gardens on L (between the N525 and the road you came up on). Continue downhill on a *camino de tierra*. 800m from the church fork L over a concrete bridge onto another *camino de tierra* through fields and new poplar plantations. 300m later turn L at a T-junction, veering R and then L again at the next, 400m later. Veer R, cross a concrete bridge and fork R on the other side. 1.5km later, at a T-junction with the river a few metres in front of you, turn R. KSO past a white building (pump house) and shortly afterwards you have the river to your L again.

When the *camino de tierra* bends sharp R turn L after first telegraph pole along track to LH side of woods, with river to your L all the time. KSO, ignoring turns, until

Santiago statue on south portal, church of Santa Marta de Tera

you reach the road coming (from R) from *Camarzana de Tera*. Turn R first, towards some gravel works, then hard L to cross the bridge over the Río Tera at

6km La Barca (684/316)
Camping/recreation area with good swimming. Bar (summer only).

Turn hard R at the end of the bridge (river is now on your R) along a *camino de tierra* in an area marked 'La Barca – adecuación recreativa'. KSO for 1km, ignoring turns. Turn R at a T-junction, veering L and the path > a grassy track. 800m later, when it veers off R, KSO ahead on a less prominent track with woods to your L. When you each a grassy track coming from back R 300m later turn L through wood to pick up a track that > clearer as you go, continuing with irrigation channel on your R. When track bends L KSO ahead on FP through trees then 500m later KSO(R) along a track joining from back L, then KSO(R) along a road coming from back L (ZAP2475).
Continue on the road for 600m and just before a bridge turn R onto a *camino de tierra* running below a small hill. Pass a fountain (L) in a stone shelter by a flight of steps. Continue ahead, cross the canal and KSO, ignoring turns, to the main street in

5km Calzadilla de Tera (689/311)
Bar, shop, panadería, though the camino does not take you through centre of village. (If shop is closed during posted opening times, ring the bell.) *Refugio*. Parish church, ermita and abandoned church of Santas Justa y Rufina.

Cross the street, turn second R towards an abandoned church (*makeshift seating in entrance*). Pass in front of it, go down a bank to its RH side, and then turn L on a track (you have done a 'loop' to pass the church). Cross another bridge over a canal and turn L along a *camino de tierra* beside it, behind the church. KSO alongside the canal for 2km to

2km Olleros de Tera (691/309)
Two bars, shop (unmarked) in Calle Fuente (near church).

Turn L over the canal bridge into the village, veering R, after which you have a choice:

a) *The shortest, most direct route (8km, but NOT for cyclists):* via the Santuario de Agavanzal, *but after this the track, though waymarked, is VERY overgrown until you reach the dam.*

After a few metres turn R at a pink house and leave the village via the **Calle de la Agavanzal**. Cross an asphalt road (ZAP2547) and continue (the road becomes a track) to the **Santuario de Nuestra Señora de Agavanzal**, set in the fields above the LH bank of the *Río Tera. You can see the dam walls in the distance ahead of you by now.*

When the road ends at a T-junction near a white building carrying the letters C.H.D. and at a *peligro* (danger) sign KSO on a small, rising path through the weeds. A little later (at a second *peligro* sign) turn R on another small and rather overgrown track which slowly takes you down to the river level (ignore a steeper variant to R after about 200m) and follows the river through rich, jungle-like vegetation (might be water-logged), then rises again to L through rocks and mossy *encinas* towards a road. When you reach the road by the dam walls turn L and L again up to the dam embankment walls (on the road) and then R to cross the dam.

b) *The second option is longer (11km):* KSO along the street to the church of San Miguel, passing to its RH side. Cross a road and continue ahead on other side (marked 'Oteros de Boda'). Fork L by well into **Calle Eras**. At end, just before school (on R, *fountain to R outside it*), fork L onto *camino de tierra* along line of telegraph poles to start with. *(The striped pole on the horizon is by the dam.)* Turn first L 300–400m later. Cross a canal diagonally and KSO. 2km later reach a wide, grassy open area. KSO ahead but 600m later, when you see a yellow arrow indicating that you should fork L, DO NOT do so but KSO ahead on less clear track through grass. Track > clearer as you proceed, until you reach a road. Fork R at the end onto a very minor road. *(Fountain to R outside old school building; the striped pole on the horizon is by the dam.)*

Yellow arrows then indicate that you should cross the road, go down the bank and then veer R by a ruined building but this is extremely fiddly and leads down to the reservoir – but on the opposite side of the river from *Villar de Farfón* (and with no means of crossing over!). **Instead** it is suggested you turn R for 1km and then turn L to cross the dam walls via the road.

Both options: after crossing the dam, turn L and L again onto an asphalted *camino agrícola* along the RH bank of the **Embalse de Nuestra Señora de Agavanzal** *(reservoir)* for about 3km, along the water's edge *(sandy beaches in places, good place to swim/paddle, as long as you are at least 200m away from the dam itself)* turning L by a small road bridge to

8km Villar de Farfón (697/303)
Church of San Pedro (porch is a good place for a rest), fountain at end of village. No other facilities at all.

Turn R at the church and cross the village square, then R once more to leave the village. In front of a small stone house turn L, past a new house and into a walled lane, then KSO for 3.5km. The *camino* leaves on a track that must have been a very old local road and along which you (quite literally) KSO in a dead straight line *(waymarks usually on the ground)*. To begin with it takes you through meadows which later alternate with rising, rocky terrain with brush until you arrive at the top of a hill from where you can already see *Ríonegro del Puente*. KSO downhill for another 1km, emerging into grassland. When you meet another track coming from L turn R downhill towards the old main road. At the bottom of the hill turn L and KSO on a track // to the road over to your R, then use a *camino de tierra* leading down to cross the river to the L of the road bridge via a concrete bridge. Continue up to road by church in

---

6.5km Ríonegro del Puente (703.5/296.5)

Bars, shop on main street (with *sello*), *panadería* on main road. Ask in Bar Palacios re. rooms. Swimming area by bridge.

Former parish church of Santiago existed until the early part of the twentieth century. Now only the tower remains (check for statue of St James in portal) and the present cemetery is on the site where the main body of the church used to be. Former hospital for pilgrims and travellers in building on RH side of main road. Santuario de Nuestra Señora de Carballada, fifteenth–eighteenth century, on the site of the original Romanesque *ermita* (traces in old sacristy); it belongs to the Cofradía de los Falifos (dedicated to looking after pilgrims and based in Ríonegro del Puente), one of the oldest such organisations still in existence (mass every evening, festival third Sunday in September). Freestanding statue of St James as pilgrim (hat with scallop shell, stick, calabash and book) on RH wall of church (inside) and freestanding statue of St Roch, also as pilgrim (hat with scallop, cape with scallop, stick, calabash, dog at his feet) on LH side wall. The Palacio de Diego de Losada (founder of the city of Caracas) diagonally across from the ayuntamiento was restored in 1992 and is now a community centre.

Note: that from Rionegro del Puente to Mombuey there is no shade at all.

Fork R up a lane // to the N525 then fork R behind the last house onto a lane, veering R towards the motorway. KSO at a crossing and turn L along a service road beside the motorway. Turn R underneath it by the SECOND underpass then L on the other side up a *camino de tierra* leading to an industrial building ahead (to RH side of road bridge). Pass in front of it (the CEPSA gas depot – *almacén de butano*) and KSO on a track // to the N525 for 3.5km.

After crossing the road coming (from R) from *Santa Eulalia* (**cyclists** *will find it easier to use the road as far as the Hotel La Ruta*), the track goes through grass but becomes clearer as you proceed. After 1km you KSO(L) on a much more prominent track joining from R. Veer gradually back towards the main road but do NOT rejoin it at a white house opposite a junction.

When you reach the **Hotel La Ruta** (*bar/rte as well as accommodation, 980.65.21.30, panadería opposite*) continue behind the hotel on the 'Vía de Servicio'. Continue behind the first houses in the town then continue on the pavement in

> **8.5km Mombuey (712/288)**
> All facilities, bank (+CD). HR Rapina (980.65.21.20, inexpensive) on main road in village centre (ask there for small, simple *refugio* nearby). Romanesque parish church of Nuestra Señora de la Asunción (restored in 1992) with thirteenth-century tower is a National Monument, its military-type construction attributed to the Templars.
>
> After Mombuey the landscape begins to change and you enter, in spirit if not in fact, into Galicia.

Cross the road via an underpass and on the other side turn L then R (**Calle Figales**) veering R towards the **Iglesia de la Asunción**. Continue past it and then KSO(R) up **Calle Rodrigo** (a lane), which leads back to the **N525**. You then continue on a *cañada* alongside it for 2km, veering L to cross the motorway.

On the other side turn R 200m later and KSO. 800m later turn R at a T-junction and KSO, veering L, into the village of

> **5km Valdemerilla (717/283)**
> Church of San Lorenzo, fountain, but no other facilities.

Turn R (**Calle Principe de Asturias**), veering L into the small square (**Plaza de la Constitución**) and turn L into a lane. KSO, ignoring turns, for 3km to

> **3.5km Cernadilla (720.5/279.5)**
> Fountain. Bar.

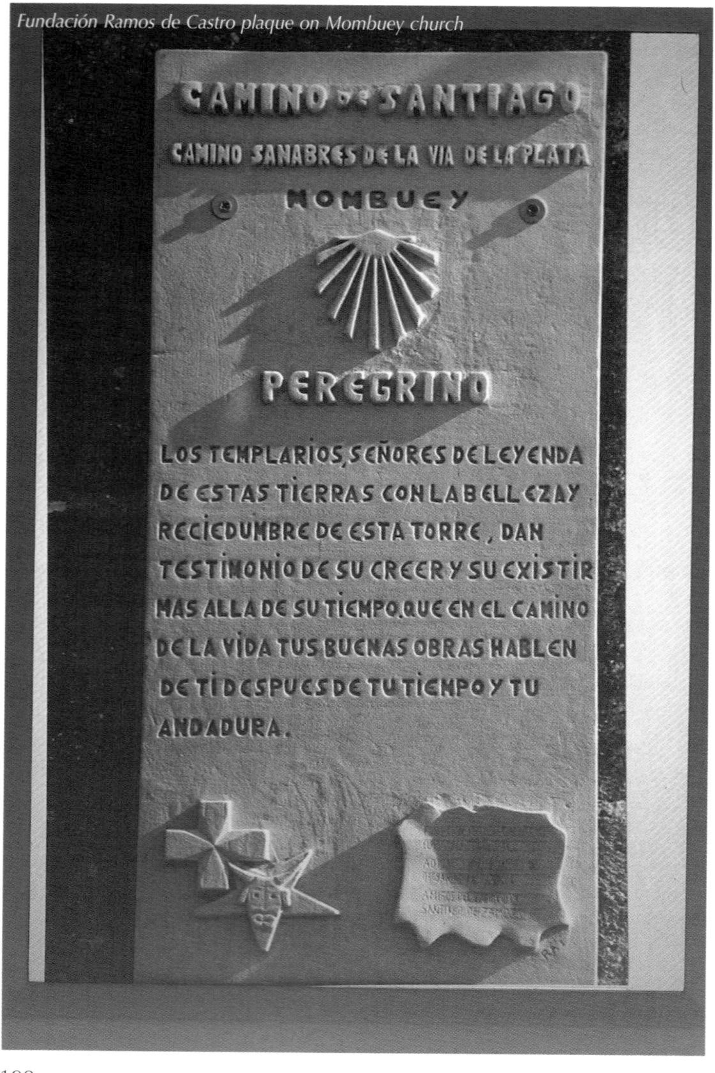

Fundación Ramos de Castro plaque on Mombuey church

Enter the village at the side of **Ermita del Cristo** *(Galician-style churches start from here onwards)* and fork L by an electric transformer down a street past the church (up on your L) and at the bottom of a hill (**Plaza de la Fuente**, *with fountain*). Turn L up the hill, KSO(R) at a fork and KSO for 2km to

2km San Salvador de Palazuelos (722.5/277.5)
Fountain.

Enter by the *ermita* (L) with fountain *(unusual bell-tower)*. Fork L to the **Iglesia de la Transfiguración** *(its porch a good place for a rest)* and pass to L of it (**Calle Transfiguración**). Go L at a fork and continue downhill into the valley *(reservoir visible ahead – you can also see where you are going next)*. Go down into the valley and then up a hill on the other side, ignoring turns. Continue ahead at a junction to a road ahead. Cross over and continue ahead on grassy track on other side, veering R, which then > a tree-lined lane. Veer L at end (600m later), continue on track to LH side of road and then on road itself for 400m, passing a stone wayside cross and enter

3.5km Entrepeñas (726/274)
Embalse de Cernadilla 300–400m away to south.

Enter the village past the *ermita* (L) and continue on the road to the church (**Iglesia de la Asunción**). Pass to R of it *(fountain on L)* and fork R out of the village. Before the end (450m later) fork L onto a *camino de tierra* which becomes a walled lane, veering L.

KSO(L) at a fork uphill and, as you approach the motorway (800m later), veer R up slope to cross the bridge, veering L on to the other side. Continue ahead, passing a football field on R, towards the church (another **Iglesia de la Asunción**, *with nice shady area with trees in front – yet another good place for a rest!*). Continue ahead to the N525 in

3km Asturianos (729/271)
Three shops, *farmacia*, fountain. Mesón El Carmen does meals.

Cross the main road and go up RH side of the **Ermita del Carmen** to the end of the street then turn L, returning to the main road. (**Cyclists: remain on road from here* *to Palacios de Sanabria**.)* Continue along it for 250m then turn R (road KM72) and 250m later turn L off road down a grassy track. KSO(R) at a fork then veer L towards woods (not well waymarked) and the track becomes clearer as you proceed. The path goes through oak woods, leading downhill to a section of old road. KSO along it for 50m then fork R uphill, veering R to pick up a track that goes alongside a wall and then to L of a hedge/line of trees. After a while it veers and then turns L, veering R again. Continue ahead and a track joins from back L, becoming clearer all the time. Reach the road at exit boards to

3km Palacios de Sanabria (732/268)
Two bars (one with rte?), shop, bank (no CD).

Continue on the other side and pass to RH side of the church *(bars on main road, 200m to L; **cyclists turn R here)*. Cross another minor road and continue on the other side, forking L onto a FP and then joining a grassy track (KSO(R)) that veers L along a line of telegraph poles.

KSO along an old walled lane *(plenty of shady trees – a very nice section)*. 1.5km later, when a track joins from back R, turn L over a bridge/causeway, cobbled (large), and continue ahead on the other side. KSO. After 800m cross a minor road and continue on a lane on the other side until you reach the road in

3km Remesal (735/265)
No facilities (but plenty of dogs!).

Cross over and KSO(R) ahead then fork L and turn L round to a fountain and *lavadero*. KSO(R) ahead, veering L, then turn R and KSO ahead down a shady green lane *(large Camino de Santiago sign)*, gently downhill.

KSO ahead in front of you all the time, for 1–2km, the motorway getting closer and closer. When you reach a wall on L veer L under HT cables and KSO(L) ahead down a grassy lane (take LH of two parallel lanes as RH one is somewhat overgrown). When you reach the motorway fence (no waymark) turn R alongside it and then turn L over a bridge. KSO on the other side, veering L (do NOT take first RH turn), then go under HT cables and turn R down a walled lane. When you reach an open grassy area KSO ahead, taking a middle course, veering slightly R (as the path you want, on R, in fact, is completely overgrown) and then KSO(L) down a walled lane (overgrown for first 100m) to a fountain (the main road – N525 – is 20m ahead) in

Wooden relief of seven sinners in the fiery furnace above south portal, parish church of Otero de Sanabria

3.5km Otero de Sanabria (738.5/261.5)
Two fountains but no other facilities. Monastery church (double-towered building outside village). Parish church has painted wooden relief sculptures on church and sacristy doors outside: two of saints Peter and Paul, a third of the seven sinners in the fiery furnace; painted reredos (inside) with San Roque.

Turn R and continue through the village to the church and then KSO to the end of the village, veering L and then R uphill by a large house in a very large garden. At the top of the hill veer L to a minor road and then turn R along it, downhill under the motorway, over a small bridge and up the other side until you reach

2.5km Triufé (741/259)
Fountain. Village still has house that was once the pilgrim hospital. Church porch good place for rest/shelter.

Just past the village nameboards turn L, veering R, turn L again at a T-junction and veer R past the church. Continue on a concrete road, past mainly abandoned houses, to a tarmac road. Turn L. Cross a bridge over the motorway and turn R onto the N525.

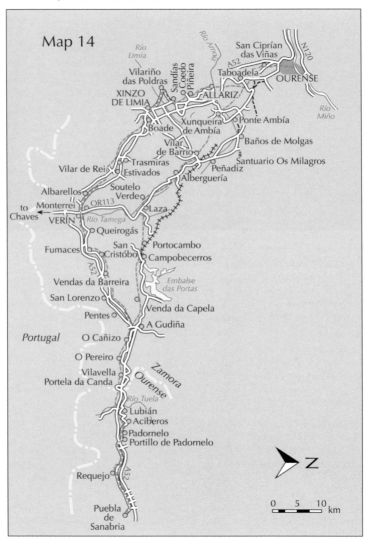

Map 14

Río Limia

Río Arnoia

San Ciprián das Viñas

N120

Vilariño das Poldras

Sandías
Coedo
Piñeira

Taboadela

OURENSE

A52

XINZO DE LIMIA

ALLARIZ

Río Miño

Boade

Xunqueira de Ambía

Ponte Ambía

Vilar de Barrio

Baños de Molgas

Vilar de Rei

Trasmiras
Estivados

Peñadiz

Santuario Os Milagros

Albarellos

Soutelo Verde

Albergueria

OR113

Monterrei

to Chaves

VERÍN

Laza

Río Tamega

Queirogás

Portocambo

Fumaces

San Cristóbal

Campobecerros

Embalse das Portas

A52

Vendas da Barreira

San Lorenzo

Pentes

Venda da Capela

Portugal

O Cañizo

A Gudiña

O Pereiro

Zamora

Vilavella
Portela da Canda

Ourense

Río Tuela

Lubián
Aciberos

Padornelo
Portillo de Padornelo

Requejo

A52

Puebla de Sanabria

N

0   5   10 km

Continue along it past a hotel (on R) then cross over and turn L up the exit/slip-road leading over the Río Tera *(swimming area)* to a newer part of the town. Turn L uphill, passing **La Cartería** (a *posada rural*) on L, then turn R at a large fountain to continue up **Calle Rúa** to the historic quarter with church, *ayuntamiento, castillo* and tourist office. *A lot of old houses with armorial devices in this part of town.*

4km Puebla de Sanabria 960m (745/245)

All facilities, RENFE 1km above the town at top of hill (Madrid, Zamora, Ourense, Santiago), buses (from petrol station on main road 1km outside town) to Madrid, Pontevedra and various parts of Galicia. Several hotels, HS la Trucha, Ctra Vieja de Vigo (in newer part of town, 980.62.00.60 and 980.62.01.50), HR Peamar, Plaza de Arrabal (980.62.01.36 and 980.62.01.07), three more hotels on main square, but NO fondas, CH. or pilgrim-only accommodation. Tourist office at side of *ayuntamiento* (open 10.30–14.00 and 16.30–19.00).

Hilltop town founded in AD 569 and which formerly had a pilgrim hospital. Castle, twelfth-century church of Santa María del Azoque with Romanesque portal and Gothic vault with sculptured scallop keystones above the altar (open July to September, 10.00 to 13.00 and 17.00 to 20.00 except Mondays, or at mass times all year).

Puebla de Sanabria

Facing the church turn L (**Calle Mayor**) then R into **Calle San Bernardo** and pass to RH side of **Colegio Santa María de la Vitoria** then turn R down a steep concrete lane beside the cemetery (on L), which then becomes a rocky track. Turn L at T-junction, pass to RH side of farm building and then veer L down bank to road at junction. Turn L on second (i.e. lower) road. Pass *hostal* and old bridge over the river and KSO for 2km until you reach the N525.

Turn L along it and stay on the road until KM91. *There are tracks to LH side of road but they involve crossing several rivers and are also very boggy if it has been raining. (Bar in Venta de Quesos next to Seat dealer at KM86.)*

80m past KM91 turn R down a lane, walled at the start. KSO(L) ahead down a shady lane. At the end KSO(L) on a gravel lane leading (800m from the N525) to the Romanesque **church of Santiago de Terroso** *(note nineteen scallop shells on doors: the twentieth is missing as its position is used for a cat-flap!).*

Continue ahead on the road, veering L to a 'stop' sign. Cross over and go down a minor road (signposted 'Terroso 500m') beside a football field with a (modern) *cruceiro* and continue into the village.

KSO(R) ahead in the village (**Calle Cabecero**) veering R and then L uphill to cross a bridge over the motorway.

9.5km Terroso (754.5/245.5)
No facilities.

KSO ahead on the other side, up a lane. Just before it turns L uphill by a HT pylon fork L along a hollow lane. KSO(L) when a track joins from R. When the lane becomes overgrown take a FP above it to R. Shortly before you reach the motorway it veers L as a grassy track. Cross an open grassy space and turn L onto a *camino de tierra* to recross the motorway.***

Veer R on the other side, continuing down a walled lane, turning L at a bend into the village. Turn R at the first house, KSO(R) to a fountain and then turn L *(second fountain on L, with 'agua no tratada')* to reach the main road opposite the *Ermita de Guadalupe* in Requejo de Sanabria.

***After heavy rain the path may be knee-deep in water so turn LEFT in village, reach N525 300m later and turn R along it for 1km to

2.5km Requejo de Sanabria 757/243)
Shops, hotel, Rte Plaza, both on main road. *Sello* in ayuntamiento (ask here for basic R&F). Church of San Lorenzo. From here onwards you will see many

houses with a *patín* (small outside stone staircase leading to balcony and/or first floor, with a landing halfway up but no banisters).

Pass to RH side of the *ermita*, in front of the *ayuntamiento (third fountain)* and KSO along **Calle Carrera**, a long street, then continuing on a minor road as far as the cemetery (L), 1.5km.

Here you have a choice: you can continue ahead (marked 'cañada'), a very quiet, shady route on an old track leading up the valley below the road, 1.5km longer than the road route but a nice option in good weather. Do NOT take it if it is (or has been) raining heavily, though, as it will be very wet and boggy underfoot and you may need to wade across streams. Alternatively you can turn R here and continue up to the pass on the N525 (not very busy now that there is a new motorway above it to the R).

a) Cañada option: with cemetery on your L, cross the road in front of you and continue on other side on a *camino de tiera*. KSO(L) 100m later, go downhill, cross river by concrete FB, continue ahead on FP for 20m then turn R onto wide stony track coming from L. KSO(R), pass farm buildings then KSO(L) at fork when *camino de tierra* to R goes steeply uphill.

KSO, climbing gently for the first 2kms, then more steeply. KSO ahead all the time, in a fairly straight line up the valley, undulating from time to time. (When you reach the beginning of a section with electricity cables overhead there may be a problem crossing a river.) *Railway line visible over to L.*

100m after cables veer L, before abandoned building, turn *hard* R up clear tack, climbing steeply. This zigzags its way uphill and after 1km reaches some gravel works, on a section of the *old* N525. Pass to RH side of buildings and continue as described below.***

Note: *if you decide to continue on the N525 when you get near to it you will have to go through the Túnel de Padornelo (the waymarked route goes over the top of it). This is 435m long and is not lit but it has a pavement on both sides and you can see the end from the start.*

b) Road route: turn R by cemetery and 200m later rejoin the N525 at KM95 *(two bars with rte, one on either side of road).*

Turn L and continue uphill for 3km, climbing gradually. *(The 'dent' ahead of you on the skyline is the pass at the Portillo de Padornelo.)*

Just past road KM98, turn L onto the old main road and stay on it. Veer R towards a gravel quarry*** and then KSO, veering L, R and L again and KSO(L) at a fork. *(See note above about continuing on the road from here.)* When you see all three viaducts ahead of you (the N525 and both carriageways of the new A52), fork L downhill underneath them all, then KSO(R) on the level (do NOT go down to the river below), veering L in horseshoe fashion. Cross an old road bridge over the river and go under the two motorway bridges again. KSO ahead uphill after that, veering R and then following the road as it zigzags up to the pass at the

13km Portillo de Padornelo 1329m (770/230)
Good views on a clear day with no haze (it can be chilly up here, even in summer).

KSO(L) ahead at a 'stop' sign and electricity mast (by a concrete hut in an enclosure). KSO(R) at a bend, down to the N525 after it emerges from a tunnel. Walk along its LH side across a bridge at the motorway and 100m later turn L down a concrete road into the village of

1km Padornelo (771/229)
Two fountains, two bar/shops on main road (one has rooms). Hotel/Rte Padornelo (980.62.01.06) by petrol station 500m after end of village.

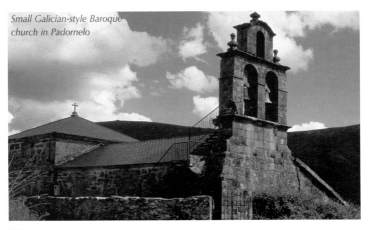

Small Galician-style Baroque church in Padornelo

Continue through the village to the church and then fork R again back to the N525. Pass the petrol station and continue for 1km then turn R onto the **old** N525, signposted 'Hedroso 4, Lubián'. *(Cyclists must continue on this old road all the way to Lubián – longer but with very little traffic and nearly all downhill.)* 300m later, at the end of the embankment wall on L, turn hard L downhill and then hard R on an old rocky track. *(Lubián visible ahead L from here; the 'dip' in the skyline now is the pass at A Canda, where you will be going tomorrow if you are on foot.)*

The track leads gently downhill alongside the hill, with the valley to L. Continue to L of an irrigation channel (may be boggy in parts) and the track becomes a walled lane, descending more steeply (with stream for 200m, though plenty of 'stepping stones'). KSO(L) on a concrete lane to the *ermita* in

3.5 Aciberos (773.5/217.5)
Another small village with fountain but no other facilities. Twelve inhabitants in winter though a lot of *emigrantes* return in July and August.

Turn R and continue through the village past a fountain *(note small old building on R – this is a watermill still in working order)*. Fork L at the end and KSO down a walled lane. KSO(L) at a fork, KSO(R) at a junction, following the lane downhill as it makes its way to the valley bottom. Cross a bridge over **Río Pedro**.

When the wall on R ends turn R uphill then 100m later fork L and then turn L onto a lane coming from R. KSO(L) ahead then veer round to R uphill and then turn L up another lane coming from R.

Go through a tunnel under the railway line and KSO ahead downhill. 200m later, when you come to some telephone cables, turn hard L downhill on a similar track. Turn hard R 100m later onto a ridge-like walled lane. KSO(R) on a track joining from back L. Continue ahead. Keep going downhill and at the bottom turn L to cross a small bridge over the river.

KSO ahead, forking R uphill. 200m later pass the first of old derelict houses and then veer L, entering

4km Lubián (778/222)
Bars, shop, Casa de Irene (a *casa rural*, 980.62.40.98) and small municipal *refugio* at beginning of village, Casa Pachaca (another *casa rural*) at end.

KSO ahead along the street. KSO(L) ahead at a fork, downhill, forking L and L again to the church. Continue past the church (L) and shop and KSO(L) at a junction. *Here you will see the first of the special pilgrim marker stones by the artist Carballo and which indicate the route all through the province of Ourense. As indicated in the Introduction, there are over 100 of them altogether, all slightly different but in the same general style.*

Cyclists: continue on the old main road from here up to the pass at *A Canda*, though you can cycle as far as the *Santuario de la Tuiza* (and back) if you wish to visit this before continuing your journey.

Continue downhill towards **Río Tuelo** and then KSO(R) ahead on a concrete road signposted 'Santuario de la Tuiza 1'. Follow it downhill, over a bridge *(picnic area to L)* and under the motorway flyovers to

> **2km Santuario de la Virgen de la Tuiza (780/220)**
> This is the church of the Virgen de la Tuiza, with *romerías* (local pilgrimages) four times a year; the most important one used to be on the last Sunday in September but has now been moved to August 5th, the feast of Nuestra Señora de las Nieves, when the *emigrantes* (from other parts of Spain, Europe and South America) take part. Eighteenth-century Baroque church replaces a former *ermita* on another site (stones brought from there) – rarely open. Fountain.

Pass the church (L) and fork R ahead down a walled lane. No waymarks for 3km at the time the present edition of this guide was being prepared. Veer L 200m later (may be wet, though it gets drier as you advance and climb). This route is a shady one in the main.

KSO(L) ahead, with the river to your L, veering round to reach it. *(Bridge broken at time of writing but water is shallow and quite a lot of large stones to step across.)* Cross the river and veer R on the other side by a wall to continue on another lane which becomes clearer as you proceed. Climb gradually more steeply, going up and down from time to time. As you continue the trees give way to heather.

Descend somewhat to cross a stream and KSO. Ford another stream at a bend in it *(roe deer may be visible here if you are attentive)* and KSO ahead. KSO(L) at a junction (that leads off to R downhill) and continue to climb.

KSO and when you are almost at the top go up bank (by telephone pylon) and turn R onto rough track coming from L. Turn R again and emerge onto a minor road *(leading to transmitter, L)* at the

5km Portela da Canda 1262m (785/215)
A pass, forming the border of provinces of Zamora and Ourense and of the autonomous regions of Castille-León and Galicia. Fountain, picnic area under trees. Another 'Ourense waymark'. Can be chilly up here too, even in summer. Good views on a clear day.

Turn hard L downhill on the other side. *Camino bollards (with distances) start here*. Turn R immediately onto a track that goes along RH side of the valley. After 1km KSO(L) at a fork, descending all the time. KSO(R) at a fork.

1.5km A Canda (786.5/213.5)
Village with no facilities apart from fountain.

KSO in the village, KSO(R) past the church and KSO(L) at the end by a bus shelter. Fork L along a minor road with crash barriers. 400–500m later, at a break in the crash barrier shortly before the road does a sharp RH bend (the track goes hard L downhill here too), continue on the inside of the crash barrier *(except for 'caballos' – horses – as the sign tells you: **cyclists** get off and push for a short distance here)*. 100m later fork L over a foot-bridge over a motorway drain and turn L downhill on an old paved track, veering R to run // to the railway line below to L. KSO ahead, veering L to go through a tunnel under the railway and KSO ahead on the other side. KSO(L) ahead down a stony track, KSO(L) at a junction and KSO ahead at a crossing, gently downhill all the time. Cross the river.
    KSO uphill on the other side. KSO where a track joins from back R and KSO(R) at a junction, veering L, and turn R to

3.5km Vilavella (790/210)
Bar, *panadería* and shop on main road. Hostal /Rte Porta Galega (988.42.55.93) and Bar 'O Carteiro' (988.42.55.99/42.56.48) are both up on N525 by petrol station and both have rooms.

Turn L into the village, fork L, fork L again and continue ahead, down a concrete lane out of the village, turning L downhill to the valley bottom *(motorway viaduct ahead above)*. Cross a bridge and KSO along the side of a hill. Ignore RH turn. KSO(R) at a fork by a barn and continue along a shady walled lane along the valley bottom.

Go through a gate (river below you to L all the time) and continue ahead on a sort of causeway to a crossing with another gate *(fountain and seat ahead L)* and KSO ahead. KSO, ignoring turns, until you reach

3.5km O Pereiro (793.5/206.5)

Pass the ***Ermita de Nuestra Señora de Loreto*** (pass to RH side of it, *porch a good place for rest/shelter)* and KSO to road. Turn L and immediately R through the village, passing the **church of San Pedro** (on R; *Romanesque but heavily restored altar, sacristy).*

KSO through the village, right to the end, coming to a wide, open area and KSO(R) alongside walls, passing to R of some enormous rocks. KSO ahead, cross the river by big stepping stones and KSO ahead in a straight line towards the ridge ahead, where you will pick up a clear track. KSO ahead and continue on a green lane, shady *(look back for good views),* then emerge on another ridge where you turn R. When the wall stops KSO in a straight line across open heathland with VERY large rocks, veering L, to the top of the ridge then down again to continue alongside a wall coming from back R.

Veer R then L to another walled lane, go over a footbridge and then continue ahead to RH side of wall that veers R and then L. When it ends KSO ahead for another 100m then turn L along a 'causeway' of large stones and a 'bridge' and continue ahead towards a wall (woods on R by now). Follow a track round to LH side of the woods. Follow it round to the top of a hill and a minor road. Turn R and L. Cross the railway line and 50m later fork R off the road onto a track leading under telephone cables. At the road KSO ahead on *a camino de tierra.*

KSO(R) 1km later at junction d 500m after that, when *camino de tierra* bends R by ruined house, KSO ahead on rocky track into village of

5.5km O Cañizo (799/201)
Shop in main square near church, bar on main road outside village. Hostal Nevada at road KM127 (988.42.10.85).

KSO to the centre of the village. KSO(L) ahead then turn R and KSO(L) on the road. Continue through the village *(shop on L)* and veer R at the end. Turn L up a short street then turn L onto a walled lane. KSO at a crossing and shortly afterwards pass a *cruceiro* (L).

KSO to the N525, turn L and continue cross over and continue on a FP downhill (motorway to R) and turn L at the bottom. Continue to a road, turn L along it and cross bridge over the motorway. Continue on the main road *(tourist office on RH side – ask here for* refugio*)*. Arrows do indicate that you can leave the road to R or L but it is not worth the trouble: stay on road instead, to centre of

> **3km A Gudiña, pop. 2200 (802/198)**
> Small town with all facilities. It takes its name from the lady (A Gudiña) who used to keep a venda (country inn) here. Refugio. Hostal/Rte Oscar (988.42.10.14) and Hotel La Madrileña (988.42.10.30) on main street in centre have rooms, as do Hostal Relojero (988.42.01.01) and Hostal/Bar/Rte Suizo lower down.
> Halfway point along the Camino meridional between Zamora and Santiago. Baroque church of San Martiño.

At a junction (on R) with the C533 (to *Viano de Bolo*) turn R and then immediately L along a street // to the main road to a square. *(For* refugio *go under the railway line at a junction and turn R; phone 696.82.07.22 for access if closed)*

Here there are two sets of waymarks as this is where the **two routes divide**: the **northern**, more isolated option via Laza, Vilar de Barrio and Xunqueira de Ambía and the **southern** one (see page 215) that goes through Verín, Xinzo de Limia and Allariz and includes more monuments to visit. Both are waymarked, the northern one in its entirety, as far as Ourense, the southern route as far as the exit from Allariz and both are equally strenuous. You can, however, pass from one to the other quite easily as there are only 13km of minor road (for cyclists, for example) between Verín and Laza and 7km (also on a minor road) between Xunqueira de Ambía and Allariz.

A) Northern Route via Laza (88km)
To begin with there is quite a lot of asphalt but it is on a small, narrow road that has almost no traffic at all and that climbs high up over the area known as the Sierra Seca, barren exposed hills with splendid views all round over the mountains and the reservoirs below you on a clear day.
From the square in A Gudiña KSO(R) ahead down the street and KSO(L) ahead past a telephone transmitter. KSO(R) and join a bigger road coming from L.

Before you reach Campobecerros you pass four of the remaining *vendas* ('*venta*' in Castilian) of a chain of them that formerly existed along this route, simple inns for travellers to rest, eat and sleep and frequently (like A Gudiña) named after the owner or some feature of its physical setting. Today they are just very small hamlets with hardly anyone living there – the terrain is so inhospitable that most of the population has emigrated, either to Ourense, to other parts of Spain or abroad, though many people return for their month-long summer holidays. Even the Venda da Capela, which was a hive of activity in the 1950s when the railway was built, is more or less 'dead' today, its station no longer in regular use and the majority of the RENFE housing deserted. The railway is only a single-track line (with over 100 tunnels between Puebla de Sanabria and Ourense) but it opened up Galicia to the rest of Spain – slowly – as a result. Nowadays there are plans to replace it with a high-speed line from Madrid (but requiring completely new track as the present line has far too many curves for the speeds envisaged by an AVE).

KSO for 3.5km to the **Venda do Espiño de Cerdeira** *(the name refers to a 200-year old cherry tree)* and fork R through the hamlet, returning to the road at the end. KSO for 2.5km more, pass a junction and fork L 200m later into

6km Venda da Teresa (808/192)

KSO towards the hamlet and fork L on a concrete road through it. KSO(R) and exit on a walled lane, along the side of a hill *(railway line below)* and KSO to join a *camino* coming from back R. KSO.

Here you are high up (1088m), with splendid views on a clear day and the Embalse das Portas visible R below. The chimney that you can see on the horizon over to the R is a ventilation shaft for a canal.

Rejoin the road coming from back R. Veer L to cross the railway line and follow the road uphill in

2km Venda da Capela (810/190)

Continue through the hamlet on a road to the end, past RENFE houses *(a line of identical buildings that formerly housed railway employees)*, and 200m later fork L up a *camino de tierra* uphill. KSO(R) at a fork then rejoin the road 600m later and stay on it for 5km to the hamlet of the

5km Venda do Bolano (815/185)

Cyclists: *KSO on road here to* Campobecerros.

KSO on the road for 2km then fork L uphill on the *camino de tierra*. Continue ahead up to the top of the hill and when you start to descend and see *Campobecerros* in the valley below look out for a milestone-*flecha* indicating a RH turn at R angles, steeply downhill to electric cables ahead. Near the bottom turn R on a track coming from L and 150m later reach a minor road. Turn hard L here and follow it round into the village, passing a *lavadero* and fountain (L) and a small church on R; *note modern statue of Santiago–pilgrim/apostle in a niche over the main door (one scallop shell on his hat, two on cape, staff and gourd in his RH and book on L).*

Pass in front of the church. KSO(R) then turn L up the main street through village, veering R to bar in

7km Campobecerros (822/178)
Bar/rte at top of hill on L, rooms in Casa Nuñez opposite (ask in bar). Fountain.

Turn L by bar up road and KSO on the road marked 'Portocambo 2.8km'. Cross a railway bridge and enter

3km Portocambo (825/175)

Turn L up the main street *(fountain on R)* and continue to the top of the hill (the pass, 1km) where there is a VERY large wooden cross at the side of the road, some 18–20ft/5–6m high. *This was donated by the monastery at the Santuario de los Milagros (some distance to the northwest of here) and positioned there on the initiative of Don José Eligio Rivas, the parish priest in Bandeira who was very active in reviving the* camino *through Galicia, in memory of those pilgrims who died whilst making their way to Santiago.*

Turn L here onto a *camino de tierra* and KSO(L) ahead. KSO(R) uphill then begins a long, gradual descent on a similar track along the side of a hill, with chestnut trees to your L and good views out over the valley to your R *(this is a very nice walk in evening sunlight)*. KSO, ignoring any turns near the end, into the village of

> **5km As Eiras (830/170)**
> Picnic area with fountain and covered seating at end of village on L.

KSO on the road, downhill. Continue on the road out of village, downhill. KSO, passing a roadside fountain on L (3km later). 2km after that, by a sharp LH bend in the road, turn R down a lane (**cyclists**: *dismount for a short distance or continue to Laza on road*). Turn L at the bottom and then R and continue on a track that crosses a bridge over a river and leads to a minor road. Turn L along it (**Carretera de Cerdedelo**), passing village place-name boards. KSO(R) at fork then L at T-junction. Turn R onto road and ether KSO ahead to continue or turn R towards church for *refugio*.

> **6km Laza, pop. 3000 (836/164)**
> Bars, shops, bank, farmacia, Rte Blanco Conde has rooms. *Refugio* (ask in Protección Civil, at side of Caso do Concello).
> Small town famous for it carnival. Late seventeenth-century church of San Xoán. Pilgrims coming from Portugal via Chaves and Verín (whether Portuguese or from Andalucía, Extremadura and parts of the province of Salamanca who had made a detour) joined the northern route here.

With *Casa do Concello* to your R and the church ahead R fork L down the street, veering L and *either* KSO to the main road, turn R and KSO along it out of village. *Or* turn R past side of shop and then veer L along main street. Pass a *cruceiro* (on L) and continue right to very end of village, // to road and then join it by village place name boards. In either case, turn R when you reach a junction marked 'Vilamea/Castro', turn L over an old bridge and then return to the road. 1km later *(pilgrim stone and marker stone are on RIGHT-hand side of road here)* fork LEFT onto a minor tarmac road and then take RH (lower) road leading to the centre of

> **3km Soutelo Verde (838/162)**
> Bar on road at entrance, fountain in centre.

KSO ahead past fountain and covered *lavadero*, forking R over a bridge and KSO(L) ahead. Cross another bridge *(ermita to R, swimming area to L)* and continue to a road (OU113). (**Cyclists** *should KSO here – even energetic ones – to Alberguería.*) KSO(L) along it for 150m then fork R onto an unpaved road leading gently downhill.

KSO, ignoring turns. Just before the village *(Tamicelas)* pass a fountain (on L) with seats then fork L and L again to the church in

> ### 3km Tamicelas (841/159)
> Fountain.

Fork L uphill by church, the beginning of a steep, continuous climb up to *Alberguería*. Continue on a *camino de tierra*, veering L and then R, and 500m later fork R onto a track through trees. 100m later KSO(L) uphill on a rough, rocky but clear track *(no shade)*, watching out for waymarks (frequent) on the ground. *This is the Monte Requeixal – nice views as you climb.*

KSO, climbing steadily. Route flattens out briefly then veers L and then R again uphill. KSO, ignoring turns, route flattening out from time to time and continuing on a ridge. Pass a large, single oak tree *(the only tree of any size on the way, offering quite a lot of shade)* and 350m later KSO(R) at a fork, veering R, until you reach the top, 600m later, by a minor road (OU113 again) by telephone cables. *Splendid views all round on a clear day.* Turn R and KSO on road for 1km to

> ### 6km Alberguería (847/153) 900m
> Bar Rincón del Peregrino.
> Site of former pilgrim hospital, as the village name suggests. Important cattle centre in eighteenth century with large population. Today it is almost empty but with interesting vernacular architecture if you look around. Church of Santa María, with statue of Santiago inside.

Fork L into the village and fork L again at the *ermita (main church is below to L)*. At the end turn L onto a tarmac lane which then > a walled lane, veering L at a fork. Continue into open countryside, KSO(R) at a fork and then KSO(L), the track following a wall again shortly afterwards. KSO(R) at a fork, pass onto open heathland, veer R past telephone cables and KSO until you reach a minor tarred road crossing at right angles.

Cross over and continue on a track on the other side, // to but not close to another road over to your R. *Very large wooden cross on the skyline ahead.* 1km later veer R to cross the OU113 and turn L up a *camino de tierra* for 200m to the

3km Cross on Monte Talariño (850/150)

Another place with splendid views on a clear day and another large wayside cross that was erected in memory of those who died on the *camino*, as well as the *segadores* (reapers) from different parts of Galicia who, until well into the twentieth century, walked this way (and back) each year with the tools of their trade, en route for work in the cornfields of Castille. This cross has a pile of stones around its base, added to by each pilgrim who passes.

Pass to L of the cross, downhill on a grassy lane leading down to a road (OU113). Turn R along it for 500m. Just before a sharp RH bend and just after the old road KM17 (OR110) fork L down a *camino de tierra* between conifers.

Shortly after LH bend (800m from road) watch out for RH right-angle turn, down to a wall. Turn R here (walled lane, often boggy) and then turn L downhill to a minor road. 300–400m later fork R downhill on a track. Turn R at the bottom on the road leading into the town. 1km later, at a LH band after passing town place-name boards, fork R up the old (main) road, // at first to the new one. Veer R uphill (*hórreo on L*) then veer L, following the road round on the level. Cross the (main) road and continue until you reach the main square (*with gardens, petrol station and* refugio*) in

5km Vilar de Barrio (855/145)

Bars, fountain, shops, bank. *Refugio* at end of main square (ask in petrol station). Meals in Bar Carmina (opposite *refugio*) or in Bar/Rte Ruta de la Plata (behind church, next to supermarket).

Town has scallop shell in its coat of arms. Parish church has a chapel given by the Marqués de Bóveda, one of the Knights of Santiago, and whose house (still standing) was also in the town. In Vilar de Barrio you will see the first of the many *hórreos* (raised granaries for corn, potatoes, etc.) that are a characteristic feature of the Galician countryside.

Cyclists may like to make a detour (12km, via the road to Macedo) to the Santuario de los Milagros (services several times a day, every day, during the month of September); you can return to the route via Baños de Molgas (hostal).

Continue past the petrol station (L) into the **Avenida Sanfiz** ahead and KSO along **Rúa da Fonte** (a very long street) out of the town, passing a church (L) and fountain/*lavadero* (R). Fork L at a junction shortly afterwards and continue on the road into

Wooden cross on Monte Talariño (photo: author)

2km Bóveda (857/143)
Bar, two fountains, shop.

Continue to the centre of the village, passing a church and cemetery (on R) and KSO(R) at a fork behind a fountain. KSO(L) along the street with three *hórreos* and then KSO(R) behind the OLD fountain (in stone casing) and return to the road at a junction by the shop. Turn R uphill, leave Bóveda and enter **Vilar de Gomareite** and at a junction, as you begin to descend, KSO ahead in front down a tarred lane.

Turn L at the bottom then immediately R by a fountain and *lavadero* and at the end turn R along a minor road between fields. 300–400m later, at a crossing, turn L down a straight *camino de tierra* lined with stone posts. KSO. Pass five crossroads, a junction and a sixth crossroads with a marble memorial cross *(to one Francisco Cid Cid)*. At the seventh crossroads (the one AFTER the memorial) turn R. KSO at a crossing 800m later then 100m after thatturn L to a road. Turn L along it then fork R immediately up a lane behind houses in

6.5 Bobadela (863.5/136.5)
Fountain.

KSO(L) ahead at a junction. Turn R at a fork then L to the end of the village and a walled lane, veering R at a fork, L at the next one shortly afterwards and L again 100m later. KSO(R) past an electricity transformer in the middle of woods and KSO ahead on a walled lane leading through woods. KSO until you reach a road. Continue ahead on the other side of the road to cut the corner, then turn L on a road into the village of

1km Padroso (864.5/135.5)

Follow the road round, passing three prominent *hórreos (middle one dates from 1933)*. KSO(R) through the village, passing a fountain (R) and KSO(R) at a fork. At the end (tarred lane turns L) KSO(R) along a concrete walled lane. When this turns L KSO(R) up cobbled walled lane. Turn L up narrow walled lane, uphill, leading to open heathland. At the top *(splendid views)* cross a track passing in front of you and continue ahead towards prominent rocky outcrop.

Pass to LH side of it (ignore RED arrows), go straight down hill for a short distance then pick up track that leads down into woods, continuing on a walled lane. Turn L onto another walled lane then L again into a lane by houses *(at the end of the hamlet of Cima de Vila)* then turn R onto another walled lane. Cross a wide track and continue straight ahead on the other side.

Continue downhill and 800m later reach a road at a bend by a large barn. Cross over and continue ahead, down grassy lane, downhill all the time. 1.5km later reach houses by road (fountain/*lavadero*) in

4km Quintela (868/132)

KSO on the road for 200m then turn R downhill on a more minor road (sign-posted 'Albergue 1km'). Pass the *refugio* (on R, next to sports centre) and a 'stop' sign at the bottom.

Continue uphill to the church *(double-sided* cruceiro *outside)* in the centre of

2km Xunqueira de Ambía (870/130)

Bars, shops, bank, *refugio* next to sports centre (ask in *ayuntamiento* or library for key. Bar (unmarked) at top of hill on R also does meals.

Twelfth-century Colexiata de Santa María la Real with Renaissance stalls, Baroque 'Virgen peregrina' in pilgrim outfit on side altar, statue of St James pilgrim on LH side altar, St Roch pilgrim on RH side altar and sixteenth-century cloisters. Palacio Episcopal, Casa Rectoral, Museo de Arte Sacro.

Continue uphill past the church, veering R to another square (and another double-sided *cruceiro*) and continue downhill (signposted 'Salgueiros' – this is **Calle Capitán Cortés**) then fork L down a steep hill to **Centro de Salud** (health centre). Go down a track to L of it *(picnic area behind)* and KSO ahead down a minor road downhill. 100m later, at a bend, KSO ahead down a track passing to RH side of a football field, leading down to a minor road.

Turn L, cross **Río Arnoya** *(swimming area to L)* and KSO (R) at a fork on the other side, uphill. 150m later fork R up a walled lane by an industrial building. KSO uphill, ignoring turns, reach a road, cross over and continue up a similar lane on the other side. Turn L on a lane coming from R then turn R along a minor road. Continue on it up to

211

2.5km A Pousa (872.5/127.5)
Two bars, shop. Note two large armorial devices on façade of small church (on R).

KSO on road to

1.5km Salgueiros (874/126)
No facilities.

Turn L at a junction (marked 'Ourense'). After approximately 1km pass LH turn marked 'Lamela' and 100m later turn L down a tarred lane signposted 'Gaspar' (just before a sharp RH bend). Follow it downhill and then up, returning to the road shortly before

1.5km Veirada (875.5/124.5)
No facilities.

KSO(L) at a junction at the top of a hill (marked 'Ourense'). *View of the city ahead.* Cross the railway and KSO ahead to **Ousende** (1km, *no facilities*). Continue on the road to **Penelas** (1km, *two bars*). Continue on the road and KSO through **Venda do Río** (2km) and

4.5km Pereiras (880/120)
Shop, bar/rte.

Follow direction 'Ourense' all the time. *600m beyond Pereiras there is a bar on L and another one, also on L, immediately after passing under railway line, plus shop 150m later on L.* KSO(L) at a fork (after a railway bridge) into

2km La Castellana (882/1180)
Two bars. Beginning of industrial suburbs at entrance to Ourense. (Note stork's nest on disused factory chimney L.)

On entering an industrial area beyond the village KSO(L) at fork, staying on the main road, then at a T-junction with a 'stop' sign and large factory opposite turn L veering R at roundabout. KSO ahead into

> **2km San Ciprián das Viñas 9884/116)**
> Bars, shops, 3 rtes.

At a fork (1km after roundabout) go R *(trees and traffic lights)* up **Estrada de Salgeiros**; at the top the road runs into OR113 at a junction, *where the variant via Verín and Xinzo de Limia joins the present route and continues into Ourense as a single* camino. KSO(R) here then, a few metres later, opposite the entrance to *Hotel Auriense*, turn L past a double-sided *cruceiro* (on L) and then immediately R down a minor road. KSO(R) on a gravel lane, downhill, with woods to LH side.

Rejoin the road at road KM549. Pass an entrance board to *Seixalbo* and a petrol station (on R). Turn R into the first street on R (**Rúa da Santa Adega**, sic) and 80m later turn L down a lane towards a hill in front of you. Reach a railway line then:

a) to visit the recently restored **Capilla Santa Agueda** do not cross the railway line but turn L alongside it, go under a railway bridge and then immediately turn hard R up a FP to the top. *Seats, good view of Ourense; large porch is good place for a rest.* Afterwards go back down the FP and turn R to pick up the *camino* again.

b) to continue without visiting the chapel veer R to cross the railway line (VERY CAREFULLY – listen as well as look out for trains) and go down a FP to RH side of a hill.

> **2.5km Seixalbo/Seixalvos (886.5/113.5)**
> Cross the road (after going down the FP at the side of the hill) and continue down Rúa de Amendo. Sign says 'Seixalbo – nucleo rural de valor etnográfico', referring to the various interesting vernacular buildings in the district.

At a complex *cruceiro* in **Praza Maior** (square) turn R into **Rúa Maior** and KSO into **Praza das Laxas** and then turn R *(Rúa da Igrexa)* to the church of *San Breixo (façade recently cleaned)*. Continue ahead past the church and cemetery on a small road, veering R, then fork L downhill.

Note: Yellow/white waymarks, starting in Seixalbo, are for a DIFFERENT walk.

KSO ahead at the bottom of the hill, joining the **Rúa de Seixalbo** (main road) at an entrance board to the city. This continues as the **Avenida de Zamora**, a *very long*

Pilgrim marker stone in Seixalbo, on the outskirts of Ourense

street *(public garden at end on R)*, and then > the **Rúa do Progreso** *(Camino de Santiago waymarking is in the form of blue and yellow stylised conch-shell tiles set into the pavement)*.

Continue along **Rúa do Progreso**. When you reach a bridge *(gardens below)* go down some steps to RH side of it and cross diagonally R past the hot springs and fork R up **Rúa As Burgas**, passing a tourist office *(no. 12, on L)*. Turn L up **Calle de la Barrera**, leading into the Praza Maior then turn L ahead along the middle of three streets (facing the Casa do Concello) – the **Rúa Arcediagos** – passing a side entrance to the cathedral. Turn R into **Rúa Ceano Vivas** and then continue up **Rúa Juan de Austria** to the main entrance of the Cathedral of San Martiño in **Ourense**.

To continue, turn to **'20km Ourense, 125m (890/110)'** page 227.

B. Southern Route via Verín (115km)

From the wayside cross *(dated 1627)* in the centre of **A Gudiña** *(with the two sets of waymarks opposite)* turn L to the N525 by the **Igrexa de San Martiño** (on your L). Cross over the main road and turn R on the other side downhill *(Bar/Rte/Hostal Suizo, Hostal Relojero and other bars 500m later)*.

KSO for 2km then, having passed the entrance to a motorway sliproad on L, fork R onto a gravel track where the N525 does a sharp LH bend. 300m later turn L at a T-junction, veering R uphill to a road. 200m later fork R and R again uphill, passing a small house, and at a T-junction 800m later return to the N525 (at KM137) and turn R along it.

KSO for 2.5km, passing **Mesón Emilio** *(bar)* on R *(with useful bus shelter if raining)* and just before road KM139 turn L down a gravel track at the side of woods (a river in wet weather), // to the A52. Pass a bridge crossing the motorway (on L) and KSO ahead downhill. Just before you reach the bottom of the viaduct turn R towards the N525 and then L to cross an old stone bridge over **Río Riberiño**.

Then you can **either a)** continue uphill on the N525 (if you are cycling, for example) to a junction at the top of the hill with a bus shelter **or b)** turn L and go under the motorway on a FP and then veer R on the other side up a wide track that emerges, at the top of the hill, onto a tarred minor road at the entrance to the small village *(no facilities)* of

10km San Lorenzo

Do not enter the village but turn R instead and recross the motorway to reach a road junction with the N525 and a bus shelter 1km later. Turn L along the N525 and 100m later turn L through a gap in the crash barrier onto a longish section of the **old** N525, downhill. Cross a bridge over **Río Xestosa** and veer L to return to the new N525.

Cross it, turn R on the other side, veering L uphill. At a T-junction at the top turn L down a forest road (the **old** N525) downhill. 300m later (after the old milestone 456) turn L downhill by a memorial to an *ingeniero de caminos* (civil engineer) who died there in a forest accident in 1927. KSO downhill to cross an old stone

---

6km Bridge over the Río Mente

100m later, on the other side, turn L and then fork R uphill on a clear track under a viaduct. A track joins from back R and when it nears the N525 (on your R) KSO ahead up a steep hill, // to the road to start with. It reaches a minor road by two white houses in **Navellos** 2km later. Turn R along it then KSO L by a fountain/*lavadero* up the main street, ignoring turns until you reach a fork in the village. Fork R downhill, leading to the motorway, and continue alongside it. Cross a bridge over the A52 (on L) and then turn R steeply uphill. Cross a minor tarred road at the top and continue ahead on a lane leading into the village, turning R to reach the N525 in

---

4km Vendas da Barreira
Shop, bakery, bars. Two bars/rte by petrol station on main road leaving town (after turn-off to *camino*); HR Bar/Rte Catro Ventos at KM150.5 has rooms. Eighteenth-century Baroque church.

Cross the A52 and continue uphill on the N525 and turn R (by road KM149) onto a small woodland track steeply downhill. When you reach a T-junction with a larger *camino de tierra* turn R downhill. When you reach a small tarmac road turn L along it, downhill to the valley floor. Pass the hamlet of **Veiguiña** and cross a bridge over **Río Mente**.

KSO(L) uphill, passing a watermill (on L) and communal oven (on R). KSO(L) at the entrance to a second hamlet (**Chaira**) by a bus shelter and then fork L almost immediately and KSO through the hamlet, ignoring turns to L or R. KSO at two sets of crossroads. Turn L at a junction and then R in **Ríos** *(third hamlet)* up the street and at the end turn L onto a gravel lane, uphill then undulating. The track stops abruptly at the entrance to a field but then starts again 80m later on the other side as a clear track. KSO along it, ignoring turns, to the lower part of

---

3km San Pedro de Trasverea

Arrows indicate that you should turn L downhill into the valley, leading you in more or less a straight line to *Miros* (visible ahead on the hilltop). However, if the weather is very wet you may prefer to continue past the church and the *casa do pobo* (community centre) to the upper part of the village, turn L on a road uphill and 500m later turn L ahead at a crossing (R to *Montelso/Piornedo*).

1km Miros (2km by road)

Fork R up a gravel lane opposite the *lavadero*. 1km later KSO ahead at a crossing, passing a sitting area shortly afterwards *(good views in clear weather)*. At the top of the hill KSO when a track joins from back L then from back R and at a five-point cross-roads turn L and KSO along a gravel lane. Pass a cemetery (on R) and descend. KSO(R) at a fork, continue ahead, ignoring turns, pass to L of a church and veer R to join the N525 in

7km Fumaces
No facilities.

Turn R along the N525 for 2.5km, forking L onto a short section of old road by two radio masts after KM158. Return to the N525 and continue on it to KM159, at the

3km Rte 'La Piscina'
Bar/rte at side of road; good views out over valley and Verín below.

Turn L off the N525 onto the OLD N525, which stays close to the new road (but not always visible), passing a picnic area and fountain 1km later. 200m after that, when you reach the new road again, turn L onto a FP behind the crash barrier to 100m (**cyclists** *stay on road*) to avoid the bend. Return to the road for 150m then fork L (not waymarked) onto a wide forest track. 300m later the OLD N525 joins from back R: continue ahead, gradually downhill all the time, until it veers R to join the new N525. Just BEFORE this fork L onto a sandy track and then 50m later turn L onto a *camino de tierra* leading downhill. Continue ahead on a small track at a crossing 200m later. KSO, ignoring turns and then 500m later, at a crossing, arrows indicate that you should fork R down a small FP; this takes you alongside the N525 above you for a while, then

217

Coat of arms above Albergue de Peregrinos, Verín

straight ahead, in a river valley (*with spectacular yellow broom in springtime*), before bringing you out at a T-junction near a farm with two large, bright orange doors, 2.5km later, where you then turn R.

However, this path is often so waterlogged as to be completely impassable so if this is the case you can continue on the track you were already on, descending gradually and veering R. After a while a track joins from back L and 1.5km (after the crossing where you continued straight ahead) another track joins from back L by the farm with the bright orange doors *(castle visible on hilltop ahead)*.

100m later cross a stream and pick up the waymarks again (the track you would otherwise have taken joins from your R here). KSO for 300m more then turn R onto a gravel lane which veers R and then L to rejoin the N525 just before the turn-off to Queirogás. Turn L along the main road for 2km *(Bar/Rte Manchego and Bar/Rte Araujo opposite petrol station both have rooms)* into the centre of

8km Verín

Small town with all facilities. Buses to Ourense, Santiago, Benavente, Madrid and other parts of Spain. Several hostales and pensiones. Tourist office (and Albergue de Peregrinos) in small restored Casa del Escudo (with large coat of arms on front of building) at junction of Avenida de San Lázaro and Avenida de Vences, on other side of Río Tamega on leaving town. Verín was formerly a spa town and origin of the Fontenova, Cabreiroa and Sousas mineral waters.

Churches of La Merced (Baroque) and Santa María la Mayor in centre of town, Capilla de San Lázaro opposite tourist office.

Continue along the **Avenida Luis Espada** through the centre of town and cross **Río Tamega**. Continue along **Avenida de San Lázaro** on the other side (this is the N525) and continue for 2km until you reach **Pazos** *(shops, bars)*.

Pass a turning to the hilltop Castillo de Monterrei. *Here you can make a detour, 3–4km each way, to the castillo to see the hilltop fortress village which looks out over the entire valley. This was built on the site of the Celtic Castro de Baronceli and three rings of fortifications enclosed a castle whose medieval walls you can still see, a palace, the thirteenth-century church of Santa María de Gracia and the fifteenth-century Torre de Homenaxe (a keep). The complex also contained a pilgrim hospital, which is now being restored for use as a refugio, and is nowadays the site of a parador (luxury hotel).*

Continue on the N525 for 5km more to

7km Albarellos de Monterrei

HS Bar/Rte San Xurxo at KM171 at entrance has rooms. Shops, bars, rte, bank. Church of Santiago, with statue of Santiago Peregrino on south wall.

Turn L off the N525 at KM172 *(first yellow arrows here)* into the village along **Rúa do Progreso** (not named at the start). Towards the end turn R opposite **Bar O'Campo** and then L in front of **Casa do Concello**. 100m later fork R down a lane through allotments, alongside **Río Rubín** back to the N525 at KM173. Cross over and go down a minor road marked 'Enfesta'.

3km Enfesta/Infesta
A long, straggling village with no facilities.

Continue through the village on **Rúa San Vicente**, then **Rúa do Progreso**, forking L later on. At a T-junction (not waymarked) turn L uphill *(Rúa de Madrid)* then immediately R by a fountain uphill. 300m later turn hard R on a rough forestry track uphill. 200m later cross over a bigger track crossing diagonally and KSO ahead on the other side, continuously uphill. 800m later cross another forest road and KSO on the other side, veering L uphill, until you reach the (new) N525 600m later.

Cross over and KSO ahead along a road marked 'Cualedro'. 300m later TURN (not fork) R onto a section of old road. 500m later fork L down a grassy/sandy lane and KSO *(often flooded in places but granite slabs down centre act as stepping stones)*. KSO(R) at LH junction. Continue along a walled lane as you approach the village, cross a flat stone bridge over a small river *(fountain on other side on L)* and veer R and then L up a concrete lane into

3km Rebordondo
No facilities.

Turn R at house no. 106, up the main street through the village, R again at no. 86 then KSO on a minor tarred road uphill out of the village, forking L by a bus shelter (on R). At the end of the village, by the last house, the road becomes a sandy track. KSO(L) at fork, over open rocky heathland. After 300m fork R uphill then turn L after 200m more. The path leads uphill and another track joins from back L. KSO on the level, turning R in order to turn L over a road bridge over the motorway in the village of

3km Peñaverde
No facilities.

100m after crossing the bridge and just before you reach a bigger junction, turn R down a street. KSO(R) at a junction, KSO ahead at a crossing, descending gradually. The tarmac stops at the last house and the road continues as a walled lane, still downhill all the time *(a very nice descent in good weather)*.

KSO(R) at a turn and 1km later an old tarred road joins from back R. 100m later KSO(L) ahead on a grassy lane *(motorway visible over to R)*. The track becomes a walled lane, winding its way down to the valley floor. 1km later cross a small river, KSO up a similar lane on the other side and 200m later cross a wide grassy bridge (for animals) over the motorway.

Turn L on the other side then immediately R onto a walled lane leading to a section of the OLD N525 400m later. KSO(L) along it and 1km (after bridge) it veers R to join the NEW N525 at the entrance to

4km Viladerrei
Bar/Rte Cesar, another bar, bank.

KSO on the N525 to

1.5km Trasmiras
Shops, bars, rte, bank.

Continue through the village (very long) on the main road and turn L opposite the church onto the road marked 'Chamusiño 4, Faramontaos 5'. 500m later, just after a lane leading to the cemetery chapel and just before a bridge over the motorway, turn R down a dead straight gravel track. *This is the first of three, leading through an area which was formerly the biggest lake in Spain until a canal was cut to drain it; nowadays it is used for large-scale potato growing.*

KSO (literally) for 2km then take the FIFTH LH turn, leading under the motorway. Turn R immediately on the other side on a track alongside the A52, also dead straight. KSO for 2km. *Be careful, however, as at the time of writing there was a 30m long and 2m high pile of rubble completely blocking the track just before the first crossroads, followed by a 10m wide cavity full of water: pass to R in the field to circumvent these obstacles.*

Turn R at a T-junction (fourth crossing), past a covered picnic area, to the village of

4km Zos
No facilities.

KSO(R) at a junction at the entrance to the village, turn L and then L again in the centre, to the end. Turn L again opposite a stone wall made of large stones and then L again (no waymarking). 200m later at a road coming from a motorway bridge turn L. Then turn R down a third dead straight gravel track and KSO for 2km. Take the fourth RH turn towards a large warehouse marked 'Patatas Paz' and then turn L 100m later, veering R to the N525.

From here you may like to turn L along the main road as the waymarked route takes you on a 2km rodeo (detour) from here, around three sides of a square, to avoid a 500m stretch on the N525. Rejoin waymarks opposite a small house on RH side with three green doors,*** just after an unmarked lane to R, forking L down a minor road along the banks of Río Limia.

Cross the N525, KSO ahead on an old tarmac road, cross a bridge over Río Limia, go under the motorway and turn L on the other side towards the village of

3km Boade
No facilities.

KSO ahead at a crossroads at the entrance to the village, go uphill ahead, veer R and then L uphill, fork L then TURN L and continue to the end of the village. Stay on the road, go over the motorway and KSO to the N525***. Cross over and continue diagonally ahead (fork L) down a tarred lane which follows the Río Limia for 2km. At a second bridge over the river turn R and immediately L along **Rúa Rosalia de Castro**. This leads to a junction with the **Avenida de Madrid**; turn (first) L here, down **Rúa de Lepanto** into the centre of

4km Xinzo de Limia
Small town with all facilities. Buses to Ourense, Santiago, Benavente, Madrid. Three hostales/rtes: Orly, Buenos Aires, Limia. HS Nazaira, Fonda Vila.
    Parish church of Santa Mariña has freestanding statue of San Roque Peregrino on RH side of chancel archway inside building and capital of a face above giant scallop shell to R of west portals outside.

Continue down **Rúa de Lepanto**, cross **Praza de Obispo Idacio** and the **Rúa Dous de Maio**, continue down **Rúa da Constitución** (not marked at start) then fork R down **Rúa Santa Mariña** (a small, curving street). Pass the church, turn L and then R (still on **Rúa Santa Mariña**) and continue ahead to the far end of a large grassy plaza (*white statue of warrior in garden is one of the typical Xinzo de Limia entroido (carnival) figures*).

Reach a road junction and fork L here along the C531, the **Avenida de Celanova**, marked 'Celanova' and 'Vilar de Santos'. KSO (*there is no option but to use the road here as the surrounding area is full of gravel pits*). After 3km cross the Canal da Lagoa de Antela. Hardly any waymarks until you reach

4.5km Vilariño das Poldras

Purple notice at entrance to village says 'Miliarios', indicating a site to R of road.
Continue ahead on the road then turn R uphill at a bend onto a very small tarred road, passing a small church on L *(porch for rest)* and sports ground (on R).

Veer R uphill through an older part of the village. Join a slightly bigger road coming from back L and KSO for 1km into

1km Couso de Limia
Small shop, bar, fountain, sign 'Albergue de Peregrinos 1km'.

KSO on the road then EITHER fork L 100m before a junction with traffic lights onto a small tarmac road, rejoining the N525 at KM205, OR continue to the lights and then turn L along the N525 in

3km Sandías
Bar on N525, bank, shop, *farmácia*. Church of San Estevo.

Continue on the road (N525) to

3.5km Piñeira de Arcos
Bar/Rte Novaiño 800m before village on N525.

Continue on the road then turn L, 100m after crossing Río Piñeira, up a minor tarmac road marked 'Coedo 2'. Pass from the *concello of Sandías* to that of *Allariz* (signboards) and continue with the river to LH side of the road, passing through the hamlet of **As Peras** and then immediately into that of

2km Coedo

Turn R by the first house after the entrance board into a sandy walled lane downhill. KSO for 1.5km and at the end it becomes tarred just before a T-junction in

1.5km Torneiros

Turn L onto a very minor road. Veer R at a fork and KSO(R) at a fountain and two *hórreos*. 100m later, at a bend uphill, a milestone post indicates a RH turn along a clear, sandy, walled lane but later the arrows disappear. Instead, continue ahead uphill onto high, open heathland. Turn R at the first bus shelter then, just before a second one, at a junction with the old N525, turn L downhill on a small tarmac road signposted 'San Salvador' into the hamlet of

2km San Salvador
Small chapel dedicated to San Salvador.

When the tarmac stops, in front of houses, KSO straight ahead down an old cobbled lane, gently downhill all the time, along the side of the valley. *This is a very nice section, with good views.* KSO, ignoring turns, down to a crossing of walled lanes in

2km Paicordero
Another hamlet with no facilities.

The tarmac starts again here. KSO ahead, following the road downhill and ignoring turns, entering the town via the **Rúa de Paicordero**. Cross the **Rúa Emilia Pardo Bazán** *(turn R uphill here if you want to go to Xunqueira de Ambía)* and continue on the other side up the paved **Rúa do Hospital**, passing the church of San Pedro (on R). At the end continue along **Rúa da Cruz** to the **Praza Maior** and the church of Santiago in

2km Allariz

Small historic hilltop town with shops, bars, rte, bank. Hostal Alarico on main street and Hostales Limia, O Mirador and Villa de Allariz on N525 at KM216. Tourist office by road bridge over river at entrance to town.

Romanesque churches of Santiago and San Estevo both have statues of San Roque Peregrino inside, church of San Pedro, sanctuary chapel of San Beito, church of Santa María de Vilanova (church of the Knights of Malta), Convento de Santa Clara with small museum of religious art. Mozárabic church of San Martiño de Pazó 2km from town. Museo Galego do Xoguete (toy museum).

Modern *cruceiro* at Piñeiro de Arcos, en route to Allariz

Turn L along RH side of the **church of Santiago** into **Rúa de Vilanova**, veering R. Pass between the church of **Santa María de Vilanova** (R) and a football ground (L) and cross the twelfth-century **Ponte de Vilanova** over the **Río Arnoia**.

KSO ahead on other side and 200m later KSO(R) ahead at a junction. Reach the N525 at KM217, by the **Allaruz factory**, and continue ahead on the other side. Go under the A52 (motorway) and turn L on the other side (this *lugar* is **Roiroz**). Turn L but then KSO on the road marked 'Santa Mariña de Augas Santas 4.8', even though the waymarking indicates that you should turn R there, as at time of writing the yellow arrows stop at the end of the village and the route is not waymarked any further.

You should therefore continue on the road to **Santa Mariña de Augas Santas** (6.5km from Allariz). Continue beyond it on the same road until you reach a T-junction 2.5km later. Turn L here into **Pereiras** (2km), where you will pick up the waymarks on the northern route coming from Laza and Xunqueira de Ambía (turn to '4.5km Pereiras (880/120)' p.212). These will take you into the centre of Ourense.

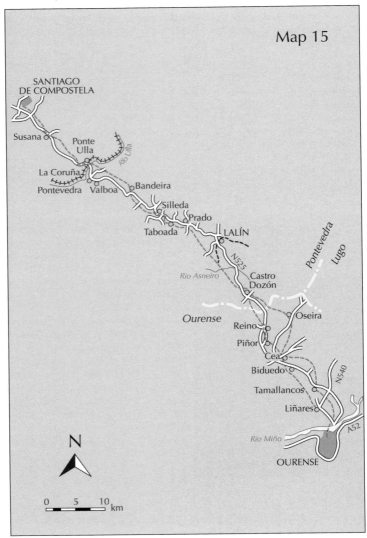

OURENSE TO SANTIAGO

20km Ourense 125m, 96,000 (890/110)

All facilities, RENFE (Madrid, Barcelona, Santiago, La Coruña, Zamora), buses to Santiago, Madrid and other parts of Spain. Plenty of accommodation in all price brackets (tourist office has separate list of pensiones). *Refugio* (with kitchen) is up on the hill above the cathedral in part of the Convento San Francisco (it shares the building with an art gallery; for opening times and contact see details on door or ask in tourist office, Rúa As Burgas 12, when open). Bike repairs: Pazo de Bicicletas, Avenida de Zamora 2.

The largest town on the route between Zamora and Santiago, situated on the Río Miño. Ourense takes its name from the Roman Aquae Urientes, its hot springs still in use today at 'As Burgas' near the market. Renamed Sedes Auriensis in the fourth century and residence of the Suebian kings in the sixth and seventh centuries, Ourense's many places of interest include the Romanesque Cathedral of San Martín, with thirteenth-century Portico del Paraíso (which includes a seated statue of Santiago), an echo of Maestro Mateo's Portico de la Gloría in the cathedral in Santiago, and various Renaissance and Baroque side chapels. It also has the fourteenth-century church of San Francisco (with interesting cloisters) and the Baroque churches of A Trinidade, Santo Domingo, Santa María la Madre (on the site of the first cathedral) and Santa Eufemia, as well as the Praza Maior, and the Ponte Vella, the Roman/medieval bridge over the Río Miño.

Hot springs in Ourense (As Burgas)

Prophets in Pórtico del Paraíso, Cathedral of San Martín, Ourense

If you would like to stay overnight in the monastery at Oseira the day you leave Ourense note that it is ESSENTIAL to telephone in advance (988.28.20.04). There is no charge but you should leave a donation.

After visiting the cathedral turn L at the exit to retrace your steps, and in front of the **church of *Santa Eufemia*** turn R into **Rúa Valentín Lamas Carvalal** and then continue along pedestrianised **Rúa do Paseo**. Cross **Rúa Cardenal Quiroga Palacios** and **Rúa Capitán Eloy** then turn L down **Rúa Concello**. Cross **Rúa Papa Juan XXII/** and continue downhill, passing to RH side of a park, to **Praza Concepción Arenal**. Veer R to cross **Avenida de la Habana**, pass in front of the **church and** *colegio* **of Don Bosco** and cross the **Río Miño** by the **Ponte Vella**. KSO on the **Avenida das Caldas** on the other side.

At the junction with the Avenida de Santiago, a pilgrim stone once more indicates **two possibilities** for continuing; both of them waymarked, both of them equally urban to start with, both of them equally strenuous and both of them described here. Variant A goes via Quintela, Liñares and Mandrás and may be easier for cyclists. Variant B is the one which turns R here to pass through Cudeiro and Viduedo (see 'Route B' below) but both meet up again at Casas Novas, 2km before Cea. And both options involve VERY steep hills!

Variant A (via Quintela)

Continue ahead (L) up **Avenida das Caldas** to the railway station. KSO(L) there and follow the direction Vigo/Pontevedra (**Rúa Eulogio Gomez Franqueira**) for about 600m. When the main road veers off L *(bus station on other side of roundabout)* KSO on the now smaller **Rúa Eulogio Gomez Franqueira** until it bends round to R to pass under the railway line. KSO ahead there (stay to LH side of the railway line) and KSO on the N120 for 2km to

4km Quintela (894/106)
Bars, rte, fountain on R by public garden.

Fork R (marked 'Castro de Beira') opposite Bodegas Arnoya (a wine factory), just after road KM573. KSO on the road and 800m later KSO(L) at a fork, marked 'Costiña de Cañedo/Castro de Beira', downhill *(on the course of an old Roman road)*. 300m later go under a railway bridge, narrow and longer than normal – EXTREMELY carefully (and quickly), listening out for vehicles as well as watching as the road on the other side is used like a race track by cars coming downhill towards you, despite humps. KSO uphill, continuously, for 1.5km to

4km Castro de Beira (898/102)

Cross the road at the top of the hill and KSO past a *bar/rte* (on L) and continue ahead on a *camino de tierra*. KSO for 2km, ignoring turns, until you come to a (tarred) minor road coming from R (buildings to either side). KSO ahead (**Carretera Cabeança Amoeiro**). *Eucalyptus trees (in bulk) begin here.* 300m later enter

1.5km Liñares (899.5/100.5)
No facilities. Main part of village over to L.

KSO on the road and KSO at a crossing (signposted 'Amoeiro') then 500m later fork R up a track, by a wall to start with, which then veers L to a minor road. Cross over and continue on a tarred lane ahead into

1.5km Reguengos (901/99)
No facilities.

Continue through the village and KSO at the end on a walled lane. Continue to the road (with a 'stop' sign) and KSO on the other side down a grassy lane. KSO straight ahead, ignoring turns, until you reach a minor road at a bend in it.

KSO(L) ahead on it for 1.5km then continue on a walled lane leading gradually downhill. Cross a grassy track and KSO on another (narrow) walled lane, widening out as you go. Then KSO until you reach the humpback bridge over the **Río Barbantiño** in

4km Ponte Mandrás (905/95)
Fountain, bar on road.

Cross the bridge and continue through the village, veering R and L to pass the fountain (on R) and then KSO(L) uphill ahead to a road *(bar on R)*. Turn R along it for 60m then KSO ahead on a walled lane *(which must have been the old 'main' road as it still has much of its original paving)*. KSO at a crossing and KSO, ignoring turns to L and R until you reach

3km Pulledo (908/92)

KSO(L) along the road for 500m to a junction with a bigger minor road and then turn R. Continue on it to the N525 at

---

1km Casas Novas (909/91)
Bar O Campo (with sello), shops. Here Routes A and B join up.

To continue, turn to '2km Casas Novas' page 233.

Variant B

Note: the first 11km of this route are continuously uphill, until 1km before Tamallancos.

Continue up **Avenida Caldas** after crossing the Ponte Vella and then turn R up **Avenida Santiago**, uphill. 1.5km later, by a petrol station on R, turn R down a small tarred road, the Camiño Real, and 100m later fork R downhill, short-cutting a bend in the N525. (*Red and white balises of other waymarked routes are also to be found in this area, from the outskirts of Ourense.*) Cross it after a bend and continue up **Camiño Real de Cudeiro** on the other side and KSO at a bend up to the *plaza* in

---

2.5km Soutelo (892.5/107.5)
Two bars. Note pazo on R, with fine coat of arms.

Continue ahead, on **Camiño Real de Soutelo**, then veering L on **Camiño Real de Cudeiro Sur**, steeply uphill all the time. *Church of San Pedro, with small plaza, has a modern cruceiro with sculpture of Santiago Peregrino on its shaft (stick in RH, book in LH, scallops on lapels).*

Reach the road (*two bars*) and then KSO on the other side on **Camiño Real de Cudeiro Norte** then 100m later turn R onto the **Camiño de Costa** (both parts paved), winding its way uphill (**cyclists** get off and push!). Modern Ermita de San Marcos da Costa and cruceiro on top of hill to R. Pass a *lavadero* and fountain and KSO.

1km Miña de Chaín (893.5/106.5)
Picnic area, information boards, fountain with very clear water.

Continue ahead, still uphill, on a sandy track. (*Lane bends sharp R here to the hamlet of Pavadura, 300m away.*) Blue waymark signs from here onwards. KSO(L) ahead,

231

ignoring turns, to a T-junction in **Sartédigos**. Turn L there onto a minor road and 100m before a 'stop' sign on the main road *(Convento de las Clarísas Reparadoras visible 350m ahead)* turn R onto a *camino de tierra* and then a walled lane. Return to the road for 50m (to skirt houses on your R) and then fork R onto another *camino de tierra*.

KSO(L) on a grassy walled lane 100m later (RH fork leads to Fonte do Santo). KSO for 300m (ahead) then, after a tarmac section starts, turn L at a T-junction. Pass below a hill on R with huge rock formations (this is *Outeiros de Forca*). KSO. 1km later KSO at a junction, on a tarmac lane (level for a change), with woods to either side.

1km later reach another local road (another hamlet, bus shelter), cross it and KSO ahead on a sandy lane. KSO downhill for 1.5km to the N525. Turn L and then 50m later fork R up a minor road. Continue to the village of

9km Tamallancos (902.5/97.5)
Bank, bar, *farmacia* on main road.

Turn L on the N525 for a bar, otherwise KSO, ignoring turns, to

1km Bouzas (903.5/96.5)
Park/bandstand, bar/tabacos, picnic area. Rte 700m to R on N525.

Continue to the N525, cross over and fork L down a *camino de tierra* past an electricity transformer and farm. 100m later turn R and then turn L, veering R downhill // to N525 over to R. *(At 'stop' sign you can turn R and then L onto main road for restaurant, 300m, then retrace your steps to continue.)*. 400m later KSO ahead on a grassy lane, passing to LH side of a *matadero* (slaughterhouse). KSO to reach a crossing. Continue ahead on small tarmac lane. 1km later reach hamlet of **Sobreira**, veering L.

Turn L at T-junction (of similar lane) and veer R at hamlet. Continue downhill and just before road bends R (600m later) fork L down lane to minor road 100m later. Cross over and turn (not fork) R on other side, downhill again. 300–400m cross an old paved stone bridge over **Río Barbantíno** *(note scrolls at each end)*. KSO and 500m later reach

2km Faramontaos (905.5/94.5)
Village that was formerly attached to the monastery at Oseira, with a pilgrim hospital.

KSO(L) uphill in centre of village then KSO(L) up walled lane, still uphill, to emerge below the N525 (to your R) in **Ermida**, by farm, 800m later. Continue ahead, // to N525, on narrow walled lane. At first houses **in Viduedo** KSO on tarmac lane then KSO(R) on minor road into

1.5km Viduedo (907/93)
Shop, bar.

Fork R past the church if you want to go to the bar on the N525. Otherwise KSO(L) ahead *(fountain)* and turn L. Reach the N525, turn L, cross over *(ignore three yellows arrows painted on this road, pointing in reverse, backwards into the village)* and at road KM258 (150m later) fork R down a walled lane. Continue ahead alongside the road for a short distance then KSO(L) onto a lane, downhill. Cross a main road 200m later, KSO, join a lane coming from back R and KSO(R) at fork. Reach another minor road and KSO, gradually uphill (shady). At a T-junction turn L (lane may be very muddy), past a *lavadero*, cross a minor road and then turn R in the village to continue. *(Turn L to N525 for a bar, with sello.)*

2km Casas Novas (909/91)

Cross the road (N525) and turn L into the older part of the village.

Continue to the end and KSO(L) on a lane that continues *(old-style paving)* through woods.

KSO at a crossing. Pass a simple *cruceiro* where another track joins from back R and continue to the road.

Cross over, continue along **Rúa do Matadoiro**, passing to L of school buildings and turn L (still Rúa do Matadoiro). Turn L opposite house no. 9 for a *refugio (42 places)*. Otherwise KSO ahead uphill to centre of

2km Cea (911/89)
Bars, shops, *refugio* and several bakeries, as Cea is famous for its bread (Pan de Cea). Parish church in centre and Santuario de Nuestra Señora de la Saleta in field to north of village.

There are **two routes out of Cea**, (A) going to Castro Dozón via the Cistercian monastery at Oseira, and (B) going there directly ('por el monte'), the first option 5km longer than the second. Read the text that follows before you make up your mind, however, not only for the routes as such but in terms of where you may want to sleep and the distances you want to cover in each of the three or four days remaining from here to Santiago. **Cyclists**: unless you want to visit the monastery you will find the direct route easier.

For a description of Route B turn to page 237.

Route A (RH route) via Oseira
Continue on **Rúa do Matadoiro** to a small square with *hórreo* in the middle. Turn R into **Rúa Bacelo** and continue up to **Praza Maior** *(bell-tower with fountains,* ayuntamiento).

With your back to the *ayuntamiento* continue R ahead up the street to RH side of the Carnicería Segundo Ventura, cross the road to Ourense and continue up **Rúa Lozairo** ahead (marked 'Campo de futbol' and 'Piscinas municipales') to the top of the hill. Turn R along a boundary fence and R again (ignore yellow arrows pointing LEFT for Route A) and then turn L at the end of the road. 100m later fork R onto a wide walled lane.

KSO, ignoring turns to R and L. (Short section may be boggy but look for stone FP to LH side by wall.) *Plenty of shade. (You will also see the yellow and white flashes of another walk – like the French-style balises; both sets indicate practically the same itinerary in this section but stick to the yellow ARROWS for security.)*

After 2–3km KSO(L) at a fork with a small pumphouse visible ahead (similar to one you passed earlier on LH side of *Camino*). KSO, ignoring turns to L or R, and about 1km later, at a crossing in open, rocky heathland, KSO ahead, following alongside a wall to L, towards woods ahead, where you will find a clear track (alongside a wall). 200m later reach a minor road. Turn L along it for 300m to the hamlet of

5km Silvaboa (916/84)
Fountain.

Fork L past the first houses and veer R uphill at the last (ruined) house, up an old, paved road, keeping to the wall on L. When the wall takes a sharp bend to L, KSO for 100m more and rejoin the road. Turn L uphill. 1km later reach a bigger minor road in

Monastery of Oseira

2km Pieles (918/82)
Fountain.

Turn R and KSO on the road and 500m later KSO(L) at a fork signposted 'Oseira'. Pass a church *(on L, dated 1789, big porch)* and cemetery and KSO on the road. Pass a monumental fountain on R, cross a bridge over **Río Oseira** and enter the village of

3km Oseira (921/79)
Bars, campsite by river.
Cistercian monastery built at different periods between twelfth and eighteenth centuries, a National Monument since 1923 and sometimes referred to the as 'Escorial of the North' due to its sumptuous reconstruction following a fire in 1552 which left only the church. Most of what is to be seen today (three cloisters, chapter house with curiously twisted columns, plateresque portals) comes from the transition between late Gothic and Renaissance style, often in an interesting mixture. Church contains Baroque altarpiece with carving of Santiago Peregrino by Gambini. Guided visits available.

Turn L up the main street. To visit the monastery turn L. To continue KSO(R) up a hill and then turn *hard* R at a fountain/*lavadero* up a steep hill, passing a wayside cross (on R). Veer R up the hill alongside a wall (to L), climbing all the time and keeping the wall to your L. Reach a minor road. KSO on the other side up a steep rocky lane. When it levels out a bit KSO(L) on a walled lane.

At the top another walled lane joins from back L. KSO, more or less on the level, for 300–400m more until you veer R to a minor road. Turn L downhill. Some 300m later, *cyclists*: KSO on road, *walkers:* look out for LH turn downhill (a short-cut) alongside a wall on R, leading back to the road in the hamlet of **Mirallos**. Turn L on the road, continue past a junction and 300m later turn R onto a second walled lane on R, downhill, veering to L and then R between walls. At a T-junction turn R onto a wider walled lane downhill, cross a bridge over a stream and turn hard L, uphill again, ignoring turns, until you reach a wide track at a crossing.

Continue ahead until you reach a minor road by a bus stop in the hamlet of **Vilarello**. Cross the road and continue down a tarred lane on the other side, turning R past an *hórreo* 60m later. Fork L between houses at a second *hórreo* then veer L and then R to the end of the village. *(Two more hórreos on R.)* KSO on lane.

Cross a bridge over a small river and follow a road round uphill *(village to R with church is Carballeidiña)*. KSO at junction, KSO at RH one, veering L to the hamlet of

4.5km Outeiro (925.5/74.5)

Turn R uphill between houses and KSO(R) ahead up a walled lane. KSO up the valley, ignoring turns. 1km later, at the top, KSO(L) at a fork, after which the lane undulates. KSO(L) at a fork ignoring any turnings, and KSO until you reach a minor road in

2km Gouxa (927.5/72.5)

Bar (marked 'tabacos'). First village on the route in the province of Pontevedra. **Note:** *galpón*, a long, low covered building with pillars, used to protect those attending the *ferias* (agricultural fairs) held here and elsewhere in the area; there are very few left now, apart from this one and another in Bouzas (on the RH route out of Ourense).

Turn L on the road then turn R in the middle of the village between houses, passing behind a bar on a lane leading to a minor road. Cross over and KSO down a walled lane (may be wet for a short section), veering L. KSO until you reach a minor road at a simple *cruceiro* then KSO(L) on it, ahead. 100m later fork R up a walled lane (just before a village on L with a tiny church) and then turn L at a junction of similar lanes 150m later. Continue to the street in the hamlet of **Vidueiro**, turn R, fork R at a *lavadero*, turn L at the end and then R onto a walled lane by a building made of breeze blocks. *N525 visible – and audible – away to L now.* KSO(R) at a fork.

236

KSOL(L), KSO(L) again, pass a *cruceiro* (R) and at a junction shortly afterwards KSO(L) at a fork, towards TV masts that you can see on the skyline and towards the N525, passing to RH side of a very long (and very smelly!) stable building.

Cross the N525, pass to a section of old road and turn R along it to avoid a dangerous bend. Then continue on LH side of the N525 for 1.25km to **Castro Dozón**. Pass **Casa de Concello** (on R) and cross to RH side by a public garden with a bandstand.

To continue: turn to '4km Castro Dozón (931.5/68.5)' page 238.

Route B (LH route) direct to Castro Dozón

Continue out of the village (of Cea) on the road, passing church (the **Santuario de Nuestra Señora de la Saleta**) on your L. Continue on the road, passing through **Porto do Souto**, to the village of

2km Cotelas
Shop, bar, fountain.

KSO in the village when the road bends R and in 200m fork R down a small tarred road which becomes a *camino de tierra*, downhill all the time. 800m later join a road coming from back L, cross **Ponte Mirela** and 200m later, to short-cut a bend, take the SECOND LH turning up a steep grassy track and return to the road 500m later. KSO ahead, uphill, passing a fountain and *lavadero*, for 500m to

2km Piñor
Shop, bar, *farmácia*.

KSO through the village on the road, running straight on into **Albarrona** *(fountain by a lavadero)*, uphill all the time. KSO for 1km more to

1.5km Arenteiro
Two bars. Capela da Nosa Senhora das Neves e Peregrina, a Baroque building restored in 1974.

KSO on the road passing the **Capela** on R *(covered sitting area, good place for a rest)* downhill for 1km to

1km Ponte
No facilities.

Cross a bridge over the river and continue uphill for 200m on the other side then, at a sharp bend, turn R up a grassy lane (short-cut for the bend) bringing you back to the road. Cross it and continue uphill on a concrete lane on the other side, veering R. Turn R, then L, pass to L of buildings and emerge on the road (N525) by a placename board for **O Reino**. Cross over and turn L (signposted 'Moire' and 'Capela da Milagrosa').

For the chapel: *(on hill, picnic area, good views)* KSO ahead for 100m then backtrack to continue.

To continue: after turning L off the road turn R IMMEDIATELY, passing to LH side of a house, cross a lane and KSO up a walled lane for 1km and reach the N525 again in

1.5km Carballeda
Igrexa da Santa María on R.

Turn L along the N525 then shortly after road KM270 turn L and immediately take RH of two forks on L, leading downhill. When the track starts to climb take the middle of three tracks ahead (i.e. RH of two leading uphill), up a walled lane with rocky heathland to either side, then veer R. When the wall stops veer L and then R to the top of the hill, veer R, join a track coming from back L and then turn L onto a minor road. KSO for 700m then, at LH bend, KSO ahead up a rough track uphill, to RH side of the road, veering R to become a clearer track as you proceed, then walled. Follow it as it undulates and KSO(L) at a fork, join a walled lane coming from back L then turn L at a junction. Veer L and then R uphill, through open heathland. 1.5km later reach a T-junction at the top of a hill *(splendid views on a clear day)*.

Turn R here and 400m later turn L and then immediately R. KSO at a crossing then KSO(L) at a fork. KSO. KSO(R) at a fork 800m later then KSO(L) shortly afterwards at the next fork. Continue downhill. Join a track coming from back L then a ROAD coming from back L. Continue to the N525 and turn L along it in

4km Castro Dozón (931.5/68.5)
Two bars, two shops, *farmácia*, but no accommodation. Twelfth-century church of San Pedro.

Fork R off the road by a square with a bandstand and pass to RH side of the church. KSO(L) uphill at a *cruceiro*. 300–400m later reach a junction at the side of the N525 (which is 80m away on your L).

Veer (do not TURN) L as if going to the main road but then, when you are 2–3m away from it, fork R onto a wide earth track above it (on its RH side). KSO(L) at a fork 150m later. Continue downhill towards the N525 (after this has done a bend), veering R, then turn R and then L 50m later onto a sunken lane. KSO(L) at a fork and continue close to, but out of sight of, the N525. Return to it at KM278 and cross over to continue on its LH side. 500m later, at a small junction at the top of the hill, cross back to RH side and continue on a section of old road, 'hide and seek' style, returning to the N525 just before the church of *Santo Domingo (note Oseira coat of arms above main door)* in

3km Santo Domingo (934.5/65.5)
Bar/rte on main road.

KSO on the road. 500m later, at a bend (just before KM280), fork L up an unpaved road. 800m later, when it levels out, fork L again down a *camino de tierra*. KSO into

4km Puxallos (938.5/61.5)
No facilities. Small *ermita* dedicated to San Roque on R.

KSO along the road on a ridge and at a crossing 200m later, KSO downhill. KSO(L) at a junction 800m later. KSO downhill then, when you see the motorway in front of you, turn L and immediately R to cross bridge. Veer R uphill on other side then KSO(R) ahead very steeply downhill. 150m later veer L away from motorway into woods, downhill all the time. 500m later reach a very minor road an turn L downhill into

1.5km Pontenoufe (940/60)
No facilities.

Turn R in the village, downhill, to cross a bridge over a small river and at a junction by a tunnel under the railway line turn R on an earth road, veering R. 200m later turn hard L up a hollow concrete lane, winding its way uphill. KSO(L) at a fork and emerge on a minor road near the top of a hill.

Church in Xestas (photo: author)

Turn R uphill // to a bigger road below L. Fork R then KSO(L) ahead and turn L at a church and continue past a modern double-sided *cruceiro* to the road in

2km Xestas (942/58)
Bar on road.

Cross over and KSO ahead down a lane through the village. Turn R by house no. 60 and KSO, ignoring turns until you reach a very minor road coming from R. KSO(L) along it and at a junction with signposting ('Medelos, Botos') KSO ahead on a minor road (*magnificent chestnut trees*).

KSO, ignoring turns, until you reach a road in

2.5km Botos de Abaixo (944.5.5/55.5)
Turn L and L again for FF.CC Mouriscade (this is Lalín railway station). Bar/rte and shop. Lalín (all facilities) is 4km away (uphill) on road to R if you want to sleep there (its *hostales* and *fondas* are nearly all in the centre of town).

To continue: turn L on the road (bar on L) and 80m later turn R downhill on a small road, cross the river and KSO uphill, forking L at a lavadero. KSO uphill again, KSO(R) at a fork and continue to

1km Botos de Arriba (945.5/54.5)

KSO past a *cruceiro* (double-sided) in the square and continue uphill on the road. KSO(R) at a fork and KSO still uphill and ignoring turns, until you come to a T-junction with a less minor road at the top. Cross over and continue down LH side of two grassy lanes, becoming walled. KSO for 1km ignoring turns until you reach a very minor road. Cross over and KSO. 200m later reach a bigger minor road and turn R. Continue on the road into the village of

4km Donsión (949.5/50.5)
Elaborate *cruceiro* with figures on base and shaft as well. Fountain. Hostal/Rte Camino de Santiago (closed Sundays) on main road.

Follow the road round to R past a fountain and a Baroque church, very large for the size of the village. Continue ahead. Fork L (signposted 'Campo' and 'Fondevila') and fork R at the next junction. Continue ahead on a stony lane leading downhill through woods. KSO(R) at a fork and KSO.

Fork L at a junction and turn L to cross a bridge over the river. KSO(L) ahead on the other side for 600m, ignoring turns, until you reach the motorway slip road. Turn L along it, pass big roundabout below you to R and continue downhill alongside the N525 in

1km A Laxe (950.5/49.5)
Fountain, *refugio*.

KSO on road then, at the top of the hill, you can either KSO on the road to Prado or fork L here, down a lane signposted 'Campo'. If you choose this option KSO, pass a *lavadero* (L) and continue down a grassy lane, veering L (you are // to the main road by now). Cross a track and KSO up a small lane alongside a hedge on L, widening out. KSO, ignoring turns, pass a high stone wall (on R) and a factory (on L) and reach a

241

minor road at a T-junction. Cross over and continue along a minor road ahead, // to the N525 (only 60–70m away). Cross another minor road, continue behind buildings and return to the N525 in

2km Prado (952.5/47.5)
Bar/Rte 'O Afilador' (on road) also has rooms (986.79.40.46), shops.

Continue ahead on the road (pavement) then 200m later, by a *tabacos* fork L down a lane and then turn R, continuing ahead on a walled lane, // to the main road some 200m away. *(To go to bar/rte turn first R to road then then turn L for 100m – retrace your steps afterwards.).* Cross a minor road, KSO and when you reach a second minor road 1.5km later, turn R to reach a section of the **old** N525 in

2km Boralla (954.5/45.5)

KSO along it, ignoring turns, for 1km until it veers R to cross the nineteenth-century bridge over the *Río Deza*. **Cyclists:** *KSO here to rejoin the N525.*
Fork L down a grassy lane (boggy in wet weather) downhill, passing under a railway viaduct *(the **Río Deza** is in a gorge below to R by now)*. 200m later cross the

1.5km Ponte Taboada (956/44)
Tenth-century bridge over the Río Deza, in very good condition, with original medieval paved surface dating from AD 912, high above the river for a bridge of this type.

Continue on a paved FP on the other side, leading up to the street in

0.5km Taboada (956.5/43.5)

Turn R and KSO(R) uphill *(note REAL scallop shells accompanying waymarks in this area)*. At the top, by houses, turn L and at a T-junction (N525 ahead across fields) turn L at another minor road. 300–400m later reach a T-junction *(note engravings on wall on R)* and continue ahead up a lane, // to the main road but at a distance. At the top turn R up a gravel track, R again and then L on a section of old road, returning to the **N525** opposite the Romanesque parish **church of Santiago** *(with a painting of Santiago Matamoros in Baroque altarpiece inside and a modern statue of Santiago Peregrino in a corner of the paved sitting area outside).*

Here you have a choice: a) You can turn L PAST a picnic/recreation area and continue on the N525 for 2.5km more (keep on LH side, a slip road, when the main road goes under a bridge) into **Silleda**. *There is quite a lot of traffic but you should take this option if it is late in the day and the light is beginning to fade.*

Alternatively, b) (this option is 1.5km longer but much quieter) *Turn L just BEFORE the picnic area, up a walled lane, veering R and continuing on lane through woods, gently uphill all the time. Reach a section of the old main road 1km later and fork L onto minor road then fork R back into woods at bend 100m later, veering R, on wide stony walled lane.*

Leave woods 700m later, veer R to small church/chapel, turn L, R and R again on small tarmac lane and continue on paved walled lane. Follow it as it veers L and L again, gently uphill, in woods, and after 1.5km go uphill to farm. Fork R and reach road by 'stop' sign. Cross over and 200m later, just before you reach another road, fork R onto a *camino de tierra*, veering R. Turn L to road and then turn R along it.

200m later turn L (**Rúa Santa Eulalia**) to church. Turn R to pass in front of it *(large sitting area)* and then continue along **Rúa Avenida do Parque** to main road (**N525**) in the centre of

> **3.5km Silleda (960/40)**
> Small town with all facilities. Hotel/Rte Ramos (Calle San Isidoro, 986.58.12.12), Café-Bar Toxa (on main road, 986.58.01.11, also has sello), Fonda Maril (Calle Venezuela 38, 986.58.09.55) and Hostal Gonzalez (Calle San Isidoro) all have rooms.

Turn L onto **N525**, downhill, and turn L down the second street after the *ayuntamiento* (**Rúa Escuadro Toriz**, signposted 'Escuadro' and 'Somoza') and turn R immediately into a lane behind an industrial building. *(Here, as elsewhere, the camino is simply playing 'hide and seek' with the N525, to avoid walking on the main road.)* Return to it after 500m, go down a tarred lane for 150m and return to the road again, then turn L down a walled lane just before KM304. KSO along this between buildings, ignoring turns, to a road fork. Fork R here uphill to a section of the **old** N525 by the *báscula pública* then turn L down a minor road opposite the **Centro Funerario** past a large factory (now on your R).

Continue down this minor road through the hamlet of **Margaride**. At the end, opposite a football field, KSO at a crossing then fork R down a lane then turn L immediately onto a track through woods. KSO at a crossing, KSO(L) at a fork and KSO(R) until you reach a minor road. Turn L and immediately R through woods again. KSO(R) at a fork, veering L. Turn L down a *camino de tierra* by a depot for 'pensioned-off' buses and trucks, pass behind a factory and KSO, ignoring turns. Cross a bridge over the river and turn L at a T-junction on the other side, turning R 80m later opposite a pumping station onto a minor road and reach the N640 *(junction with N525 150m over to your R)*.

Cross over and continue ahead on minor road, cross motorway and KSO. At crossing by small bus shelter *(small church to L uphill)* KSO. However, if you want to go to the **Albergue de Peregrinos** (signposted here but over 1km away and more than 1km from Bandeira) turn R here. Go to N525, turn L and then turn R before exit board for **Chapas**.

Otherwise: turn R 300m later down tarmac lane by farm, turn R at T-junction down *camino de tierra* and then turn L up another. 200m later fork R to return to the N525 and turn L along it into

7km Bandeira (967/33)
Small town with all facilities which originally had a Hospital de Peregrinos. Hostal/Rte Conder Rey (986.58.53.53), Hostal/Rte O Portón, Casa Cuiña (a *fonda*) on main road and Hotel Vitoriño (986.58.53.30) all have rooms. *Refugio* (outside town).

KSO on the main street and at the end turn R down a minor road signposted 'Dornelas/Piñeiro/Cira', leading downhill to a bridge over the river 1km later. KSO(L) ahead on the other side. Turn R at a junction then L shortly afterwards, veering R. KSO(R) twice and continue on a minor road with houses at intervals. Cross three minor roads and then, at a farm, where the tarmac stops and a lane veers R, KSO(L) ahead to R of buildings, continuing straight ahead downhill. Pass to RH side of some vines where a lane veers L, down a gravel lane through woods down to a minor road. Turn L, KSO(L) at a fork. Turn R 400m later at a T-junction with a minor road.

KSO and KSO(L) onto the road into the village of

5km Dornelas (972/28)
Fountain. Romanesque church with rounded apse (typical of many in this area).

KSO past the church, KSO(L) at the first T-junction and KSO(R) at the second onto a bigger minor road. KSO(L) twice (at two T-junctions) and KSO on a minor road. Turn L at the next junction then 50m before you reach the N525 turn R down a shady lane through woods.

From here you can make a detour to visit the Pazo de Oca, one of the largest and most palatial manor houses in Galicia, with its own chapel, lakes and landscaped gardens; continue up to the N525 and turn R onto it at KM315, continue along it for 2km and turn L beside Hostal América onto a minor road into a thickly wooded valley with the Pazo de Oca at the bottom.

Otherwise: KSO(L) at a fork and KSO(R) at the next fork, uphill. *N525 over to L all the time, audible as well as visible.* Turn R at a T-junction then turn L at the next junction and KSO(L) at the next. KSO at a crossing. Reach a road by a very long farm building *(view of Pico Sacro from here – see Introduction)* and KSO(R) along the road to a junction opposite a sawmill in

3km Carballeida (975/25)
A lot of very large blue as well as white (wild) hydrangeas in this area.

KSO down the road opposite (signposted 'Castro') and KSO to

1km Seixo (976/24)
Bar/shop.

KSO through the village and turn R on a road ahead, downhill for 500m, then fork L, veering R down to a crossing and turn L (down a very minor road). Continue steadily downhill, ignoring turns until you reach (on your R) the

2km Santuario de Gundián (978/22)
Small chapel in a park with a pavilion and sitting/picnic area; good (shady) place for a rest.

Fountain with Santiago sculpture, next to Capilla de Santiaguiño

To continue: turn L on the road (when coming from above) or, from the Santuario, KSO ahead out of the site and continue downhill on a minor road, ignoring turns, for 1.5km until you reach the old bridge over the **Río Ulla**.

This river forms the boundary between the provinces of Pontevedra and La Coruña (which you are now entering). There are several impressive pazos *in this area, which is also reputed for its good-quality* aguardiente *(a type of brandy).*

2km Ponte Ulla (980/20)
Bars, shops. Rte Ríos (by bridge, 981.51.23.05), Rte Donostiarra Txolo and Bar Tanis all have rooms.

Turn R and cross a bridge and then turn L towards a viaduct but before it turn R up a newly-paved walkway then fork L to the side of a substantial house up an old paved road under pergolas of vines. *(Notice in gallego – which you should heed as well as read – says 'Ollo con os cans' – 'Beware of the dogs'.)* Turn L at the top under an old wooden footbridge. *(The building to your L is the Pazo de Vista Alegre.)*

KSO(L) on a lane coming from R for 150m to the N525 just below KM322.

Cross over and continue on LH side for 500m then fork L at end of crash barriers on a short section of old road. Continue for 200m more on road then cross the N525 and turn hard R on the other side. Turn L under the railway line and L again on the other side up a forest road.

Turn R uphill at T-junction at the top of the hill, then turn R again up a tarmac road at crossing, veering L, and then, 300m later, turn L uphill on gravel track. KSO, ignore LH turn, KSO at a crossing and KSO(L) at RH junction. When the road comes to an end shortly afterwards KSO ahead on a track. KSO at a crossing and 250m later continue through woods. At the end of another gravelled road 250m later KSO(R) ahead on a track through woods. Reach a minor road 400m later and turn L to the

---

4.5km Capilla de Santiaguiño (984.5/15.5)
Chapel dedicated to Santiago, built in 1696 and restored in 2000. Fountain with statue of Santiago Peregrino in niche above it. (Note: a VERY aggressive small dog lives in the house opposite.) *Refugio.*

Pass to RH side of the chapel and KSO on a gravel lane through woods, more or less level, then rising gradually for 2km, ignoring turnings. *Another view of the Pico Sacro on a fine day.* 2.5km from the chapel pass a large modern house and reach a T-junction with a minor road.

247

Here the Pico Sacro (550m) is some 500m away from you, clearly visible ahead, with the ninth-century Ermita de San Sebastián just below the top; turn R to visit and then retrace your steps (see below). This is the place where, according to legend, the bad Reina Lupa (Wolf Queen) lived and who intentionally misled the two disciples seeking a final resting place for the body of St James, sending them to a place she knew to be full of wild bulls that she hoped would kill them all. Instead, however, these animals all calmed down miraculously when the disciples arrived and let them pass unhindered and, as a result, so the story goes, the queen was converted to Christianity.

To go there (1.5km each way but worth it for its splendid 360 degree views on a clear day) turn hard R here and then L uphill at a junction after 1km. The big cleavage in the rocks – the passage is known as the Rúa da Reina Lupa – was reputedly hacked out by an irate giant but a more probable explanation is that it was made in Roman times to facilitate access to and the removal of iron ore from the other side of the hill. Retrace your steps to continue – unfortunately the path off to the R as you descend will not take you in the direction you need to go next.

Otherwise (i.e. if you continue without visiting the Pico Sacro) turn L and continue to a crossroads with a TV mast. KSO and 100m later, by a cruceiro, turn R by a more minor road. KSO at a crossing (church over to L) and at the next crossing (this is Ardois/Lestedo) **there is a choice of waymarks**:

a) The option to KSO ahead is slightly shorter but not so quiet as it passes closer (though not right next to) the N525 for much of the time.

KSO ahead, ignoring turns until you veer L and pass under a railway line. Turn R along a tarred lane on the other side. 150m later, when this bends R, KSO ahead on a track (also tarred). When this bends R KSO, through woods (the N525 is quite close, over to L, by now). KSO at a crossing of grassy tracks, after which the track narrows and veers L down to the main road.

Cross over to a section of old road and fork L down a camino de tierra // to the road. Cross a humpback bridge, the **Ponte de Busacos**, over the river (another – bigger – aggressive dog lives at house on the other side) and KSO ahead. Cross a road and KSO behind a mineral-water factory, returning to the road by a sawmill just before the entrance to **Susana**. Turn L and continue on LH side of the N525 then fork L onto a minor road (signposted 'Marrozos') at the side of the petrol station. KSO(R) at the first junction, turn L at the second and KSO(R) down a lane under pergolas of vines at the third. Reach a minor road, cross it (the two options meet up here) and go through a tunnel under the N525. Continue as described at *** below.

Capilla de Santiaguiño (photo: author)

b) Turn R, veering L downhill, and KSO ahead at a crossing (*Rubial*). Turn R at junction, uphill, and 300m later reach crossing of minor road by *cruceiro* and bus shelter. Turn L downhill and KSO at next crossing on gravel track leading into woods. KSO at crossing (no waymarks), continue downhill, veering R, and go under the railway line. KSO ahead on other side, cross concrete bridge over river and reach crossing (no waymarks).

KSO, turn L *(KSO here if you want to go to the bar/rte 150m away on the N525, and then retrace your steps)* and then turn R uphill (and pick-up waymarks again) veering L and then R, // to N525. Veer R at T-junction turn R on gravel track. Reach a tarmac road 500m later and turn L. 100m after that reach junction with two other roads (marked 'Estación FFCC Susana') and turn L. 150m later reach junction with N525 at the end of Susana *(Rte and* farmacia; *this is also the terminus for the Santiago city buses).*

Cross over and go up street ahead, veering R (**Rúa da Sombra**). Cross road and go through the tunnel under the N525.

7km Susana (991.5/8.5)
Bars, rte, supermarket, *farmacia*. City buses into Santiago.

KSO ahead on the other side of the tunnel***. KSO(L) on a very minor road downhill, cross a bridge over a small river, turn L at a T-junction and then turn R up a bigger minor road uphill. 200m later, by house no. 46, turn R up a tarmac lane, turn L on a minor road at the top and 100m later turn L to cross a bridge over the railway. *(This area is the Lugar da Cañoteira de Marrozos.)* Turn L at the end then 200m later, in a dip, turn L again, veering R uphill.

KSO, ignoring turns, to a T-junction and turn R (*cruceiro* on R) by a fountain/*lavadero* in **Aldrei**. Turn L at a T-junction, go under the railway again (**Rúa do Carballade de Aldrei**) and turn R on the other side (this *lugar* is Vixoi). Turn L down a road, KSO ahead at a crossing and veer R downhill, leading to the

4.5km Capilla de Santa Lucia (996/4)
Small church dating from 1829. Seats, trees, good place for a (final) rest.

Turn R in front of the church and continue on the walkway (**cyclists** *stay on road, turning R).* Cross a road bridge, KSO on the road then KSO ahead on the middle of three lanes *(more* pergolas*).* KSO ahead at a crossing by a *cruceiro*, cross a minor road by an electricity transformer and continue ahead on a minor road. After this bends R continue on a *camino de tierra*. Pass under the motorway and continue ahead, on a very minor road between fields. KSO(R) over the railway again and continue on **Rúa Camiño Real de Angrois** *(bar on L)*. KSO to the end of this (very long) street, continuously uphill, to a crossroads at the **Cruceiro do Sar** *(with cruceiro). Bar and bar/shop on R.*

Cross the road (**Rúa do Sardiño**) and KSO(R) ahead down a cobbled lane *(**Calzada do Sar**)*, with a view of Santiago Cathedral. At a junction at the bottom KSO(R) along **Rúa da Fonte do Sar**, entering the **Sar** district of Santiago *(bars, shops)*.

Cross a bridge over **Río Sar** and turn L (**Campo do Sar**) to visit the church and cloisters of

3km Colexiata de Santa María do Sar (999/1)
Twelfth-century Romanesque collegiate church with inclined internal pillars and very fine cloisters, part of a monastery originally founded in 1136.

Colexiata de Santa María do Sar (photo: author)

Santiago Peregrino arrives in Compostela

Continue ahead (**Calle do Sar**), pass under the railway line and continue uphill via the **Rúa do Sar de Afora**, **Rúa Castron Douro**, **Patio de Madres**, **Rúa da Virxe da Cerca** and the **Porta de Mazarelos**, the only surviving entry gate of the seven the city originally had. Continue along the **Praza da Universidade**, **Calle Caldería**, **Costa de Xelmírez** and the **Praza de Praterías** to the cathedral in

1km Santiago de Compostela 264m, 80,000 (1000/0)

All facilities, RENFE, buses to Madrid, Barcelona, Seville and many other parts of Spain. Plenty of accommodation and in all price ranges. Two campsites: one on the main road to La Coruña, the other at As Cancelas (on outskirts). There are many places to eat in Santiago but for somewhere cheap, filling and with plenty of choice go to the Café-Rte Casa Manolo, now in the Plaza Cervantes. Two tourist offices, both in the Rúa do Vilar (near cathedral).

The most important of the many places of interest in Santiago (all in the old town) is the cathedral, part Romanesque, part Baroque, with its magnificent Portico de la Gloria and façade giving onto the Plaza del Obradoiro. Raised up behind the main altar is the seated statue of St James the apostle to whom it is customary to give the traditional *abrazo* (hug) when visiting the cathedral for the first time (and which people you encountered along the *camino* may have asked you to do on their behalf). The cathedral also houses what is probably the world's

252

biggest censer (incense burner), the famous Botafumeiro. It is made of silver and weighs nearly 80kg, requiring a team of eight men and a system of pulleys to set it in motion after mass, swinging at ceiling level from one end of the transept to the other. Guidebooks (in English) are available from the bookshops in the Rúa do Vilar (near the cathedral) or in the new town (such as Follas Novas, Calle Montero Ríos 37). There are also many interesting churches, the Museo de las Peregrinaciones, the Museo do Pobo Galego as well as many large-scale temporary exhibitions. Try to spend two or three days in Santiago as there is much to see and do.

If you have time two pilgrim destinations outside the city are worth visiting. **Padrón** is the place where the boat bringing St James to Galicia in AD 44 is believed to have arrived and also contains the *museum of Rosalía de Castro*, the nineteenth-century Galician poet; it can be reached easily by bus (some 20km) from Santiago bus station (frequent services). **Finisterre,** the end of the known world in former times and the end of the route for many pilgrims in centuries gone by, can also be reached by bus (95km) from Santiago bus station, returning the same day if you leave early in the morning. If you prefer, however, you can continue there on foot, a three to four day journey (for walkers) described in Appendix A, four to five if you decide to walk on after that up the coast to **Muxía**.

Puerta Santa (Holy Door), Santiago Cathedral

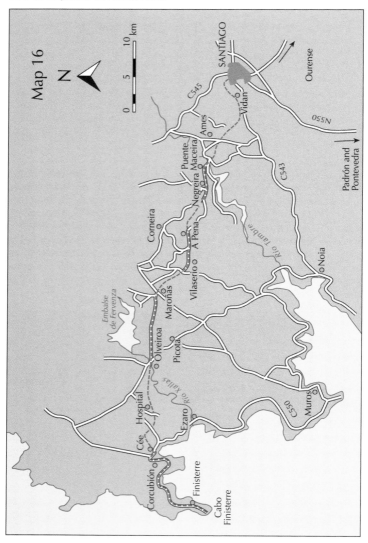

APPENDIX A
Santiago to Finisterre/Muxía

Finisterre ('Fisterra' in Galician) was the end of the known world until Columbus altered things, and was the final destination of many of the pilgrims who made the journey to Santiago in centuries gone by. There are various explanations as to how this continuation came about (one such is that it was based on a pre-Christian route to the pagan temple of the sun god Ara Solis in Finisterre) but it is also known that a pilgrim infrastructure existed, with 'hospitals' in Cée, Corcubión, Finisterre itself and elsewhere. There are also several Jacobean and other pilgrim references along the way: a *cruceiro* with a figure of Santiago in Trasmonte, the church of Santiago in Olveiroa with a statue of St James inside and a bas-relief on the tympanum outside, a probable pilgrim hospital in the place of that name (apart from those already mentioned in Cée and Corcubión), the church of Santiago at Ameixenda 2km south of Cée with a relic reputed to be of one of St James's fingers, a large statue of San Roque in pilgrim gear in the church of San Marcos in Corcubión, a statue of St James in the church of Santa María das Areas in Finisterre with a cemetery chapel that formerly belonged to its pilgrim hospital, and two references to San Roque in place names: the *Encrucijada* or *Alto* de San Roque at the top of the hill leaving Corcubión and the San Roque area at the entrance to Finisterre. Then, 4km before Muxía on the route direct from Hospital, the Capilla San Roque has a statue of San Roque as a pilgrim inside the building while in the altarpiece of the Santuario de Nosa Señora da Barca in Muxía itself there is a figure of St James praying. And after accounts of their journeys along the Camino Francés, the route that those pilgrims in the past most frequently wrote about was the continuation Finisterre–Muxía. These writings came from various European countries and were in several different languages, including an account by the seventeenth-century Italian Domenico Laffi, four times a pilgrim to Santiago, who describes his visit to the church of Santa María das Areas 3km before the 'end of the earth' itself.

It has always been possible to walk there avoiding main roads but, although numbers have increased quite a lot in the last few years, at present only a very small percentage of those who make the pilgrimage to Santiago continue on to Finisterre. This has no doubt been in part due to lack of information and route-finding difficulties but now that the entire route has been re-waymarked and that there are *refugios* and other accommodation available at convenient intervals along the way those who feel their pilgrim journey would be incomplete without continuing to the 'end' will find it much easier to do so. As already indicated, pilgrims in past centuries also continued to the Santuario de Nosa Señora da Barca in Muxía, 28km further up the Atlantic coast, to the north of Finisterre. This route has now been fully waymarked, both directly from Hospital and from Finisterre (and back) and is also described here.

Like your journey along the Vía de la Plata, you may have to be more alert to route-finding than you probably needed to be on the Camino Francés but continuing to the coast on foot is definitely worth the effort. Finisterre is the real end of the journey, both in the physical sense and the religious and historical one. You will pass a number of interesting small churches, *pazos* (large Galician country houses) and old bridges along the way, apart from (if you have already walked *to* Santiago) the now familiar *hórreos*, and the scenery is often beautiful. It is very peaceful and, as there are still relatively few walkers, the route is quite different from the often *autopista*-like Camino Francés before Santiago in July and August. It does rain a lot in this part of Spain of course and it is often misty in the mornings, but on the walk to Finisterre (and especially if you continue on to Muxía), you will have the opportunity to see something of the real Galicia, away from the big towns.

How long does it take?

Allow at least three days, preferably four, to walk to Finisterre, with possible overnight stops in Negreira, Olveiroa and Cée, plus a day for the (recommended) continuation to Muxía. The actual walking is not hard but there are a lot of climbs and descents.

Continuation to Muxía

There are two ways to continue to Muxía: from Finisterre (28km), northeast, parallel to the coast, or directly from Hospital (29km). (If you take this second alternative you can then continue southwesterly to Finisterre as this section is waymarked in each direction.) Both of these options are described here.

Waymarking

The route is waymarked with the familiar yellow arrows and they lead you from the first one, on the pavement in the **Rúa das Hortas** in Santiago, all the way to the town of Finisterre. (Watch out carefully, however, as in the past the route to Finisterre was waymarked in both directions – there and back as well). The route is also marked with concrete bollards with both the blue and yellow stylised ceramic shell familiar from parts of other *caminos* (and whose rays normally indicate the direction you should take). Some of these bollards also indicate the distance remaining to Finisterre while others give the number of kilometres left to reach Muxía.

Pilgrim marker post (photo: author)

Maps

Some maps are available in Santiago bookshops, such as the 1:250,000 map of Galicia (published by the Xunta de Galicia) and the relevant sheets (*hojas*) of the IGN's 1:25,000 series of the Mapa Topográfico Nacional de España: 94-IV (Santiago), 94-III (Negreira), 94-I (A Baña), 93-II (Mazaricos), 93-I (Brens), 92-II (Corcubión) and 92-IV (Fisterra). For the Finisterre-Muxía section you will need 67-IV (Touriñan) and 67-II (Muxía) (*hojas* 93-1, 93-2 and 92-2).

Accommodation

(in *hostales, pensiones*) is available in Negreira, Cée, Corcubión, Finisterre itself, Lires and Muxía and there are now *refugios* in Negreira (21km from Santiago) and Olveiroa (34km further on), as well as the one in the centre of Finisterre (34km from Olveiroa) It is also possible to sleep in the old school (no facilities) in Vilaserio and sports halls in Cée and Muxía. A further *refugio* is planned for Corcubión.

Please note that if you wish to stay in the *refugios* you will need your *credencial* (pilgrim passport), normally the one you used to walk/cycle **to** Santiago. Note, too, that the *refugio* in Finisterre is **only** available to those who walk or cycle all the way there from Santiago – **NOT** to those who arrive by bus.

Food

You will pass some shops and bars along the way but it is better to take at least some reserve supplies with you.

Fisterrana

This is a certificate of pilgrimage given by the Concello (town hall) in Finisterre to those who have completed the route and have had their *credenciales* (pilgrim passports) from the route they walked prior to Santiago stamped at intervals along the way. You can make enquiries about this in the *refugio* in Finisterre. A similar certificate *(Muxiana)* is also available for those who have walked to Muxía (ask in town hall), whether from Finisterre or direct from Hospital.

As on the main *camino*, a **stick** is very useful, for brambles, wet grass, testing the terrain and for frightening (but not hitting!) DOGS.

SANTIAGO – FINISTERRE 92km

Leaving Santiago (260m) From the **Praza do Obradoiro** and with your back to the cathedral, pass in front of the **Hostal de los Reyes Católicos** (on your R), go down the slope in front of its garage (this road is the **Costa do Cristo**), then down some steps and along the **Rúa das Hortas** ahead *(first yellow arrow on manhole cover on RH pavement ahead)*. Veer R at the end into **Rúa do Campo das Hortas** and turn L at traffic lights to cross **Rúa do Pombal** via pedestrian crossing. Continue ahead along **Rúa do Cruceiro do Gaio** (the first of two streets in front of you) and then along the **Rúa da Poza de Bar**; this then > the **Rúa de San Lourenzo**.

At the **Carballeira de San Lourenzo** *(a small, shady park with seats, a fountain and some 30–40 old oak trees)* there is the first *camino* milestone. **Here you can either:**

a) KSO ahead to visit the (former Franciscan monastery) church of San Lourenzo de Trasouto *(normal visiting hours Tuesdays and Thursdays 11.00 to 13.00, 16.30 to 18.30, otherwise open at mass times)* then retrace your steps, veering L alongside the monastery garden wall (on the **Costa do Cano**) to pick up the *camino* ahead, **or**

b) Turn R (coming from the cathedral, signposted 'Sanatorio') and then fork L diagonally across the park and continue alongside monastery garden wall. Turn L down a cement road (still the **Costa do Cano**) leading you downhill to cross a bridge over **Río Sarela** in

> **1.5km Ponte Sarela 195m**
> The first house by the bridge has a sign 'Parroquia de San Fructuoso, Lugar de Puente Sarela' (the old buildings by the bridge were tanneries and the mills used to power them). From here for the next 7km to Ventosa, in order to avoid the main road, the route is extremely fiddly, with constant changes of direction.

Turn L on other side of the bridge, KSO(L) at fork along the bottom of two lanes, gently uphill, and cross the stream by large stepping stones. KSO ahead uphill on other side. KSO(L) at fork shortly afterwards and KSO at crossing 200m later, uphill through a meadow. Go under telegraph wires and veer L uphill, to reach minor road by modern houses (500m after Ponte Sarela). Turn L downhill *(good views of cathedral over to L on a sunny day)* and 200m later on turn R onto a tarred lane uphill.

This continues as a shady walled lane through eucalyptus woods, gently downhill all the time. KSO(L) at fork then KSO(R) at another junction 400m later. KSO(R) when track joins from back L, then turn L downhill at a staggered crossing and then turn L at a crossing at the bottom 250m later. Turn R onto a minor road then 60m later KSO(L) at a staggered crossing. Cross small river, KSO(L) at two junctions, then turn R at third (still on minor tarred road), veering R to crossing with 'stop' sign. Turn L and reach five-point junction with bus shelter in hamlet of

> **2km Piñeiro 170m**

Turn R in front of *hórreo*, veering R. KSO(L) at fork, turning L and then R to a very minor tarred road. Turn L along it for 300m, crossing small river on the way, then 50m before a bigger road and 'stop' sign, turn R uphill on another minor road which then > a CT. When it > a gravelled road and turns sharp L turn R onto track into woods, veering second R on clear forest track. KSO along this, ignoring turns. Cross very minor tarred road and KSO ahead, gently downhill all the time, then KSO(R) ahead at junction.

KSO ahead all the time, ignoring turns, until you reach the edge of the woods. KSO ahead, on tarmac road, KSO(L) at junction, and 300m later reach T-junction with 'stop' sign. Turn L to bus shelter then immediately turn hard R down lane, veering L. Fork R at junction and 200m later on turn R at road junction (football pitch to L ahead) and cross

3.5km Bridge over Río Roxos 155m

Pass picnic area (on L) then KSO(L) at fork. 200m later turn R uphill. 500m later, shortly after an industrial building on R, turn R when road bends L, into woods. Turn L at T-junction 200m later, along walled lane. KSO to minor road at entrance (on L) to village of **Roxos**. (*This is the Alto do Vento* (178m), *bar/mesón opposite*). Turn R (*passing park on L, seats*), downhill, into

1.5km Ventosa 60m

Turn R by a bus shelter and KSO, veering L downhill on an old road. Cross the road again (by another bus shelter) and KSO on the other side under pergolas. Pass between buildings, follow lane round, turn R and then turn R again in front of a huge electricity pylon and continue down lane. Turn L onto a very minor road then immediately L on a bigger one. At junction (*shop on L*) KSO ahead, downhill into

2km Augapesada 60m
Mesón on R. Medieval bridge (recently restored), picnic area.

Just *before* road junction (signposted 'Bertamirans 3') turn L onto paved lane past old (restored) bridge (*seats*), then continue on to road at 'stop' sign. Cross over and then turn R uphill on other side (*bar 50m further on L, past turning*) up small concrete road uphill (*bar 50m further on, on L after turn*) which then becomes a forest track. KSO at crossing (*two handy seats on R*), continuously uphill.

When you reach a minor road 500m later (to L), turn R (*third seat on R shortly afterwards*). KSO, passing 4th seat and 5th (on L) just before the road (on L). Turn R here and continue on a track uphill. Return to the road by 6th seat and TV mast and turn R uphill along it. Pass a second TV mast and 200m later on R (by a sign 'Trasmonte-Santa María') pass a fountain. 200m later begin to go downhill and enter

2km Carballo 260m

Continue on the road, passing a wayside cross on a wall (R). KSO at a junction and continue to

1km Trasmonte 220m
Baroque church of Santa María and *cruceiro* (with figure of Santiago) to L. Bar/shop.

Continue on the road, passing through hamlets of **Reino** and **Burgueiros**. KSO on the road, turn L at a junction and reach

2km Ponte Maceira 160m
Bar/rte. Picturesque village in two parts with stone bridge (five main arches) over Río Tambre, constructed late fifteenth/early sixteenth centuries and restored in medieval style in the eighteenth. Chapel of San Blas and large neo-medieval *pazo* on other side of bridge and several stone houses with armorial devices. (Romanesque church of Santa María de Portor 1km to north – tower visible from here.)

Weir at Puente Maceira (photo: author)

Turn R over a bridge (**Calle del Puente Maceira**), turn L uphill at the end and 200m later fork L downhill by house no. 22. Turn L down minor road, // to river then, 100m before a 'stop' sign, fork L down track into woods, to river, and go under arch of nineteenth century bridge (*Ponte Maceira Nova, bar on other side*). KSO ahead on a *camino de tierra* leading through fields (*road above you to R*), returning to the road after 1km in

2km Barca 150m

KSO on the road for 600m, then fork L (signposted 'Logrosa') past factory buildings, uphill, ignoring turns to R or L. KSO(L) ahead to

1.5km Chancela 190m

Pass the entrance gates (L) to the large **Pazo de Chancela** (also known as *Pazo de Capitán* – watch out for VERY large, loose dogs here) and KSO ahead, ignoring turns, following the road down to a 'stop' sign at bottom of hill. Turn L, pass the large statue of a pilgrim (L), then pass a second statue (*of Minerva and the bulls*) and a fountain, veering R uphill (**Avenida de Santiago**).

1.5km Negreira 160m
Small town with all facilities. *Refugio* (20+ places, with kitchen) 1km away, on outskirts (follow camino waymarking). Hostal Mezquito (Rúa do Carmen 2, in centre) has rooms.

Turn L (signposted 'Campo de Feria') down the **Carreira de San Mauro** and continue to the bottom, passing under an archway linking the **Capilla San Mauro** (on R) and the **Pazo de Cotón** *(a medieval fortress restored in the seventeenth century)* on L. (*Modern statue on R is of the* emigrante/segadora – *itinerant harvester* – *figure, with a boy pulling at his father's trousers through a window and mother and child seated.*)
Cross a bridge over **Río Barcala** and at a fork turn L uphill. (*Yellow arrows directing you to R here, on road, miss out church*). 200m later, at next fork, either KSO(L) for *refugio* or bear R, marked 'Negreira-Iglesia,' to continue. Turn R at a *cruceiro* to visit eighteenth century **church of San Xulián** (otherwise take the second R turn to pass in

front of it.). Turn L up some steps, go through a gate and turn R along a lane, continuing straight ahead onto a tarred lane, on the level. When this bends hard R downhill *(this is where the RH road option rejoins the route)* KSO(L) ahead on RH of two // grassy lanes on L, still on the level, then climbing gently, through eucalyptus woods, with the road away to R below. Pass a concrete (public services) building on R and KSO, reaching the road (CP56031) 200m later. KSO on the road (uphill) for 500m, passing a turning to Cobas (R) and then turn R opposite unmarked *bar/shop* and bus shelter in

3km Zas/Xas 260m

KSO along the lane, passing tiny church (R), KSO(R) at a fork, KSO(L) at the next fork and 100m later KSO(R) again to end of village. Pass to L of house no. 21 then take LH of 2 grassy walled lanes at fork.

KSO(L) at a junction and KSO when a track joins from back L. KSO(R) at a fork, then KSO(L) immediately afterwards on a track coming from back L. KSO, then 200m later turn L. When you reach T-junction (1.5km from Zas) near a main road over to your L in **Camiño Real** (*bar on road*), turn R along an earth lane. 200m later turn L down a walled lane, gently downhill. At a junction 300m later KSO ahead then KSO(L) at the next. Cross a minor road 150m later and continue ahead on the other side on what looks like a FP but is, in fact, a walled lane. *(This is a very old, historic route, completely overgrown and impassable until the late 1990s, becoming wider as you proceed, // to the 'main' road all the time.)* Cross another very minor road and KSO ahead, in a straight line all the time.

KSO when a track joins from back L, veering R and almost immediately turn L, again in a straight line ahead, // to the road. Turn L at a crossing 150m later. KSO(R) ahead when a track joins from back L, becoming a walled lane leading downhill. KSO(L) ahead when a track joins from back R and continue to a very minor road in

4km Rapote 330m

Cross over and continue on a concrete lane ahead, turn L and then R through the village to continue ahead at the end down a sunken walled lane downhill, ignoring turns, until you reach the bottom. Turn R then KSO(L) uphill on a walled lane, ignoring turns until you emerge just below a minor road in

2.5km Peña/A Pena 260m
Bar on road (turn L, R and L by first house, simple meals; if you go to the bar you can stay on the road afterwards and rejoin the route in Porto Camiño – see below).

Otherwise (to continue) continue ahead (below road), KSO(R) ahead below a church and turn L at a *cruceiro* uphill, then turn L again to the road and turn R. KSO (this is **Porto Camiño**, 380m, a pass) for 400m on the road then just after a turning to **Xallas** (on L) turn R onto a track and then immediately L ahead (on the third from L of the four tracks in front of you) by a concrete water tank. KSO(L) at a fork and continue downhill, ignoring turns. Cross a stream, veer R and then L uphill again and at a T-junction turn L. Return to the road and turn R. 2km later, just before a sharp LH bend, turn L down a walled lane into

4.5km Vilaserio 360m
Bar (on road) on R. Ask here if you want to sleep in the old school (no facilities).

Fork (not turn) R downhill behind the bar and turn L on the road. Pass a turning (L) to **Pesadoira** and KSO on the road, veering L up to a crossroads and turn R into

2km Cornado 332m

Turn L in the village then 150m later fork L uphill on an earth road. At a fork SO(L) ahead until you reach a road (CP5604, KM18). Turn R here, KSO for 300m, then turn L down a lane. KSO, ignoring turns, gently uphill.

At the top (marker stone 50,266) KSO ahead, gradually downhill, then 150m later fork L at a fork uphill. At a T-junction 250m after that turn R and fork L at a fork after another 250m. *(Shell and 'Maroñas' on one side of marker stone, 'Neria' and shell on other.)* KSO at a crossing, KSO at the next, cross a bridge over the river and enter

5km Maroñas
Bar(?), shop on road.

Turn L in the centre of the village, following the road round and turn L at the end (a very long village), continuing on the lane to a T-junction, then turn L at a *cruceiro* in the centre of

1km Santa Mariña 330m
Twelfth-century Romanesque church.

Continue to L and turn R along a lane to the 'main' road. Turn L and continue on the road for 500m (*two bars on R: first one is Casa Vitoriano, simple meals*), then turn R uphill (signposted 'Bon Xesús and Guiema'). Continue on the road for 3km to three scarcely separated hamlets and turn L in the first one (**Bon Xesús**, 371m). KSO uphill into the second (**Gueima**, 388m, *with simple cruceiro on LH side of road*) and turn R when you get to **Vilar de Xastro** *(420m)*, veering L, then:

a) *in good weather*: fork L up a track along RH shoulder of *Monte Aro* (555m), climbing steadily (*good views as you go on a clear day*). KSO at a crossing 100m later, veering L (*views out over embalse when track levels out*) and veering R, to a junction 500m after that. Turn R then 100m later turn L, downhill, on an unpaved road. Part way down turn hard L. Veer R at bottom into **Lago**.

b) *in bad weather*: KSO(R) on road. Turn L at T-junction. Continue uphill and KSO ahead at crossing at top. KSO(L) at fork. When you reach **Lago** KSO at crossing in village then KSO(L) at junction. At next junction (with road coming from back L) you will meet up with the route coming over the Monte Aro.

6km Lago 340m

Turn L and continue out of the village on a very minor road. 300m later turn L at a T-junction.

Continue on the road for 400m and turn R (marked 'Corzón') downhill by a bus shelter. KSO(R) at a junction then KSO(L) ahead at a fork. (*Sudden view of line of 20–30 modern windmills on the horizon ahead*.) 700m later turn R then, 250m later, veer L KSO on the road and KSO(R) at fork until you reach the small church of

3km San Cristovo de Corzón 286m

Continue on the road, past the church (*with separate bell-tower*), a *cruceiro* and cemetery, then 100m later turn L. KSO, ignoring turns. Cross a bridge over the small river and KSO.

Reach the 'main' road in **Mallón**. Cross a bridge over **Río Xallas** (and enter *Concello de Dumbría*, leaving the *Concello de Mazaricos*) in

2km Ponte Olveira 270m

KSO(L) at a fork 100m after the bridge. KSO for 2km, passing turning (R) to *Santiago Olveira*. KSO and then opposite road KM22, fork L down a minor road into

2km Olveiroa 270m
(Not to be confused with Olveira, another village nearby.) Village with several *hórreos* and interesting examples of vernacular architecture, church of Santiago with statue of St James (inside) and a bas-relief on the tympanum (outside). *Refugio* (30+ places, with kitchen and hot showers) in centre of village. No shop but Bar Mueriños 50m off route to R uphill at entrance does meals.

KSO through the village (turn R for *refugio*) and 500m later turn L by a *lavadero* (public washing facility) crossing a small river then, at a junction by a telephone pylon, **fork** (not turn) L up a small concrete road (near the 'main' road) uphill. 300m later fork R onto a *camino de tiera*. When you reach telephone cables fork L up another track. *From here to Cée is a very nice section, apart from the two large, belching carbide factories on the skyline, the first of which is just outside the village of Hospital. The* camino *undulates on a wide track high up, with the mountains all around and the Río Hospital below you to the L.*

Descend fairly rapidly and cross the river – carefully. *The stone bridge has now collapsed but is due to be replaced. In the meantime you can cross fairly easily via the stepping stones in dry weather but when there has been a lot of rain you will need to remove your boots and wade across; it is suggested that you wear sandals if possible, to avoid slipping or cutting your feet. The water is not deep but watch out for the current.*

Continue on a FP on the other side, uphill. Turn R at junction with another FP at marker stone 32,066, onto a wider track. KSO ahead into

Unusual rock formation near Logoso

3.5km Logoso 295m
Small hamlet with only a few houses.

Continue to end and take upper of two tracks, undulating, high up, across the shoulder of the mountain. Reach the top of the hill (*and a view of the carbide factory ahead, L*) and turn R onto the unpaved road in

1km Hospital 330m
A village likely, given its name, to have had a pilgrim hospital here in centuries gone by, though no evidence remains.

Turn L immediately and L again onto the road by KM27 (P340A) towards the factory. (*Bar/Rte Casteliño on L at top of hill does sandwiches.*) Turn R onto an old minor road at marker stone 29,353, veering R to the 'main' road by the factory and 100m later cross it.

Here there is a double marker stone and **you can either**:
    a) turn R for the direct continuation to Muxía, 27km. See page 280 for a description of this route **or**
    b) turn L to continue directly to Finisterre, 29km.

For option b) turn L and KSO on the road for 600m then, at a bend just past the factory gates, turn R onto a track which becomes an old walled lane. *This is the old Camino Real, the beginning of 9km of drove road leading through the mountains to Cée, more or less in a straight line, and with splendid views all round on a clear day.* Pass marker stone 27,967 and KSO. KSO for 1km then KSO(L) at a fork 100m later. Cross tarmac road (*cruceiro* in middle) and KSO on the other side. Pass marker stone 26,285 and KSO(L). Veer gradually L and KSO on the wide track with open vistas to all sides, 'roof of the world' style. The *camino* turns L 1km later, at marker stone 25,883. Descend gradually, reach a T-junction 2km later and turn R. KSO then turn L downhill 400m after that and 100m later reach the

5km Santuario de Nosa Señora das Neves 270m

Small church in shady grounds (nice place for a rest), restored in 1997. The Fonte Santa, a fountain below the road to the L by the *cruceiro*, is well known for its curative properties. A *romería* (local pilgrimage) takes place here annually, on September 8th.

Turn R below the church, veering L then R uphill, ignoring turns. KSO. KSO at crossing, KSO(R) at fork. Ignore turning at staggered crossing 1km later. Turn L at junction 100m later (marker stone 21,878) then KSO(R) at next fork shortly after that. 400m later pass the church of

3.5km San Pedro Mártir 310m

Small chapel set in a field, with its own *fonte santa* (water reputedly cures rheumatism, painful feet and verrucas), focus of local pilgrimage and another good place for a rest (covered pavilion useful in bad weather).

Turn R to visit, then retrace your steps. KSO, ignoring turns, for nearly 2km, until you reach a square, pointed marker stone on your L. *From here (on a fine day!) you have your first view of the sea and Cape Finisterre, Monte de Gozo style.* After this the *camino* begins to descend.

At a fork, with a paved section to R and earth track to L, KSO(L), descending steadily. Veer R, turn L and descend steeply. *(View of another belching factory below, in Cée.)* Reach a minor road at marker stone 16,918 and turn L. Turn hard R immediately, downhill, R again at the bottom to *a cruceiro* and KSO(R), after a 'stop' sign, along the 'main' road (**Campo do Sacramento**), past old cemetery (on L). Fork L

Church of San Pedro Mártir (photo: author)

downhill *('Albergue' indicated as straight ahead – ask in Protección Civil)*. Veer L then go down some steps and turn R at bottom into **Rosalia de Castro**. At end reach **Praza da Constitución** *(trees, seats)* and take LH far corner exit to **church of Santa María de Xunqueira**. Pass between this and the **Casa do Concello** and then turn L to cross grassed area with trees, cross canal and reach waterfront in

6km Cée 5m
Coastal town with all facilities. Hostal Vitoria, Hostal Galicia (on road to Corcubión). Hospedaje Crego (in Avenida Finisterra) is inexpensive and owner speaks excellent English. Pilgrims also report sleeping in the Protección Civil facilities, near bus depot (beds, showers).

Church of Nosa Señora de Xunqueira (with Gothic section). 2km to south, in hamlet of Ameixenda on coast (in direction of Ezaro), church of Santiago has a relic reputed to be one of the saint's fingers.

Continue (R) along waterfront and then, when the road starts to go uphill, cross over and 200m later fork R up a steep concrete street at the entrance board for **Corcubión**. KSO uphill, KSO(L) at a fork (the **Calle Rafael Juan** but not named at the start) and then continue along it when it becomes **Calle Antonio Porrúa**. Pass the **Capilla del Pilar** (1931) and a fountain (L) and reach a small square (**Plaza de Castelao**, *seats, trees, taxi rank*). Leave by the top LH corner (**Paseo de San Marcos**) veering L to the thirteenth-century **church of San Marcos** *(large statue of San Roque in pilgrim gear in niche in RH wall)* in

1.5km Corcubión 12m

All facilities. Bar Sirena has rooms. Church of San Marcos in 'gótico-marinero' style. Many interesting old houses in the town centre (whose *casco antiguo* – old centre – is classified as a historic monument).

Facing the church door, turn hard R up some steps and up the street ahead (**Calle de las Mercedes** – *note houses with armorial devices*) to another square (**Campo de Rollo**). Cross over, pass to L of walled garden and turn L between houses nos.11 and 12 up narrow lane with high walls on either side. KSO(R) at fork. *Nice views back over the port as you climb.* Turn L, uphill again, at T-junction with wider path. At next T-junction (in front of a house), turn L onto wider track, veering R to (tarmac) road in a hamlet. Turn R uphill and emerge at junction with main road (C552) opposite a sports ground at the **Encrucijada de San Roque** (*trees, shady place for a rest, cruceiro and fountain on LH side – the* Fonte de Vilar).

Cross over and continue on an old road on the other side. At a junction KSO ahead down a FP. Continue along a boundary wall (with fountain) on R, downhill, down a grassy lane, descending gradually. Return to the road 500m later in the hamlet of

2km Amarela 90m

Approaching Finisterre

KSO on the road for 400m until it bends sharp L, then cross over and KSO(R) on a section of old road. 80m later turn R down a wide grassy lane, reaching the road again 100m later near the sea. Turn R and KSO on the road into

1km Estorde 50m
Nice beach, campsite (Camping Ruta Finisterre – shuts October), Hostal Playa de Estorde, bars.

KSO on the road for 1km to

1km Sardiñeiro 20m
Another nice beach; shops, bars, Hostal Nicola has rooms. Eighteenth-century church of San Xoán.

Just before you enter the village, at end of section on old road, cross over, turn L onto old tarred road and then R by village name board between houses. This short-cuts a bend and then returns to the road. Cross over and fork L down **Rúa do Mestre Barrera** and return to the road by **Hostal Nicola** (L). 200m later, by house no. 31, turn R up **Rúa do San Xoán** (signposted to 'Praia do Rostro' and church) then turn L immediately (**Rúa Nova**) and continue uphill (**Rúa de Fisterra**). At a T-junction 200m after the last house, turn L up a grassy walled lane uphill through eucalyptus woods.

KSO (R) at a crossing 600m later and at another (marker stone 7627), and shortly afterwards emerge with a view out to sea and 'the end of the world' on the second hill ahead of you. Veer R to return to the road just past a lay-by with a picnic area. Cross over and continue ahead downhill and then up *(quiet secluded beach 50m below you)* and return to the road after a bend (300m later).

350m after that (at marker stone 6484) fork L down the **Corredoira de Don Camilo** *(named after the Nobel prize-winning Galician novelist José Camilo Cela). This is a paved paseo that runs alongside the sea for 2km, tarmac at first, leading down to and then along the Praia de Langosteira (beach). It continues along the sand dunes all the way to the entrance to the town of Finisterre (2km), ending at a viewpoint with a cruceiro, and has cafés and chiringuitos (snack bars) at points along it in summer. Or, if you want, and if the tide is suitable, you can walk along the beach itself (seawater good for tired, sore, blistered feet...).*

When you get to the end of the *corredoira* (this area is known as **San Roque**) go up the slope to a wayside cross and *mirador* (viewpoint) and continue on LH side of

271

Fishing port, town of Finisterre

the road. KSO along **Calle de Coruña**, then down **Calle Santa Catalina**, veering R downhill to centre of town (port to L).

4km Finisterre
Population 3000. Small fishing port with all facilities. Refugio in town centre, near port (20+ places, kitchen, opens 17.00). Several *hostales* and *pensiones*, including Hospedaje Lopez in centre of town and Casa Velay. From the town of Finisterre it is a further 3km to the lighthouse ('el faro') and the real 'end of the earth'. Twelfth-century church of Santa María das Areas, eighteenth-century Capela do Bo Suceso, remains of eigth-century Ermita de San Guillermo, eighteenth-century Castillo de San Carlos.

To walk to the lighthouse: cross the street and continue ahead up *Rúa Real* (refugio *on LH corner*) to **Plaza de la Constitución** then straight on down **Calle Plaza** to **Plaza de Ara Solis**. Turn R and then turn L in front of **Capela do Bo Suceso** (*note house with armorial device, cross and sundial to R*). Continue along **Calle Ara Solis**, veering R uphill. Cross **Calle Manuel Lago Paris** and continue uphill to join the **C552** coming from back R and reach the church of

1km Santa María das Areas

Twelfth-century parish church of Saint Mary of the Sands, Romanesque in part, with statue of St James as pilgrim in the nave. Originally only a rectangular building, several side chapels were added later, including one built at the end of the seventeenth century to house the Gothic statue of the Santísimo Cristo, the focus of an annual *romería*. Gothic cruceiro outside and a building that was formerly a pilgrim hospital. The church has its own Porta Santa (Holy Door) and jubilee years. Open 10.00 to 13.00, 15.00 to 19.00 (summer only?).

Continue for 2km more on the road to the lighthouse *(fountain – Fonte Cabanas – on R, halfway along). A rocky outcrop known as the 'Piedras Santas', a possible focus of pre-Christian worship, is to be found on the north shore of the peninsula.*

Hospedaje O Semáforo (in former observatory and morse radio station) with rooms (expensive) and rte (981.72.58.69), Bar O Refugio. Bronze sculpture of pair of broken boots on rocks behind lighthouse. As the weather is often misty until about midday in this part of Spain you may well have better views from here in the late afternoon and evening.

Return to Santiago

By bus (from the long, low building in the port) – three or four journeys a day, the last one leaving at 16.00 Mondays to Saturdays (18.00 Sundays and holidays). Journey time 2½–3 hours, though the service is not always direct and you may have to change in Vimianzo or Baio to connect (coordinated) with another bus. Space permitting, it is also possible to take one or two bikes.

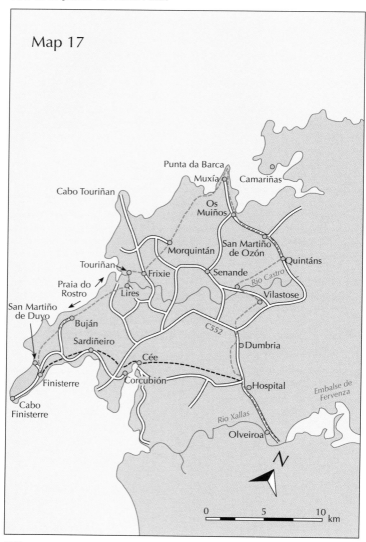

Map 17

Punta da Barca
Muxía
Camariñas
Cabo Touriñán
Os Muiños
Morquintán
San Martiño de Ozón
Quintáns
Touriñán
Frixie
Senande
Río Castro
Praia do Rostro
Lires
Vilastose
San Martiño de Duyo
Buján
C552
Sardiñeiro
Cée
Dumbria
Finisterre
Corcubión
Hospital
Embalse de Fervenza
Cabo Finisterre
Río Xallas
Olveiroa

N

0   5   10 km

FINISTERRE–MUXÍA 28km

The continuation to Muxía is waymarked in **both** directions – there and back – but economically. That is, there is only one marker stone at each manoeuvre, set at an angle to indicate which way to go, so you will need to watch out carefully at turns and junctions. These bollards have the shell **upright** on this route but have no kilometre indications, simply 'Fisterra–Muxía' (or 'Muxía–Fisterra'), according to where these two places are situated.

Take food and water with you – the only place with any facilities is Lires (2 bars, one selling food).

Note: until the footbridge they are planning to build has been built, you will have to remove your shoes/boots and wade across the Río Castro (500m past Lires), via the stepping stones. This is not a problem in very dry weather but when it has been raining they will be partly submerged. It is better to put your boots in your rucksack to avoid them dangling and unsteadying you (and roll up your trousers if you are not wearing shorts) and it is suggested that you wear sandals to avoid slipping or cutting your feet. Stick(s) recommended. The water is very clear and not very deep but watch out for the current. However, a longer, road alternative is also available and is described later.

From the centre of Finisterre, retrace your steps to the *cruceiro* (where the walk into the town along the beach ends) and then continue along the main road (**Calle de La Coruña**). Pass town exit boards and then turn second L uphill onto minor road, passing the place-name boards for **San Martiño**. Veer R and then KSO(R) ahead, on the level, at fork by bus shelter. Pass cemetery and then church of

> **2km San Martiño de Duyo**
> Duyo (Latin Dugium) was the former Roman city where, according to medieval tradition, the disciples bringing St James's body sought permission from the authorities to bury it in this area.

KSO, pass *lavadero* (L) and KSO ahead, gently downhill, // to sea and ignoring turnings. 800m after church reach T-junction and the hamlet of **Escaselas** (1km). Turn L.

At crossing 100m later turn L at slightly bigger road and 500m later reach village of

2km Hermedesuxo de Abaixo

KSO then at five-point junction at end of village fork R ('one o'clock' style) ahead and KSO ahead, on concrete lane, through hamlet of **San Salvador** 600m, *HR Dugium (rooms) on R*. KSO ahead, rising gently at first, then more steeply. Track joins from back L – KSO here but then fork L 100m later, gently downhill, ignoring turns. *View of sea over to L, through trees.* Continue until you reach a minor road at entrance to hamlet of

2.5km Rial

Cross over and KSO on other side along walled lane. KSO(R) ahead at junction shortly afterwards, // to sea over to your L. Fork L after first house in hamlet (*aggressive dog?*) between *hórreos*, veering L onto tarmac road at entrance to

0.5km Buxan

Turn R at junction 50m later and then watch out for RH turn by sawmill *(this is, in fact, waymarked, but it is only obvious if coming from the other direction)*. Turn R here onto *camino de tierra* into woods, gradually downhill, leading down to a tarmac road at a forked junction. KSO(L) here and then turn L down *camino de tierra*, steeply downhill *(sea over to L)* and then up, in a dead straight line. KSO(R) up lane at end and then veer R into

1.5km Castrexe

Turn L onto *camino de tierra*, undulating through fields. Reach tarmac road at bend, turn R up it and 250m later, at top of hill, reach junction in hamlet of

1km Padris

Turn L on road, then fork L along *camino de tierra* under electricity cables. This leads into the woods. KSO ahead in a straight line all the time, ignoring turns for 800m, then fork R in a small clearing along lane with walls to either side. 500m later veer R, then L, then 100m after that **you have two options**, as the bollard ahead indicates a RH turn but the arrows painted on it also indicate a LH turn. The RH route goes through the village of Canosa, the LH one misses it out and goes straight to Lires, nearer to the sea.

a) Route via Canosa *(marked with bollards throughout)*. Fork R here along walled lane. At end fork R, steeply downhill, down gravel lane towards village, leaving woods. Turn hard R at junction at bottom, onto concrete lane, then turn L steeply downhill again, in

2.5km Canosa

Turn L again, second R and then L onto concrete walled lane, still downhill. Turn L at junction onto *camino de tierra*, KSO(L) at next junction and KSO(R) at the next and continue alongside a small river (on your R). At junction by a bridge turn L then 100m later turn R at T-junction of similar tracks. KSO along side of hill (// to road over to your R) then veer R to road. Turn L along it for 200m to junction with a bridge to L and church to R and turn R uphill in

1.5km Lires.

b) Route direct to Lires *marked (rather sparsely) with yellow arrows. Splendid views on a nice day.*

Fork L here, along walled lane alongside edge of woods *(view of sea over to L ahead)*. KSO ahead at first two junctions then fork L at third. Descend to junction with short stretch of tarmac road, near sea. Turn R here then fork R onto *camino de tierra*, into scrubby woods, veering R and then leading downhill. Turn L at junction then R along very minor road alongside the **Río Lires**. Pass cemetery (R) and turn L to cross bridge over river and KSO(L) uphill by church in

1.5km Lires
Two bars (one, As Eiras, does food and has rooms, 981 74 .81.80). Fountain. Two CL (*casas de labranza* – i.e. bed and breakfast) Casa Raul and Casa Lourido. Many interesting *hórreos*. Church of San Estevo.

Fork L at *cruceiro*, veering L, fork R uphill then turn L on the level by *hórreo* with six sets of 'legs' *(turn R here for the two bars and to turn L for road option via Ponte Nova***)*. Fork R onto concrete lane which then > a walled *camino de tierra*, leading down to the Río Castro. Cross over via stepping stones and veer L on other side to a *lugar* (consisting of a single house), **Baosilveiro**.

***To avoid having to wade across the Río Castro turn L in Lires on road to side of *Bar As Eiras*, turn L to **Porcare** (another hamlet) and cross bridge at **Pontenova** (another *lugar* with a single house) and then turn L to **Frixe**.

0.5km Baosilbeiro

The marker stones lead you up a lane straight ahead (L), then turn R uphill at bend (to L) into woods. KSO(L) at crossing of similar tracks (not marked), which leads you to a minor road where you turn L. However, in bad weather the lane may be completely waterlogged so continue on the minor road ahead of you to the R (at *Baosilbeiro*) as the two options join up again shortly afterwards anyway. KSO on minor road to

1.5km Frixe
Bar/tienda 500m away, Romanesque church of Santa Leocadia.

Turn L in hamlet and then almost immediately R, up concrete lane which then > walled *camino de tierra* and then veers L. KSO in a straight line all the time, ignoring turns, and reach a tarmac road (road to *Touriñan*). Cross over and KSO on gravel road on other side, through woods. KSO, in a straight line, very slightly uphill all the time, ignoring turns, for 1km approx., after which tracks begins to descend. 200–300m later turn L by barn and then R alongside it, down grassy paved lane *(may be boggy)* and reach road in

2.5km Guisamonde

Turn R then KSO ahead at crossroads, on road uphill through woods. KSO for 2kms, passing *cruceiro* and fountain (both on RH side) and enter

1.5km Morquintián
Romansque church of Santa María.

KSO(R) on upper of two lanes, then KSO(R) on road at fork. 1km later reach T-junction where, once again, **you have two options**:

a) Turn L and 60m later turn up *camino de tierra*. This option is 2km longer and goes alongside the sea *(splendid views on a clear day)* via **Marineto**, **Figueiroa** and **Lourido**, marked only with bollards *(no yellow arrows)*;

b) Turn R on road, then turn L 500m later up wide *camino de tierra*, uphill, veering L and then R *(very good views on a clear day)*. Track levels out after a while. KSO along it. Track then veers R and begins to descend, gradually. KSO(L) at fork and continue to descend.

After about 2km turn R down wide track and then L some 800m later. Reach T-junction with concrete lane at first houses and turn L in

5km Xurarantes

Turn R at minor road in hamlet, downhill. Pass **fountain** on L and 60m later turn R downhill to junction with bigger road. Turn L. KSO on road for 2km (fork L down *camino de tierra* and continue to beach at bend in road 1.5km later) and enter

3km Muxía
Small coastal town with all facilities, founded in the twelfth century and whose main activities are fishing and bobbin lace-making. Hostal Cruz on sea-front near entrance to town. Pilgrims can sleep in the sports centre (in middle of town – gym mats, hot showers – ask at Protección Civil for key). Tourist office. Romanesque parish church of Santa María, many interesting old houses in town centre.

Continue ahead and after houses start road > **Avenida Doctor Toba**. Reach *plaza* with modern statue in middle, cross over and KSO(L) along paved walkway then KSO(R) ahead along short unnamed street. This continues as the **Rúa Atalaia**, a very long street. KSO along it, crossing a square part way, along to the very end and then KSO ahead along wide *camino de tierra* leading below **Monte Corpiño** on the **Camiño da Pel** *(so named because the existence of a nearby fountain allowed*

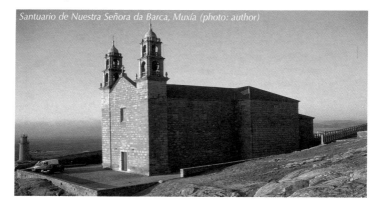
Santuario de Nuestra Señora da Barca, Muxía (photo: author)

*pilgrims to perform their ablutions (a symbol of purification) before entering the
Santuario).* This track leads directly to the

1km Santuario de Nosa Señora da Barca
The church's name derives from the stone boat in which the Virgin Mary is said
to have journeyed there in order to encourage St James in his preaching and
evangelising mission in Spain. The church dates from the twelfth century and has
a large Baroque altarpiece inside. A Gothic statue of the Virgin Mary, reputed to
have been brought there in a boat guided by two angels. The Santuario is the
focus of one of the most popular *romerías* in Galicia, held each year on the first
Sunday after 8th September.

You can return to Santiago (or A Coruña) by bus twice a day, either directly or by
changing in Cée. Buses leave from *Bar Día y Noche* on the seafront.

HOSPITAL–MUXÍA 27km

In this section the direction to proceed in is indicated by the rays of the 'shell' on
the bollards (and which indicate the number of kilometres remaining to *Muxía*).
(**Note:** as this section is only waymarked in **one** direction (towards *Muxía*), it is
more difficult to follow in reverse.)

Hospital

At marker stone 29,730, turn L into road by bus shelter. Continue to **Bar Casteliño** *(bar, rte)*, cross main road and continue on old road to junction with **two** marker stones: 'Fisterra 28,807, Muxía 27,005.'

Fork R on road (marked 'Dumbría 4.5'), go down hill and 1km later, just before bend, turn L down FP, downhill. Cross small river by solid granite FB and veer L uphill on old track that > a walled lane. Return to road at 600m later, cross over and continue on wide, clear grassy track *(good views)*, descending gradually and veering L to return to road after 500m. Turn R along road for 300m, then turn hard L down forest track, veering R downhill into hamlet of **Carizas**. Turn R on a very small road then R again at a 'stop' sign 500m later. Return to main road at entrance to

6km Dumbría
Several bars, supermarket, bank (CD), Bar 'O Argentino' (below bank) does meals, fountain.

Turn L, passing sports ground and sitting area and then Baroque **church of Santa Eulalia** and two-sided *cruceiro (note* hórreo *with eight pairs of 'mushroom-style' legs and two crosses on top)*. Continue through town and turn L by **Centro de Saude** (health centre).

KSO at 'stop' sign and continue to main (Cée–La Coruña) road, crossing road bridge over the **Río Fragoso**. Cross over *(very carefully)* and KSO ahead up walled lane on other side, with eucalyptus woods to either side. 400–500m later reach minor road (to your L) and turn R here along another walled lane, into woods. KSO, ignoring turns, keep to LH side of wall, turn R at end and 50m later (marker stone 20,416) turn L on lane alongside another wall (on R), turning R, L and R, downhill, to minor road in

3km Trasufe
A lot of *hórreos*, small church of N–S de Arantazu/Virxe do Espiño.

Turn R and KSO on road, veering L past *cruceiro* and church. Turn L at junction and then R by bus shelter. KSO, cross bridge over Río Castro and 60m later turn R behind house (in **Cadeiro**) up wide *camino de tierra*, veering L uphill. Turn R at

281

T-junction of similar tracks 500m later, turn L 75m afterwards then turn R 60m after that. Continue ahead until you reach the village of

2.5km Senande
Two bars, shop/tabaco.

KSO(R) on main road coming from back L to square with seats and then turn L on minor road marked 'Agrodosio/Vilastose/Casanova.' Pass turning to **Agrodosio** (on your L) and then KSO(L) ahead at junction marked 'Vilastose' then KSO(R) at entrance to **A Grixa** (marker stone 16,134). *Cruceiro opposite.* Pass church (on L) and its separate bell tower (on R) of **San Cibrán de Vilastose**. Turn L on road at end of village. *Note house on RH corner with large* hórreo *(with nine pairs of legs) on its roof!*

KSO on road then 250m later turn R onto walled lane, then L at fork 150m later, leading towards woods. KSO ahead at first crossing and at second 700m later.

At next junction, 650m after that, take second of 2 LH forks, onto wide walled lane. KSO, undulating, to outskirts of village then turn R downhill to junction and KSO ahead to school and church *(seats, shade)* in

4km Quintáns
Two bars, shop, fountain, Rte Plaza (also has rooms).

Cross road and fork L down street. KSO(L) at turn and KSO(L) ahead at junction, pass barn and reach minor road. Turn L along it. Continue ahead at crossing on CT between fields. Reach a road, turn L, and almost immediately turn R down walled lane, forking R and R again downhill. *(View of VERY large* hórreo *ahead to R).* KSO ahead at crossing, pass the very long *hórreo (with 22 pairs of legs)* and turn R at second *cruceiro* into hamlet of

1.5km San Martiño de Ozón
Church with Romanesque apse, site of former Benedictine monastery. Note capitals under eaves of apses at rear of building.

Pass church *(shady seats – good place for a rest, fountain).* KSO to end of village and after last (industrial) building on R KSO ahead on road. KSO, gently uphill, semi-shaded, then climbing increasingly steeply. (*View of small town of Camariños on the other side of the bay from Muxía ahead through trees on LH bend at top.*)

1.5km later turn L at unmarked junction. KSO(L) down to road and KSO ahead, // to sea. Fork R downhill after house no. 117 and pass a marker stone. 50m before junction and, shortly before place-name board for **Merexe** (*Casa Carmelo does meals*) KSO on road for 2.5km to large village of

> ### 4km Os Muiños
> So-named because of the large number of mills there in the past. Bars, rte, shop, hotel, *panadería, farmacia*.

KSO ahead at junction and entrance to village then turn R at junction in centre, veering L, then turn R over bridge over stream and reach a main road at a junction (*several bars to L*) where road divides for Cée/Corcubíon and Muxía. *Aparthotel Los Molinos (by day or longer, 612-709-625).*

Fork L and then R again, downhill. KSO(R) downhill at next fork then, 350m later, fork L up paved grassy lane uphill. Cross main road and go up paved FP on other side to church of

> ### 1km Moraime
> Twelfth-century church of San Julián, former Benedictine monastery.

Turn R up steps and turn L on road uphill. Turn R uphill. Reach minor road at top at junction, cross over and go straight ahead, uphill into woods to the

> ### 1km Capilla San Roque
> Statue of San Roque Peregrino inside, with wound on RH leg, angel/child and dog at his heel, hat (and shell), stick.

Fork L onto *camino de tierra*, pass in front of chapel (*recently restored*). Track > tarmac road when houses start. Reach T-junction and turn R. Turn L at junction 100m later, then L at fork, then fork L at last house onto wide walled lane, descending steadily.

Pass concrete building and watch out for arrows on the ground 20m later, then fork L down FP (*view over to Muxía, L, as you go down*). Continue downhill, veering L, to continue along walled lane. This leads downhill, turns R by eucalyptus woods and reaches road by the **Playa de Espiñeirido** (beach). Turn L.

Pass (smart) bar/rte (on L) and then, opposite a second one, turn R onto sandy track (marker stone 2278). 250m later fork L, pass between two sets of boundary posts and KSO on FP to road ahead. Turn R and KSO, continuing ahead when it > the **Paseo Maritimo** (*HS/Rte La Cruz on L at start*). Fork L onto **Avenida López Abente** (*named after a local poet*) and then continue along the **Rúa Real** to a square with a fountain and continue ahead on the **Rúa Virxe da Barca**.

> ### 3km Muxía
> Small coastal town with all facilities. Founded in the twelfth century and whose main activities are fishing and bobbin lace-making. Hostal Cruz on sea-front near entrance to town. Pilgrims can sleep in the sports centre (in middle of town – gym mats, hot showers – ask at Protección Civil for key). Tourist office. Romanesque parish church of Santa María, many interesting old houses in town centre.

Pass tourist office (on L) and turn hard L opposite *Casa Rectoral* (no. 34) and continue along **Rúa Encarnación** then turn hard R at *cruceiro* to parish church. Pass to L of it and continue on paved walkway, high up, descending, at end, to

> ### 1km Santuario de Nosa Señora da Barca.
> The church's name derives from the stone boat in which the Virgin Mary is said to have journeyed there in order to encourage St James in his preaching and evangelising mission in Spain. The church dates from the twelfth century and contains a large Baroque altarpiece inside, with a Gothic statue of the Virgin Mary, reputed to have been brought there in a boat guided by two angels. The Santuario is the focus of one of the most popular *romerías* in Galicia, held each year on the first Sunday after 8th September.

You can return to Santiago (or A Coruña) by bus twice a day, either directly or by changing in Cée. Buses leave from **Bar Día y Noche** *on the seafront.*

MUXÍA–FINISTERRE 28km

The continuation from Muxía to Finisterre is waymarked in **both** directions – there and back – but economically. That is, there is only one stone at each manoeuvre, set at an angle to indicate which way to go, so you will need to watch out carefully at turns. The marker bollards have the shell **upright** on this route but have no kilometre indications, simply 'Fisterra–Muxía' (or 'Muxía–Fisterra'), according to where these two places are situated.

Take food and water with you – the only place with any facilities is Lires (two bars, one selling food).

Note: until the footbridge scheduled for 2004 has been built you will have to remove your shoes/boots and wade across the Río Castro (500m before Lires), via the stepping stones. This is not a problem in very dry weather but when it has been raining they will be partly submerged. It is better to put your boots in your rucksack to avoid them dangling and unsteadying you (and roll up your trousers if you are not wearing shorts) and cutting your feet. Stick(s) recommended. The water is very clear and not very deep but watch out for the current. However, a longer, road alternative is also available and is described later.

With your back to the church of **Nosa Señora da Barca** and the sea, fork R along a wide, unpaved road (sea to your R). This > the **Rúa Atalaia**, a very long street. KSO along it right to the very end, passing a small square on the way. Continue ahead along another street (short, unnamed) and then along the pedestrianised walkway by the sea, leading to a plaza with a modern sculpture in the middle. Cross it and continue L ahead up the **Avenida Doctor Toba**, which leads you out of town, alongside the sea.

KSO. 1km later pass turning to Praia de Lourido (a beach). 2km from town reach a road junction and fork R uphill (on same road) then turn L uphill at a T-junction, passing fountain (on R, with cross) into

4km Xurarantes

Fork L onto concrete lane in hamlet, slightly downhill then, 100m later, turn R onto wide *camino de tierra*, leading past a *nave* (industrial building) on R, uphill into woods. Turn R at T-junction then second L 50m later on, up wide, sunken lane uphill. Ignore turning hard L downhill when you reach the top. KSO and then KSO(L) at fork shortly afterwards, when track levels out a bit.

5km Morquintián
Romanesque church of Santa María.

KSO(R) through hamlet at fork and continue ahead past *cruceiro* and fountain (both on L) at end. KSO on road for 1km to

1.5km Guisamonde

KSO ahead at road junction with bus shelter and 50m later fork up grassy paved lane between *hórreos* (may be boggy). 100m later turn R onto gravelled walled lane and KSO, gently downhill all the time, ignoring turns, until you reach a road. Cross over and continue on other side. KSO, leading downhill, as concrete lane at end, to hamlet of

2.5km Frixe
Bar/tienda 500m away, Romanesque church of Santa Leocadia.

Join road leading through village but then turn R almost immediately onto small tarmac road leading uphill into woods. *However*, to avoid having to wade across the Río Castro you can KSO ahead here (instead of turning R), turn R to cross the bridge at **Pontenova** (another *lugar* with a single house), continue to **Porcare** (another hamlet) and then turn R onto road leadng to Lires, passing to the side of the Bar As Eiras.

Otherwise: KSO, descending gradually at first and then more steeply, and some 800m after Frixe, when you see a house through the trees ahead, fork (not turn) R into woods, alongside wall on L to start with. (In very wet weather continue along road to **Baosilbeiro**). KSO ahead (i.e. third from L – not marked) at crossing of similar tracks then turn L at bottom along lane coming from R (may be waterlogged) and KSO down to

1.5km Baosilbeiro
Lugar consisting of a single house.

Continue ahead down shady lane, passing to R of house, veering L and then R down to banks of the **Río Castro** 300m later. Wade across and then fork L up lane on other side. Continue on concrete lane, veering L. Turn L along street in

0.5km Lires
Two bars (one, As Eiras, does food and has rooms, 981 74 81 80). Fountain. Two CL (*casas de labranza* i.e. bed and breakfast), Casa Raul and Casa Lourido. Many interesting *hórreos*. Church of San Estevo.

Fork R downhill (*continue L ahead here for bars*) and follow road down to church and turn L on road just before a bridge. 200m later turn R up walled lane, veering L alongside of hill. At T-junction of similar tracks turn L and then, 100m later, turn R onto track just before a small bridge and continue alongside river. KSO(L) at junction then KSO(R) up hill at next. Reach a concrete walled lane and turn R up it, uphill into

1.5km Canosa

Turn R, turn L and then R again, steeply uphill, then R at top to leave village, all on concrete lanes. Turn hard L at top, up gravel lane, steeply uphill again, towards woods, and at top fork L along stony walled lane. At junction at end turn L (*this is the place where the deviant route via the sea rejoins – yellow arrows only – in Fisterra–Muxía direction*).

Turn R at fork 100m later and then L 50m after that. Turn L at next junction (of similar tracks). KSO ahead, ignoring turns, until you reach a road in the hamlet of

2.5km Padris

Turn R along it then, 100m later, turn R at junction, downhill (marked 'Praia do Rostro'). 250m after that, at bend, turn L onto *camino de tierra*, undulating through fields. Turn R onto road 500m later in

1km Castrexe

Veer L, then KSO(L) down long, dead straight *camino de tierra*, downhill and then up. KSO uphill, ignoring turns, then at T-junction at top, turn R along tarmac road. 200m later fork R onto *camino de tierra* leading into woods. Continue gradually uphill and turn L onto road by sawmill in hamlet of

1.5km Buxan

Turn L at junction, veering L. Fork R up lane between *hórreos* and then KSO(R) on walled lane coming from R. KSO, veering R, with woods to either side. KSO, ignoring turns, until you reach a minor road at entrance to

1km Rial

Cross over and KSO on other side, above hamlet. KSO. At junction with a large forest track coming from L turn R downhill. Fork L shortly afterwards, downhill all the time. Leave woods and continue on concrete lane in hamlet of **San Salvador.** KSO(R) ahead at crossing with *cruceiro* and reach junction with a more main road at entrance to

2.5km Hermedesuxo de Abaixo

KSO on road then turn R in minor road (marked 'Fisterra/Escaselas'). Turn 1st R on old concrete road, veering L uphill, and follow it round. KSO(R) uphill at junction, then turn L at next one, passing in front of church of

2km San Martiño de Duyo
Duyo (Latin Dugium) was the former Roman city where, according to medieval tradition, the disciples bringing St James's body sought permission to bury it in this area.

KSO. KSO ahead at junction by bus shelter and veer L downhill to main road. Turn R and continue on, past *cruceiro* (on L), to centre of

2km Fisterra
See description on page 272.

Typical hórreo

APPENDIX B
Summary of Santiago and Pilgrim References

(a) Seville to Astorga

Seville 1. Cathedral a) Puerta de San Miguel has carving of Santiago Peregrino b) Capilla de Santiago has painting of St James the Great at the battle of Clavijo by Juan de Roelas, 1609, on R as well as stained-glass window of Battle of Clavijo. 2. Hospital de la Caridad has statue of San Roque with scallops and staff in chapel, on RH side of main altarpiece.

Almadén de la Plata formerly had church dedicated to Santiago.

Calera de León Conventual de Santiago, monastery of Order of Santiago founded by Pelay Pérez in 1275, master of Order of Santiago a) Painting behind high altar in monastery church of Nuestra Señora de la Asunción depicts knights carrying banner of Order of Santiago in battle against Moors b) Stained glass of apse contains swords of Santiago.

Monasterio de Nuestra Señora de Tentudía Belonged to Order of Santiago. Italian tiled altarpiece in RH Santiago chapel with Santiago Matamoros.

Fuente de Cantos Church of Nuestra Señora de la Granada has statue of San Roque inside on R and statue of Santiago Apóstol (with shells on each lapel) on altar mayor.

Calzadilla de los Barros Town coat of arms contains scallop shell and sword of Santiago.

Zafra 1. Hospital de Santiago (now mental hospital), founded by los Condes de Feria in 1457. 2. Colegiata de Nuestra Señora de la Candelaria has statue of Santiago Apóstol to upper R of main altar. 3. Arco del Cubo, Campo de Rosario, has equestrian Santiago bas-relief.

Los Santos de Maimona 1. Town coat of arms with Cruz de Santiago. 2. Palacio de la Encomienda (command headquarters of military Order of Santiago) is now *ayuntamiento*. 3. Church of Nuestra Señora de los Angeles has a) Puerta del Perdón and b) lion with sword of Santiago above door. Town formerly belonged to Knights of Santiago and had five *ermitas,* including one from 1504 onwards dedicated to Santiago.

Villafranca de los Barros Church of Santa María del Valle has a) much shell decoration inside: shells on collars around pillars of south porch, south nave and around south nave portal b) statue of San Roque with very large scallop shell, staff and big leg wound in south porch c) Santiago Apóstol with book and shell in main altarpiece on RH side, centre, of main altarpiece. (Town also belonged to Knights of Santiago.)

Almendralejo Another town reconquored from Moors by Order of Santiago (1241). 1. Church of Purificación de Nuestra Señora has escutcheon incorporating scallop and sword of Santiago in apse. 2. Capilla de Santiago. 3. Church of San Roque in western suburbs.

Torremegía Palacio del Marquesado de Torremegía has ring of huge scallops around Renaissance main portal.

Mérida 1. Church of Santa María (church of last Master of the Order of Santiago) has escutcheon incorporating scallops and cross of Santiago on west door. 2. Church of Santa Eulalia has stone bas-relief of Santiago Peregrino with hat and staff on pulpit.

Aljucén Church of San Andrés (inside) has Santiago crosses on all its pedestals.

Casas de Don Antonio 1. Ermita de Nuestra Señora del Pilar at exit to village has a) relief sculpture of Santiago Apóstol, with hat, on altarpiece and b) tiny statue of Santiago Matamoros on prancing horse, taken on annual romería on May 1st. 2. Ermita de Casa de Santiago Bencaliz (which has small Roman bridge behind it).

Cáceres 1. Town coat of arms includes sword of Santiago, scallop shells. 2. Escutcheon of sword of Santiago and scallop shells on façade of a) Palacio de Hernando de Ovando, Plaza Santa María and b) in cloister in Casa de Lorenzo de Ulloa, Calle Ancha. 3. Iglesia de Santiago a) bas-relief of pilgrim with staff, scrip, hat, shell above north portal (first pilgrim figure on journey) b) collars of scallop shells encircle north portal pillars c) Baroque main altarpiece has huge Santiago Matamoros at Clavijo d) south chapel has wooden chairs with scallop shells on back e) stained glass in apse contains sword of Santiago. 4. Iglesia de Santa María a) relief sculpture of Santiago Matamoros in main altarpiece (sixteenth century, possibly by Roque Balduque) b) wooden sculpture of Santiago Peregrino.

Casar de Cáceres 1. Iglesia de la Asunción in centre of village has Baroque wood painted Santiago on LH side of main altarpiece with fine Santiago Peregrino complete with staff, gourd, hat and scallop. Modern but inverted black scallop in grille of southwest chapel. 2. Ermita de Santiago, at end of village, has modern Santiago Matamoros with giant sword above altar.

Cañaveral Sixteenth-century Ermita de San Roque.

Galisteo Church of Santa María has scallops in groups of five in decorative ironwork in north portal.

Carcaboso Modern church of Santiago Apóstol with glass roundel of Santiago Matamoros above west door.

Plasencia 1. New Cathedral: Santiago Peregrino on main altarpiece (bottom R). 2. Old Cathedral: scallop shell decoration on pillars in its cloisters. 3. Old Cathedral museum has eighteenth-century statue of Santiago Apóstol. 4. Sculpture of Santiago Peregrino in town walls.

Aldeanueva del Camino San Servando, one of its two parish churches, has modern tiled Santiago panel above high altar.

Baños de Montemayor A casa-hospital belonging to *ayuntamiento* in Plaza de la Alberguería existed here until nineteenth century.

Valverde de Valdelacasa 1. Iglesia de Santiago. 2. Calle Camino de Santiago. 3. Remains of former hospital, 1704 in lintel, with Santiago cross in coat of arms.

Fuenterrobles de Salvatierra Formerly had both ermita and hospital dedicated to Santiago; latter was demolished in 1770 due to bad condition. Was also Santiago fountain in area, near Sierra de Tanda.

Pico de la Dueña now topped by sword of Santiago.

Salamanca 1. Twelfth-century brick church of Santiago by Roman bridge with sword of Santiago in escutcheon on west front. 2. Old Cathedral a) Talavera chapel: shield with scallop shells b) Salas Capitalinas: statue of Santiago Apóstol with book, dressed in white c) Santa Catalina chapel: statue of San Roque d) Anaya chapel has marble bas-relief of Santiago Peregrino on base of tomb of Don Gutiérrez de Monroy and tiny alabaster bas-relief of heavily bearded Santiago with other apostles along base of alabaster tomb of Bishop Anaya. 3. New Cathedral: painted wood statue of Santiago Apóstol in north aisle of Capilla de Santiago. 4. Convento de Sancti Spiritu, its church associated with the Order of Santiago: a) Santiago Matamoros in pediment of north portal b) Santiago Matamoros in pediment of south portal with medallion of head of Santiago Peregrino L, above south portal c) painted Santiago Matamoros in centre of main altarpiece d) stone Santiago Apóstol in north aisle. 5. Colegio Arzobispo Fonseca

(Irish College): medallion of Santiago Matamoros above main portal and frieze of scallop shells. 6. Corner of Calle Cervantes and Calle Rabanal: shell escutcheon. 7. Convento de las Dueñas: medallion of San Roque and shell motifs in lower cloister. 8. University – Patio de las Escuelas: shell decoration in ironwork of main doorway. 9. Casa de las Conchas, civilian residence so named for its shell-covered facade, built c. 1490 by Dr Rodrigo Arias Talavera Maldonado, knight of the Order of the Knights of Santiago in Salamanca. 10. Museum has statue with attributes of Santiago Apóstol with shell on hat.

Calzada de Valdunciel Statue of Santiago Peregrino in church of Santa Elena, in sandals and with no hat.

Villanueva de Campeán Calle de Santiago.

Zamora 1. Twelfth-century Romanesque church of Santiago del Burgo has painted bas-relief of Santiago Matamoros above painted wooden statue of Santiago Apóstol with staff and book on main altarpiece. 2. Second Santiago church, outside town walls, tiny Romanesque Ermita de Santiago de los Caballeros. 3. Church of San Claudio de Olivares has statue of San Roque Peregrino. 4. Cathedral: gilded statue of Santiago Peregrino with hat, scallop, gourd and staff in niche on RH side of chancel. 5. Cathedral museum: painting of head of Santiago on RH side of predella of wall-mounted San Ildefonso altarpiece.

Castrotorafe Ruins of Castillo, seat of Order of the Knights of Santiago.

Benavente Former Hospital de la Piedad has pilgrim doorknocker and scallops incorporated into arms of founder on main facade. Modern church of Santiago in suburbs.

Alija del Infantado Modern Cruz del Orden de Santiago on hill high to R above village at exit.

La Bañeza Hospital donated to church of El Salvador in 932 for pilgrims and other needy.

Astorga contained twenty-two pilgrim hospitals in the Middle Ages, the last of which, the Hospital de las Cinco Llagas (the Five Wounds), burned down early in the 20th century. 1. Cathedral: a) tiny statue of *Santiago Peregrino* above main west portal b) bas-relief of procession of pilgrims, tympanum of west portal c) statue of Santiago, chapel of north wall d) painting of Santiago among other apostles on the side of a wooden chest from the Cistercian monastery of Carrizo de la Ribera, in the diocesan museum. 2. Museo de los Caminos, Palacio Episcopal has several stone/poly-chrome/wood statues of Santiago. 3. Church of San Pedro, main facade covered in pilgrim themes: mosaics – route, churches, hospitals and pilgrims – prepared for *Las Edades de del Hombre* (exhibition) in 2000.

(b) Granada to Mérida

Granada Iglesia de Santiago, sixteenth century, in the Calle Marques de Falces (off the Gran Vía). Statue of 'hybrid' St James over entrance door. Hat, with shell at front, stick missing, book. (Nothing re. St James inside the church.)

Alcalá la Real Fortaleza de la Mota has 1. Puerta de Santiago. 2. Iglesia Mayor Abacial (abbey church) has a) LH door to side room (on upper level when facing altar) has 15 convex *conchas* round its frame b) Capilla la Peregrina has large (concave) scallop shell in wall (where an altar would be) in chapel (to L of door on entering church) plus 14 (concave) scallops on arch at entrance.

Córdoba Iglesia de Santiago, with tile Matamoros figure in the porch and a painting of Santigo Peregrino/Apóstol over the altar.

Don Benito Thirteenth-century Iglesia de Santiago, in the Plaza de España, has a) painting of Santiago Matamoros in the middle panel of the lower row of paintings in the reredos and b) an almost life-size statue of Santiago Peregrino on RH side altar, with both a halo and a hat (with a scallop shell on it), stick, gourd and scallops on his cape.

Medellín Iglesia de Santiago, closed as a place of worship, is now a *centro de interpretación* (visitors' centre) for the Parque Arqueológico.

(c) Tábara to Santiago

Santa Marta de Tera Santiago Peregrino statue in LH portal of south door.

Pumarejo de Tera Church dedicated to Santiago.

Olleros de Tera Formerly had pilgrim hospital.

Rionegro del Puente 1. Former pilgrim hospital (building still exists). 2. Former church of Santiago (only tower left) is now cemetery chapel. 3. Cofradía de los Falifos, oldest such organisation devoted to looking after pilgrims, still functioning. 4. Santuario de Nuestra Señora de Carballada has freestanding statues of St James as pilgrim on RH side wall inside and St Roch as pilgrim (on left).

Triufé House that was formerly pilgrim hospital still standing.

Terroso Church dedicated to Santiago.

Campobecerros Church dedicated to Santiago with modern statue of Santiago pilgrim/apostle in niche over front door and representation of Santiago Matamoros inside building.

Laza Church contains depictions of Virgen del Rosario, Santiago and San Roque Peregrino on main altarpiece.

Albergueria Site of former pilgrim hospital. Statue of Santiago inside church of Santa María.

Vilar de Barrio Scallop shell in town coat of arms.

Xunqueira de Ambía 'Virgen Peregrina' in Baroque pilgrim outfit on side altar of twelfth-century church. St James pilgrim on LH side altar, St Roch pilgrim on RH side altar.

Ourense 1. Cathedral a) Pórtico del Paraíso has seated statue of Santiago, against pillar; sword in RH, open book in LH, with text facing viewer, no hat, three scallop shells at base of column b) Statue of Santiago Matamoros in interior over north door c) Sixteenth-century polychrome Santiago Peregrino set in grille d) Tiny stone bas-relief of Santiago Peregrino above north portal (part of Deposition scene). 2. Claustro de San Francisco has statue of Santiago Peregrino with scrip, scallop, tau and book on north-east pillar in cloister. 3. Tiny statue of Santiago Peregrino (stone, modern) above a Romanesque tympanum built into modern building on LH side of Avenida de Zamora (on way into town).

Albarellos de Monterrei Church with statue of Santiago Peregrino on south wall.

Monterrey Ruins of eighteenth-century pilgrim hospital in hilltop castle complex.

Xinzo de Limia Romanesque church of Santa Mariña has a) freestanding statue of San Roque on LH side of chancel arch b) capital of a face above giant scallop to RH side of west portal.

Piñeira de Arcos Modern *cruceiro* with statue of Santiago Peregrino on shaft.

Allariz Church dedicated to Santiago. Both this and church of San Estevo have statues of San Roque Peregrino inside.

Faramontaos Village formerly had pilgrim hospital.

Oseira Formerly had pilgrim hospital a) Monastery church of Santa María la Real has Baroque altarpiece with painting of Santiago Peregrino b) Monastery cloister has polychrome statue of Santiago Peregrino in niche in north-east corner of upper Galeria de Claustro Procesional.

Puxallos Ermita de San Roque.

Taboada Church of Santiago has a) painting of Santiago Matamoros in Baroque altarpiece inside building b) modern statue of Santiago Peregrino in sitting area outside.

Bandeira Formerly had pilgrim hospital.

Capilla de Santiaguiño (between Ponte Ulla and Susana) 1. Chapel dedicated to Santiago, built 1696, restored 2000. 2. Fountain with statue of Santiago Peregrino in niche above it.

Santiago de Compostela 1. Cathedral
   a) Statue of St James and his companions Anastasius and Theodore above the Puerta Santa
   b) Platerías facade – spindly Santiago Apóstol is to Christ's R in the Apostles frieze above the portal
   c) Azabachería facade – *Santiago Peregrino* flanked by kneeling figures of Alfonso VI and Ordono II at the very top of the facade above the doors
   d) Obradoiro facade: centre top *Santiago Peregrino;* above entrance to crypt – tiny bas-relief of *Santiago Matamoros*
   e) Pórtico de la Gloria: St James seated with tau cross on the trumeau and scroll; *Santiago Apóstol,* right panel of Apostles
   f) *Santiago Matamoros:* west side of north Azabachería arm of the transept – statue in glass case; Clavijo tympanum – stone bas-relief of *Santiago Matamoros,* west side of the south, Platerías arm of the transept
   g) Polychrome statue of *Santiago Peregrino,* altarpiece of Capilla de San Bartolomé, northeast ambulatory
   h) Capilla de las Reliquias, south aisle has: Gilded statuette of Santiago Coquatriz; gilded statue of *Santiago Peregrino* of Don Alvaro de Isorno; *Santiago Peregrino* – tiny silver statue

i) Niche statue of *Santiago Peregrino*, west wall of the south (Platerías) arm of the transept above the door to the Sacristy

j) Stained glass seated *Santiago Peregrino* in the ambulatory above the Holy Door (the inside one)

k) Chancel – Capilla Mayor has: *Santiago Matamoros* crowning the baldechín; *Santiago Peregrino* standing on top of the Camerín; Seated *Santiago Peregrino* in the camarín – the 'hug' Santiago

l) Neo-Romanesque silver casket containing the body of St James and his disciples Anastasius and Theodore in the crypt under the Capilla Mayor

m) Cloister: *Santiago Peregrino*, left side of the altarpiece of the Transfiguration of Christ, Capilla de Alba, NW corner of cloister

n) Polychrome statue of *Santiago Peregrino*, left side of altarpiece of Capilla del Salvador (chapel of the Kings of France), axial chapel of ambulatory

o) Museum of the Cathedral: seated stone polychrome Santiago with tau cross and crown; bronze relief of the Translation of the body of the Apostle to Galicia; polychrome wood and alabaster retablo of the Life of St James, donated by John Goodyear – the Calling, Martyrdom and Translation; gilded wood panel of Queen Lupa's stubborn oxen and the apostle's body in the cart in Galicia; gilded wood rerdos of pilgrims climbing the hill to Santiago; gilded wood panel of Moors returning the bells from Córdoba to Santiago; polychrome wood relief of Santiago preaching in Galicia.

2. Colegio de San Geronimo – north portal, statue of *Santiago Peregrino*, left side.

3. Palacio de Rajoy: *Santiago Matamoros* crowning a triangular pediment of bas-relief of *Santiago Matamoros* at the Battle of Clavijo - main facade.

4. Hostal de los Reyes Católicos: a) statue of *Santiago Peregrino*, top left upper frieze above the main south portal b) statue of *Santiago Peregrino* - centre of the lower frieze of the Apostles above the main south portal c) statue of St James, right jamb of main south portal.

5. Monasterio de San Martín Pinario (in its museum) a) statue of the Virgen del Pilar and Child appearing to a kneeling *Santiago Apóstol* b) statue of *Santiago Matamoros*.

6. Colegiata de Santa María del Sar a) statue of *San Roque Peregrino* in vestry b) statue of *San Roque Peregrino* in north apse.

7. Pilgrimage museum a) Wood relief, *San Roque Peregrino* b) Wood statue of a pilgrim c) Polychrome wood panel painting of Christ as a pilgrim d) Polychrome wood statue, *San Roque Peregrino*, back of a chest e) Santa Isabel, 'Reina de Portugal Aragonesa' – dressed as a lady pilgrim f) Polychrome *Santiago Peregrino* – eight wood ones g) Polychrome granite *Santiago Peregrino* h) Polychrome wood 'Virgen Peregrina' with child i) Stone statue *Santiago Peregrino* three stone ones j) Tapestry/embroidery of *Santiago Apóstol*.

8. Statue of St James above a fountain near Santo Domingo de Bonneval

9. Colegio de Santiago Alfeo/de Fonseca – statue of *Santiago Peregrino* above main portal

10. Huge modern statue of *Santiago Peregrino* in middle of roundabout outside the Xunta de Galica headquarters in the San Caetano area of Santiago (near bus station).

Façade of the Casa de las Conchas, Salamanca

APPENDIX C
Suggestions for Further Reading

General

Fernando Alonso Romero, *Historia, Leyendas y Creencias de Finisterre*, A Coruña: Briga Edcions, 2002.

Donald Atwood and C.R. John, *Penguin Dictionary of Saints*, third ed., Harmondsworth: Penguin, 1995.

Nancy Louise Frey, *Pilgrim Stories*, Berkley and Los Angeles: University of California Press, 1998.

This refers specifically to the experiences of modern pilgrims along the road to Santiago de Compostela, before, during and after making their pilgrimage, but the questions raised confront any modern pilgrim on a route where the journey itself, rather than the destination, is the real issue at stake.

Martin Robinson, *Sacred Places, Pilgrim Paths: an anthology of pilgrimage,* London: Fount, 1997.

An anthology reflecting the experiences of pilgrims through the ages, dealing with places of pilgrimage, preparation for the journey, the journey itself, the inner journey, worship on the way and on arrival and the questions raised once the pilgrimage is over.

David Stancliffe, *The Pilgrim Prayer Book,* London: Continuum books, 2003.

Collection of prayers drawing on many christian traditions.

The Way of a Pilgrim, trans. R.M. French, London: Triangle, 1995.

First published in English in 1930 this book was written by an unknown Russian pilgrim in the nineteenth century, telling the story of his wanderings from one holy place to another in Russia and Siberia in search of the way of prayer.

Camino Mozárabe/Vía de la Plata

Actas. Congreso sobre o Camiño Xacobeo na Provincia de Ourense, Xunta de Galicia (Consellería de Cultura, Dirección Xeral de Promoción do Camiño de Santiago), 1995.

Collection of papers (in Spanish) given at a conference in 1993 on the history, geography and tradition of the Camino de Santiago in the province of Ourense.

Joaquein Miguel Alonso and Juan Luis Rodríguez, *La Vía de la Plata*, León: Editorial Everest, 2004.

Walkers/cyclists guide book to the original *calzada romana* from Mérida to Astorga (not the waymarked pilgrim route), containing extensive bibliography on Roman roads (in Spanish).

María Cuenda and Darío Izquierdo, *La Virgen María en las Rutas Jacobeas. Ruta meridional – Vía de la Plata*. 1999

One of a set of three volumes (the other two deal with the Camino Francés and the Camino Portugués) that examines representations in art and architecture of the Virgen Mary along the Vía de la Plata, many of them linked with the theme and portrayals of St James. Contains excellent photographs.

Hermenegilde de la Campa Martínez, *De Granada a Santiago. Una ruta andaluza*, Granada: Grupo Editorial Universitario, 1999.

An account of the experiences of the pilgrimage on foot made by members of the Granada Association during the summers of 1994, 1995, 1996 and 1997. (Note, however, that they made this before the route was changed between Villaharta and Monterrubio de la Serena.]

José Eligio Rivas, *Camino meridional de Santiago, continuación de la Vía de la Plata*, Xunta de Galicia.

History of the places the route goes through in the Galician section.

Salvador Llopis, *Por Salamanca también pasa el Camino de Santiago*, Salamanca, 1965, reprinted 1998: Fuenterroble de Salvatierra (Salamanca), Asociación de Amigos del Camino de Santiago 'Vía de la Plata'.

As its title indicates, this book describes the route in the province of Salamanca, including variants. Originally published in 1965 but reprinted in 1998 by the 'Amigos' in Fuenterroble de Salvatierra.

La Ruta de la Plata a pie y en bicicleta: monumentos, gastronomía, refugios, etapas, Madrid: El País Aguilar, 2000.

Practical guide to the route but only from Mérida to Astorga. Contains very good maps and information on the Roman aspects of the route (roads, bridges, history) but very little on the Vía de la Plata as a pilgrimage route.

La Ruta de la Plata, Camino Mozárabe de Santiago, Bilbao: Sua Edizoak, 1996.

A guide to the route for motorists but with background information and photographs of interest to all types of pilgrim.

La Ruta de la Plata de Sevilla a Gijón, León: Ediciones Lancia, 1993.

Guide to the history of the route and its monuments, with good photographs.

La Ruta de la Plata: Guía práctica del viajero, Madrid: Editorial Everest, 1994.

Another guide to the route for motorists but with background material and photographs of interest to all types of pilgrim.

José Sendín Blázquez, *Calzada y Camino de Santiago – Vía de la Plata – Historia, Mito, Leyenda*, Zamora: Fundación Ramos de Castro, 1992.

As its title suggests, this is a collection of writings pertaining to the local history, myths and legends surrounding the southern route to Santiago.

José Sendín Blázquez, *Mitos y leyendas del Camino de Santiago del Sur*, Plasencia: Ediciones Lancia, 1996.

A further collection of history, myths and legends about people and places along the Vía de la Plata.

APPENDIX D
Useful Addresses

Associations
Confraternity of Saint James
27 Blackfriars Rd,
London SE1 8NY
☎ (020) 7928 9988
www.csj.org.uk
office@csj.org.uk

Amigos del Camino de Santiago de Sevilla: Vía de la Plata
Calle San Jacinto 25, Portal 6, Local 4,
41010 Sevilla.
☎ 95 433 5274 or 696 600 602
viaplata.org.es
sevilla@viaplata.org.es

Asociación de Amigos del Camino de Santiago de Granada,
☎ 958.49.93.06/670.85.65.71/607.54.25.16.
www.iespana.es/amigoscaminosantiagodegranada

Asociación de Amigos del Camino de Santiago en Córdoba,
Casa de Galicia, Plaza de San Pedro 1,
14002 Córdoba.
☎ 957.47.64.64.
www.caminomozarabe.es.vg

Asociación de Amigos del Camino de Santiago 'Vía de la Plata'
Calle Larga 37
37768 Fuenterroble de Salvatierra
(Salamanca)
☎ 923.15.10.83

Federación Asociaciones Amigos del Camino de Santiago - 'Vía de la Plata'
Calle Santa Clara 33
49002 Zamora

Websites

As well as those listed above, all of which have links to other sites, you may find the following useful:

www.caminomozarabe.com
www.terra.es/personal6/caminomozarabe/etapas
www.caminosantiago.org/cpperegrino/cpcaminos/caminomozarabe
www.godescalco.com/iphp/etapas.php?via=plata

Bookshops in Santiago

Librería Egeria, Plaza de la Inmaculada 5, 15704 Santiago de Compostela.
　　Up-market religious bookshop.
Librería San Pablo, Rúa do Vilar 39, 15705 Santiago de Compostela.
　　Religious/general bookshop.
Librería Encontros, Rúa do Vilar 68, 15705 Santiago de Compostela.
　　General bookshop.
Librería Gali, Rúa do Vilar 66, 15705 Santiago de Compostela.
　　General bookshop.
Follas Novas, Montero Ríos 37, 15706 Santiago de Compostela.
　　University/general bookshop.
Abraxos Libros, Montero Ríos 50, 15706 Santiago de Compostela.
　　University/general bookshop

Other

Manfred Zentgraf – Verlagsbuchhandel, D-97332 Volkach/Main, In den Böden 38, Germany.
Walking books. Specialises in pilgrim guides.

APPENDIX E
Glossary

One or two linguistic hints may help to equate the Galician words to the Castilian ('Spanish') ones you probably already know (Galician is sometimes described as 'Portuguese with Castilian spelling'). For example:

- dropping intervocalic consonants *(media/meia, salud/saude, arena/area)*
- e = ei *(crucero/cruceiro)*
- ue = o *(puerta/porta, puerta/porta)*
- j = x *(junta/xunta, Jesús/Xesús)*

Plurals of abbreviations: the letters are doubled *(FF.CC: ferrocarriles – seen on road signs crossing railway tracks)*

Words beginning with al-, a- are usually of Arabic origin *(azúcar, alcalde, algodón, albericoque, almacén, almohada)*

agua (non) potable	(not) drinking water
agua non tratada	'untreated' (chlorine-free) water
alameda	poplar grove, avenue, boulevard
albergue	inn; also used to refer to a pilgrim refuge/hostel
alcalde	mayor
alcazaba	citadel, castle
alcázar	fortress, castle
aldea	hamlet
almacén	warehouse, store
alguacil	constable, municipal employee
aljibe	cistern, tank
alto	*hill, height*
arcén	hard shoulder, verge
arroyo	stream, small river
atalaya	watch tower, observation post
ayuntamiento	town hall
barrio	suburb, district
bascula pública	public weighbridge

bodega	wine cellar, tavern; also used to describe a storage place for wine and other items located in hillsides and elsewhere, in the open countryside
cafetería	a café that also serves snacks (not a self-service restaurant for hot meals)
callejón	alley, passageway
calzada	(paved) road, causeway
camino	track, path
camino de tierra	earth road/track
cañada	widest category cattle track, drover's road
cancela	outer door/gate; wrought-iron/lattice gate
capilla	chapel
carretera	(main) road, highway
Casa Consistorial	town hall in small places
Casa do Concello	town hall in small places (in Galicia)
casa huéspedes (CH)	guesthouse
casco antiguo	historic quarter (of a town)
churrería	shop or stall selling *churros* (tubular flour fritters)
cierren la puerta	'close the gate'
cigüena	stork
circunvalación	by-pass, ring road
colegiata/colexiata	collegiate church
cordel	middle category of old cattle/drover's road
corredoira	walled lane (Galicia)
cortefuego(s)	firebreak (in forest)
cortijo	farm, farmhouse (in the south)
coto de caza	hunting/game preserve
coto de pesca	fishing preserve
cruceiro	wayside cross
¡cuidad con el perro!	beware of the dog
dehesa	estate; pastureland
depósito de agua	water tower
desvío	detour, diversion (on roads)
embalse	dam, reservoir
encina	holm oak (an evergreen variety)
ermita	originally a hermitage but nowadays frequently used to describe a small church or chapel
estanco	kiosk (selling tobacco, stamps)
estrada	main road, highway (Galicia)
finca	smallholding

fonda	guesthouse, inn
frontón	pelota court
fuente	fountain, spring
gallego	Galician
gasolinera	petrol station
'la general'	'main road' (= carretera general)
hogar del pensionista	bar/social club for senior citizens
hórreo	(raised) granary
hospedaje	a fonda (in Galicia)
hospedería	inn, hostelry
hostal	hotel (less expensive than a hotel)
humilladero	cross or statue often placed at entrance or exit to village and used for devotional purposes
igrexia/eirexa	church (Galician)
jacobeo/xacobeo (adj.)	of St James
jara	cistus (bush)
latifundio	(very) large estate
lavadero	outdoor washing-place, (public) wash-house
lugar	small collection of houses (a subdivision of a pueblo)
merendero	picnic area, refreshment stall
meseta	plateau, tableland
mesón	restaurant (often simple, with period decor)
minifundio	smallholding, very small farm
molino/muiño	mill
mosteiro	monastery (Galician)
nave	nave (in church); hangar, industrial building
¡ojo al perro!	beware of the dog! (Castilian)
¡ollo o can¡	*beware of the dog! (Galician)*
palmero	*pilgrim who has been to Jerusalem*
panadería	bakery
pantano	marsh, swamp (natural); reservoir, dam (artificial)
pasadero	causeway, stepping stones (in river)
paseo	stroll, walk; avenue
paso canadiense	cattle grid
peregrino	pilgrim
perros sueltos	loose dogs (not tied up)
plaza de toros	bull ring
presa	dam; weir, barrage
posada	inn (simpler than a fonda)
praia fluvial	swimming area (in river)

pueblo	village, small town
puente	bridge
puerta	door, gateway
puerto	mountain pass; port
repetidor	TV mast, transmitter, antenna
rollo	stone wayside cross, often at junctions; raised up and may be highly decorated
rodeo	roundabout or indirect route
romería	pilgrimage to a local shrine
romero	pilgrim (originally one who had been to Rome)
rúa	street (Galician)
santuario	church where, originally, relics of a saint were believed to be kept
sellar	to (rubber) stamp
sello	stamp, seal
senda	(small) path, track
señal	waymark, signal
tapas	light snack taken with drinks in a bar
torre de homenaje	keep
travesía	cross-street, short street which joins two others
ultramarinos	grocer's shop
vega	fertile plain, lowland area, valley (often found in placenames)
venta/venda	country inn (in former times)
vereda	smallest category of cattle/drover's road
villa	small town

For pilgrims who attend mass and who would like to be able to join in at least once during the service the Lord's Prayer is given below in Spanish:

Padre nuestro, que estás en el cielo,
santificado sea tu Nombre;
venga a nosotros tu reino;
hágase tu voluntad en la tierra como en el cielo.
Danos hoy nuestro pan de cada día;
perdona nuestras ofensas,
como también nosotros perdonamos
a los que nos ofenden;
no nos dejes caer en la tentación,
y líbranos del mal.

APPENDIX F
Index of Principal Placenames

APPENDIX G
Index of Maps in this Book

NOTES

NOTES

NOTES

NOTES

LISTING OF CICERONE GUIDES

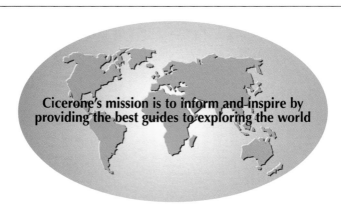

Cicerone's mission is to inform and inspire by providing the best guides to exploring the world

Since its foundation over 30 years ago, Cicerone has specialised in publishing guidebooks and has built a reputation for quality and reliability. It now publishes nearly 300 guides to the major destinations for outdoor enthusiasts, including Europe, UK and the rest of the world.

Written by leading and committed specialists, Cicerone guides are recognised as the most authoritative. They are full of information, maps and illustrations so that the user can plan and complete a successful and safe trip or expedition – be it a long face climb, a walk over Lakeland fells, an alpine traverse, a Himalayan trek or a ramble in the countryside.

With a thorough introduction to assist planning, clear diagrams, maps and colour photographs to illustrate the terrain and route, and accurate and detailed text, Cicerone guides are designed for ease of use and access to the information.

If the facts on the ground change, or there is any aspect of a guide that you think we can improve, we are always delighted to hear from you.

Cicerone Press
2 Police Square Milnthorpe Cumbria LA7 7PY
Tel:01539 562 069   Fax:01539 563 417
e-mail:info@cicerone.co.uk   web:www.cicerone.co.uk

CICERONE